FIRST FREEDOM

The Baptist Perspective on Religious Liberty

First Freedom

Edited by Thomas White, Jason G. Duesing, and Malcolm B. Yarnell III

B&H Academic
Nashville, Tennessee

Thirteen-Digit ISBN: 978–0–8054–4387–5

Published by B&H Publishing Group
Nashville, Tennessee

Dewey Decimal Classification: 261.72
Subject Heading: FREEDOM OF RELIGION

1 2 3 4 5 6 7 8 9 10 11 12 • 15 14 13 12 11 10 09 08 07
VP

★ ★ ★

This volume is dedicated
to the saints of God
who gave their lives
to gain the religious liberty
that we enjoy today.

"The blood of the martyrs is the seed of the church."

—Tertullian

★ ★ ★

Contents

Acknowledgments

This volume would not be possible were it not for the efforts of the Center for Theological Research and the Smith Center for Leadership Development at Southwestern Baptist Theological Seminary. Both of these centers put time and resources into the first Baptist Distinctives Conference held at Southwestern's Fort Worth campus during September 2005.

The Smith Center for Leadership Development is a fifty-five-thousand square-foot conference center with fifty-five guest-housing rooms. It attempts to bring positive change to the local churches through hosting theologically organized events addressing culturally significant topics. More information on the Smith Center, including information for scheduling conferences, may be found at www.swbts.edu/center.

The Center for Theological Research is currently engaging in a monumental task which will benefit all Baptists. The Web site www.BaptistTheology.org will make available to the broader public both white papers addressing current theological issues and rare or out-of-print Baptist works online. By readily providing access to these important Baptist resources, the Center for Theological Research seeks to preserve the Baptist heritage and help educate a new generation in the biblical ways of our forefathers.

The editors wish to express their deep appreciation to the administration of Southwestern Baptist Theological Seminary for its support of the Baptist Distinctives Conference and this publication. The Baptist Distinctives Conference is scheduled to occur each fall at the Fort Worth campus of Southwestern Seminary.

Finally, a special thanks must be extended to Anthony Moore and Dusty Deevers for their dedicated work indexing this volume. If these two students represent the future of Southern Baptists, then our future is bright indeed.

Introduction

Earl Grey, the cost of turnips, and the early crowds milling about the shops of High Street were probably the only things on Edward Bean Underhill's mind on that morning in 1833. Unbeknownst to Underhill, a significant event in the struggle for religious freedom was taking place an ocean away. The fruits of the labors of Underhill's Baptist kinsmen had finally seen religious liberty spread throughout America with the end to the establishment of the Commonwealth of Massachusetts as the last state in the union maintaining an official religion. Underhill, a grocer in Oxford like his father before him, had yet to leave his significant imprint on the heritage of Baptists at this time when Baptists in America were celebrating. However, soon thereafter, health-related issues with his wife caused Underhill to leave the city of spires to take up the new occupation of devoting "himself to the study of the history of the Baptist denomination."[1] Underhill would learn well of the Baptist struggle for religious liberty.

The produce of Underhill's new labors would culminate in what is arguably his chief contribution to Baptist heritage, the founding of the Hanserd Knollys Society.[2] This society had as its aim the publishing of early works of significant Baptist writers, the focus of which often concerned the advancement of religious liberty. At the beginning of several of the ten total volumes published between 1846 and 1854, Underhill penned a continuous historical survey, *Struggles and Triumphs of Religious Liberty,* that chronicled the advocates of the "rights of conscience," many of whom were Baptists, from the time of Henry VIII to the settlement in New England.[3]

1. W. B. Owen, "Underhill, Edward Bean (1813–1901)," rev. Brian Stanley, *Oxford Dictionary of National Biography,* Oxford University Press, 2004. See also http://www.oxforddnb.com/view/article/36611; accessed 25 Jan. 2006.
2. In addition to these early historical studies, Underhill would have a significant career as secretary of the Baptist Missionary Society and later president of the Baptist Union in England.
3. The Hanserd Knollys Society published ten volumes from 1846 to 1854, including *Tracts on Liberty of Conscience,* vol. 1, and Roger Williams's *The Bloudy Tenet of Persecution,* vol. 3 (London: Hanserd Knollys Society), Archives, A.W. Roberts Library of Southwestern

Underhill saw these Baptists, and rightly so, as heroes worthy of honor because they "sounded the note of freedom for conscience as man's birthright" even while paying the ultimate price with "holy tears and the martyr's blood."[4] Underhill's survey of Baptists' role in the advance of religious liberty served to remind his readers of the price that was paid for their freedom and to challenge them in the vital work of the ongoing protection and promotion of the freedom of religion for all.

Following the example of Underhill, the editors of this volume have sought to gather a collection of essays from current Baptist authors of note that will serve to edify and encourage local churches, their pastors, and citizens at large in their understanding of and actions in response to the gift of religious liberty. What began as a collection of the presentations at the first annual Baptist Distinctives Conference, "The First Freedom: A Conference on Religious Liberty," at Southwestern Baptist Theological Seminary in September 2005 has resulted in the present publication.

Barrett Duke's chapter on the Christian doctrine of religious liberty served as the first presentation at the Baptist Distinctives Conference and fittingly takes the same place in this volume. Duke's careful and constructive work argues that the doctrine of religious liberty is, in essence, a biblical articulation of a fundamental human right. Duke sets the stage for the chapters that follow by providing several definitions of religious liberty including the entire article from the Baptist Faith and Message 2000.

Paige Patterson provides this volume with a biblical foundation as he seeks to answer the question whether the positions of religious liberty and the exclusivity of salvation in Jesus Christ are coterminous or paradoxical. With a characteristically clever style, Patterson's penchant for making the Scriptures come alive is vividly displayed. Concluding with an interaction with the views of the Anabaptists of the Radical Reformation, Patterson gives a clear and biblical answer to the question of supposed paradox that builds strongly upon the theological foundation put forth by Barrett Duke.

Baptist Theological Seminary, Fort Worth, Texas. In 1851, Lewis Colby Publishers in New York reprinted Underhill's introductions to Volumes 1, 2, and 4 under the title *Struggles and Triumphs of Religious Liberty. An Historical Survey of Controversies Pertaining to the Rights of Conscience, from the English Reformation to the Settlement of New England.* Citing Underhill's introductions as works of "great historical value," Lewis Colby explained in their preface that "it is to be regretted, that they have attained no wider circulation in this country."

4. Underhill, *Struggles and Triumphs,* 201.

Thomas White follows Patterson's biblical introduction with the first of three historical treatments. White's work lays the necessary historical foundation and framework for any discussion of religious liberty as his presentation portrays the advancement of the doctrine from the Swiss and South German Anabaptists to the early Baptists in England. Of special significance is the contribution White makes by drawing six areas of common agreement among all of these early Baptists as they advanced their belief in the freedom of religion in their respective contexts.

Malcolm Yarnell continues the historical inquiry by giving a sweeping, yet entirely thorough, look into the traditions that shaped the expressions of the relationships between religious liberty and political involvement among Southern Baptists. He distinguishes between the Virginia Tradition and the South Carolina Tradition of political theology. Yarnell's chapter specifically serves the twenty-first-century reader as he provides clarity to the multifaceted religio-political concerns competing among Baptists in America that often confuse rather than instruct.

Richard Land's chapter complements the historical section in this volume with an insightful narrative that emphasizes the events that led to the establishment of the doctrine of religious liberty in America. Land's vast experience as president of the Southern Baptist Convention's Ethics and Religious Liberty Commission adds an enlightening dimension to the ways in which these historical events relate to the present political climate.

Craig Mitchell takes a close look at the various contemporary arguments surrounding the belief that there exists an external natural law by which all of humanity is governed and judged. Mitchell draws from a broad field of research that enables him to apply with careful erudition the concept of natural law to the doctrine of religious liberty. This helps communicate religious liberty's universal nature and resulting implications for America's citizens.

Daniel Heimbach's contribution is arguably one of the most important in this volume for the contemporary discussion that surrounds the doctrine of religious liberty because he provides detailed definitions to often misunderstood terms. Heimbach seeks to unravel the complexities of the appropriate role of government with regard to the freedoms granted to its citizens for religious expression. The four views Heimbach provides on the meaning of religious liberty combined with his four concluding principles shine like a light in the often dark and confusing discussions that surround this first freedom.

Russell Moore's chapter stands beside those that interact with contemporary concerns as they relate to culture and Christianity. Moore contributes a message that combines alacrity, wit, and a truth-telling edge as no stone in our contemporary garden of conservative Christianity is left unturned. In didactic fashion, Moore reminds the reader that the struggle for religious liberty is a struggle that can be reduced to a simple matter of priority: Christ before culture.

Emir Caner's essay brings a timely inquiry into whether religious liberty could exist in Muslim nations. Drawing from personal experience and church history, Caner interacts with both the Bible and Islamic texts to advance a bold and hope-filled view of the possibility for true freedom to exist in places where many would think such to be impossible. This chapter provides the reader with a much-needed but rarely heard perspective on a subject that increasingly dwells closer and closer to home.

The Honorable Paul Pressler concludes the volume with a unique and valuable personal perspective on his involvement in the cause for the preservation of religious liberty in contemporary culture. In a priceless conversational style, Pressler provides several snapshots of court cases that have implications for the current state of religious liberty in America. There have been few Southern Baptists who have had the years of experience and influence both in the civil and denominational worlds as Judge Pressler. Having his personal perspective as a part of this publication is a privilege not only for today's readers but also for many students and pastors to come.

The purpose of this collection of essays, therefore, is first to provide an introductory look at the biblical and historical foundations of religious liberty and also at several instances of contemporary expression and defense. Second, however, both the editors and contributors wish to play the role of Edward Bean Underhill and many historians like him by reminding Baptists in the twenty-first century of the price that was paid by their forefathers for the establishment and defense of religious liberty. To be sure, there were people of various religious and denominational preferences that Providence used to implement the religious freedoms now enjoyed by all, but for Baptists to overlook the contribution of their own would be a travesty.

Underhill said it well:

> Thus the [B]aptists became the first and only propounders of "absolute liberty, just and true liberty, equal and impartial liberty."[5] For this they suffered and died. They proclaimed it by their deeds, they propagated it in their writings. In almost every country of Europe, amid tempests of wrath, stirred up by their faith, and their manly adherence to truth, they were the indefatigable, consistent primal apostles of liberty in this latter age. We honor them.[6]

May those who read this volume not only honor them but also the Creator who made them, redeemed them, and gave them hearts to establish the first freedom.

Jason G. Duesing

5. Underhill notes that a portion of this sentence is from "Locke on Toleration, p. 31, 4th ed.," in *Struggles and Triumphs,* 201. The location of Underhill's inset quotation marks here are of significant historical significance as many later historians and Baptists regrettably failed to notice this distinction and claimed the entire sentence as Locke's. However, as Conrad Henry Moehlman reveals, nothing could be further from the sentiments of the mind of Locke, who apparently did not hold Baptists and other dissenters in high regard. See "The Baptists Revise John Locke," in *The Journal of Religion,* 18, no. 2 (April 1938): 174–82.
6. Underhill, *Struggles and Triumphs,* 201.

CHAPTER 1

The Christian Doctrine of Religious Liberty

Barrett Duke

Recently, the United States Bureau of Immigration Appeals (BIA) argued that a Chinese man who had been arrested and beaten in China for operating an unregistered house church could not remain in the United States but would have to return to China. The BIA denied his request to remain because it believed that the treatment the man received from the Chinese authorities was related to his illegal activity of operating an unregistered place of worship, not his religious beliefs.

Essentially, the BIA made a distinction between religious belief and religious practice. For them, persecution for religious belief merits protection, but persecution for religious practice born out of that belief is not necessarily protected behavior. The BIA made this decision in spite of the fact that it is clear that this man refused to register his church because he knew the Chinese government would not permit him to teach anything contrary to party doctrine. In other words, the Chinese government was engaged in restricting religious liberty, and this man considered the restriction to be a violation of his religious beliefs, which his conscience would not allow.

The BIA did not see it that way. They saw only a man who refused to obey the law set forth by his government. Incredibly, a three-judge panel of the United States Fifth Circuit Court of Appeals upheld the BIA distinction, arguing, "While we may abhor China's practice of restricting its citizens from gathering in a private home to read the gospel and sing hymns, and abusing offenders, like Li, who commit such acts, that is a moral judgment not a legal one."[1]

It is frightening that supposedly enlightened individuals, in significant positions of power, could make such erroneous distinctions between religious belief and practice. Evidently, it is time to reopen the issue of religious liberty and reclarify its meaning for a new generation. While many religious groups can claim the right to speak on the topic of religious liberty because of their own experiences as a persecuted people, Baptists approach this topic from their own uniquely qualified position. Baptists, as a distinct group, lived and died through more than two centuries of religious persecution. In fact, their earlier spiritual brethren, the Anabaptists, were among the first to speak out against the Reformers' use of the power of the state to punish those whose religious practices were at odds with their own beliefs.[2]

While the persecution dilemma has subsided in this country with the cessation of the official state church, people of faith are finding a new intolerance of their faith and their convictions born of that faith with the emergence of fundamentalist secularism in the West. Furthermore, in many areas in the rest of the world, persecution for religious faith remains a serious and deadly problem for millions of people of faith, especially, but not limited to, Christians.

Religious liberty is threatened on at least four fronts today.

First, a new religious fundamentalism has gripped many countries where it is bringing the power of the state to its aid in suppressing those of other faiths or even different sects of the same faith. The rise of religious fundamentalism among Muslims, Hindus, and Buddhists around the world—coupled with the direct assistance, sympathy, or apathy of the civil powers—has made the issue of religious liberty one of the

1. *Xiaodong Li v. Alberto Gonzalez,* 420 F.3d 500 (5th Cir. 2005). This decision was appealed subsequent to the delivery of this paper in September 2005. Due to significant pressure from the religious and human rights communities on the Department of Homeland Security, DHS petitioned BIA to reopen its removal proceedings against Li. On October 6, 2005, BIA reversed its previous decision and granted Li permission to remain in the United States. On November 1, 2005, the Fifth Circuit panel responded by vacating its previous decision, and Li was not forced to return to China.

2. Harold Bender notes that the Anabaptist Balthasar Hubmaier's 1528 pamphlet, *Von ketzern und iren verbrennern,* "has been called the first Protestant declaration for religious freedom." Harold S. Bender, *Anabaptists and Religious Liberty in the Sixteenth Century* (Philadelphia: Fortress, 1970), 9.

most pressing concerns of the last decades of the twentieth century and the first decade of this century.

Second, religious liberty is threatened in some countries by certain Christ-confessing groups that believe in the superior nature of their sect or who consider other Christ-confessing groups as nuisances or threats to their dominance—in the former Soviet countries, for example.

Third, the world's remaining totalitarian states still see religious belief as a threat to the state's dominance of every aspect of life. China still imprisons, tortures, and murders Christians who choose to follow the dictates of their conscience in matters of faith. North Korea's attitude toward unsanctioned religious groups is even more brutal.

Fourth, but probably not finally, a fundamentalist secularism has emerged in many countries that considers the church's denouncement of certain sins to be unacceptable. A growing movement is afoot to label certain religious speech—speech against homosexuality for example—as hate speech. In response, these people have begun to marshal the civil powers to restrict and punish undesirable religious speech. In other quarters a new militancy against the involvement of people of faith in political life is emerging such that moral convictions are being equated with religious beliefs and deemed an unconstitutional intrusion of faith in the body politic.

As the church seeks to speak to these new and old threats to religious liberty, she must also contend with a postmodern mind-set among Western intellectual elites that no longer believes in absolute moral truth. This abandonment of the concept of absolute moral truth has led many people to question whether any culture can demand certain behaviors of any other culture. After all, if one accepts the postmodern model that each community constructs its own reality, and that one community's construction of reality and its attendant absolutes are as valid as another's, within certain humanitarian boundaries, then it is nearly impossible for someone from one community to insist that another community change. The problems postmodernism creates for those who are attempting to promote religious freedom throughout the world are immense. Just consider the scope of postmodernism's reach. Gene Veith provides a superb summary of its tenets:

1. Social Constructivism. Meaning, morality, and truth do not exist objectively; rather, they are constructed by the society.

2. Cultural Determinism. Individuals are wholly shaped by cultural forces. Language in particular determines what we can think.
3. The Rejection of Individual Identity. People exist primarily as members of groups. Identity is primarily collective.
4. The Rejection of Humanism. Values that emphasize the creativity, autonomy, and priority of human beings are misplaced. There is no universal humanity since every culture constitutes its own reality.
5. The Denial of the Transcendent. There are no absolutes.
6. Power Reductionism. All institutions, all human relationships, all moral values, and all human creations—from works of art to religious ideologies—are all expressions and masks of the primal will to power.
7. The Rejection of Reason. Reason and the impulse to objectify truth are illusory masks for cultural power. Authenticity and fulfillment come from submerging the self into a larger group.
8. Revolutionary Critique of the Existing Order. Modern society with its rationalism, order, and unitary view of truth needs to be replaced by a new world order.[3]

The implications of these tenets for religious liberty are obvious. If our concept of religious liberty is merely a construct of our community but not universally valid for the myriad reasons suggested in the above postmodern tenets, then the postmodernist will argue that this is a relative value and not binding on all cultures.

This is the environment with which people of faith must contend today. As Christians relate to these various pressures, we can respond in one of two general ways. We could accept the postmodern construct and simply write off people of faith being persecuted by other cultures and take a Star Trekkian "prime directive" attitude toward them. Or we could reassert the universal nature of religious liberty and insist that all cultures, our own as well as others, respect the faith of the various faith groups in their midst and protect them and their right to practice their faith as they choose, within reason, of course, including their right to engage in religious speech and the life of their community and nation.

The first option is hardly acceptable. To sit idly while people are murdered, raped, imprisoned, dispossessed, displaced, and margin-

3. Gene Edward Veith Jr., *Postmodern Times: A Christian Guide to Contemporary Thought and Culture* (Wheaton: Crossway Books, 1994), 158.

alized because of their faith is an act of cowardice tantamount to the barbaric acts themselves. The second option is the only responsible option. However, it seems necessary to regain some lost ground in order to press the cause of religious liberty around the world, as well as in our own nation. Of foremost concern must be the ideological basis for this "interference" and advocacy on behalf of persecuted people of faith. A number of approaches can be taken to establish the ideological ground for universal religious liberty.

First, one may argue the case from natural law. Proponents of natural law theory argue that universal moral absolutes are deduced by observing the created order or human behavior and social systems. While natural law theory has seen its share of triumphs and defeats, it still provides a solid footing for many. The recent work by J. Budziszewski, *What We Can't Not Know,* promises to reassert the importance of this approach to moral values in general and, consequently, to the case for religious liberty in particular. Budziszewski does not argue that people know moral law inherently, as though they are born knowing it. He argues that a morality is inherent in the created order and that humans cannot prevent themselves from learning it. Four evidences or "witnesses" are at work in every human that "provide real moral knowledge." These "witnesses" are: deep conscience, design as such, our own design, and natural consequences.

Budziszewski does an excellent job in a brief space of demonstrating how these witnesses lead to the understanding of certain moral truths. However, he has not proven whether men discover these moral laws or produce them in response to these inner witnesses. He even admits this failing: "I have not proven that they do; I have only declared it. There is no way to prove the obvious."[4] But even if one were to assume he need not prove that these moral laws are already present, there is yet another problem with natural law theory. Whether people discover certain moral truths or produce them, there is no certainty that they will come to the right moral conclusions as they respond to the "witnesses." It is expected that they will, and fortunately, they usually do; but left to their own faulty reasoning capacities, they are likely going to miss something at the very least.

---

4. J. Budziszewski, *What We Can't Not Know: A Guide* (Dallas, Tex.: Spence, 2003), 103.

Natural law theory eventually succumbs to the same argument opposing postmodern formulations of moral values; it is dependent on the reasoning capacity of the individual or collective. Unfortunately, pure objective reasoning is not easy to achieve or maintain. In most cases a person's cultural exposure affects his deductive reasoning. A perfect example can be found in a later section of Budziszewski's volume where he answers the objections that people raise to natural law arguments. At one point he notes that people discount the credibility of natural law arguments because some of its proponents have been wrong about what they considered to be natural laws. For example, one of the greatest natural law proponents of all time, Aristotle, among many others, argued that slavery was natural. To this Budziszewski retorts rather glibly, "They were wrong."[5] Yes, Aristotle and the others were wrong, but they were preconditioned by their own experiences, cultures, and limitations to arrive at their conclusion.[6]

The question this example begs from us is, why should we believe Budziszewski or anyone else is right on every count? And when are they right, and when are they wrong? Carl F. H. Henry responded to these same concerns:

> The sin-warped predicament of man in whom God's creation-image is now flawed raises questions also about a body of commonly or universally perceived ethical imperatives. It is not in question that humans are confronted in general divine revelation by the will of the Creator, and that such revelation contains both formal and material elements. What is in question is the ability of sinful humanity to translate the moral revelation into a universally shared body of ethical truth. If, as champions of natural morality insist, human nature is inherently structured with imperatives, how can humans know that these requirements are ethically legitimate? . . . The predicament of man in sin includes a propensity for perversion of religious real-

5. Ibid., 108.

6. In his defense, Budziszewski admits humans may not know these moral truths "with unfailing perfect clarity, or that we have reasoned out their remotest implications: we don't, and we haven't." That is the point, however. How can we know when we have attained "perfect clarity" or the "remotest implications"? Future generations, or other cultures, can always argue that current moral formulations are either incomplete or mistaken. Ibid., 19.

> ity. What humanity affirms solely on the basis of inherent instincts and philosophical reasoning lacks normative force; only what God says in Scripture and has disclosed in Christ is normative.[7]

Second, one may also take a strictly humanist approach to the question. In this case, the issue isn't so much whether certain moral absolutes are part of the warp and woof of the natural world but whether men must choose to adopt a certain universal morality simply to be able to form a brotherhood of man that respects all men. The *Humanist Manifesto 2000* takes this approach.[8] The author of the *Manifesto* recognizes that postmodernism has destroyed the notion of universal absolutes. Consequently, there is no longer a solid foundation for arguing for certain shared moral values from natural law. However, because men must respect a certain moral code if they ever hope to live together in peace, the author appeals to his readers to adopt his proposed set of moral values as a reasonable approach to civil life together.

The question this approach raises is, of course, why should anyone accept this set of values? The values are based on the author's perception of the way things ought to be, but they have no authoritative basis beyond the strength of the arguments used to promote them. One can easily dismiss the author's proposal as a product of a particular culture and reject the *Manifesto's* system as inferior to his own.

The third approach is to argue for a theological basis for religious liberty. In this case religious liberty will be said to rest on the foundation of deity itself. Given the severe weaknesses of the other two options, I believe the most dependable foundation for the promulgation of a doctrine of religious liberty is deity. However, this proposal has some obvious shortcomings. First, not everyone accepts the same deity. Because I happen to believe in the God revealed in the Bible, this does not make my belief in him or my subsequent conclusions based on that belief legally binding on anyone else. The second problem with this approach is the need for an authoritative source that reveals unerringly the thoughts of this deity.

7. Carl F. H. Henry, "Natural Law and Nihilistic Culture," *First Things* 49 (1995): 59.
8. Paul Kurtz, *Humanist Manifesto 2000: A Call for a New Planetary Humanism* (Amherst, N.Y.: Prometheus Books, 2000).

I resolve both of these problems for myself by appealing to the person of Jesus Christ as he is revealed in the Bible. His message, actions, miracles, and life demonstrate a believability that satisfies my need for verification of his deity. Others must either show that their deity is as believable or give serious consideration to the claims of Jesus Christ and the moral values that naturally follow from that belief. I resolve the issue of an authoritative source by starting with Jesus Christ. His supreme confidence in the veracity and inerrancy of the Hebrew Scriptures instills confidence that I can trust those texts to reveal the mind of God. The New Testament texts are another issue, of course. However, these texts have withstood the scrutiny of the critics, bear the marks of men of integrity and veracity, and have the support of two millennia of church history such that they also pass the authority test.

In this chapter we will follow the theological approach to the question of religious liberty. Our task is to present a biblical doctrine of universal religious liberty that will by its very nature establish religious liberty as a fundamental, universal, human right. The difficulty, of course, is that nowhere in Scripture does God say, "I want all people to be free to worship or not to worship whatever they want." In fact, scholars are pretty much in agreement that such a doctrine of religious liberty is not immediately identifiable in Scripture. Luke Johnson comments, "The Christian Scriptures, in short, do not in any direct or obvious way provide support for the contemporary proposition that 'it is a human right to be religious.'"[9]

Consequently, we are left asking if this is what God wants. While direct references to religious liberty are lacking, there are sufficient implications in the major theological doctrines of the Christian faith to demonstrate that God has granted mankind the freedom to choose who or what he wants to worship in the way that he pleases.[10]

---

9. Luke Johnson, "Religious Rights and Christian Texts," in *Religious Human Rights in Global Perspective: Religious Perspectives,* ed. John Witte Jr. and Johan van der Vyver (Boston: M. Nijhoff, 1996), 66.

10. This has been recognized elsewhere, perhaps in fuller and more eloquent ways. Certainly one of the greatest statements on the foundations of religious liberty, natural and theological, is the Vatican "Declaration on Religious Freedom," adopted on December 7, 1965. The declaration noted, "Revelation does not indeed affirm in so many words the right of man to immunity from external coercion in matters religious. It does, however, disclose the dignity of the human person in its full dimensions. It gives evidence of the respect which Christ showed toward the freedom with which man is to fulfill his duty of belief in the Word of God." The declaration itself, while arguing for religious liberty principally from natural law theory, includes a chapter entitled "Religious Freedom in the Light of Revelation" in which it demonstrates that the Bible

J. D. Hughey, former president and professor of church history at the Baptist Theological Seminary in Ruschlikon, Switzerland, took this approach. He agreed that "religious liberty is not a truth explicitly revealed in Scripture." He continued, however, that "religious liberty is implicit in Christian teaching" and then provided a succinct, well-argued case for religious liberty from the doctrines of God, man, Christ, salvation, and the church. He followed that by developing an ethic of religious liberty built on man's creation in the image of God, the "fundamental Christian teaching of love," and the Golden Rule.[11]

This chapter, of course, is indebted to Professor Hughey, and others, for their careful work on this important topic.[12] We begin by looking at the doctrine of man, beginning with his creation. The book of Genesis states that God created man in his image (Gen. 1:27). Theologians have many opinions about what it means to be created in the image of God. While many of these suggestions seem credible, absolute certainty is not possible. About all that can be said is that the phrase does not refer to a physical similarity. The Bible teaches that God does not have a specific physical form (Deut. 4:15–18). If God does not have a physical form, then there is no physical image to replicate in man.

The other certainty is that only humanity possesses this image. Nothing else in creation is said to be created in God's image. Evidently, this image is fundamental to what it means to be human. It separates us from all of the rest of creation. While we cannot state categorically what this image entails, we do understand that it means that humans possess something of the divine that nothing else in creation possesses. What we must also recognize is that all humans possess this image to the same degree. There are not greater and lesser image bearers. Consequently, there are no superior people in the eyes of the Lord. Scripture states, "There is no partiality with God" (Rom. 2:11).

Given this truth, it would be inappropriate for someone to claim that he possesses an inherent spiritual superiority that entitles him to

---

teaches the principle of religious liberty. The document affirms, "What is more, this doctrine of freedom has its roots in divine revelation."

11. J. D. Hughey, "The Theological Frame of Religious Liberty," *Christian Century* 80 (November 6, 1963): 1365–68.

12. I am indebted to the research assistance of Andrew Lewis, a summer intern in the Washington, D.C. office of the Ethics & Religious Liberty Commission and student of Southeastern Baptist Theological Seminary in Wake Forest, N.C., whose efforts to gather relevant materials for this paper were invaluable.

suppress another's spiritual freedom. All people bear the same image of the divine; therefore, all have equal spiritual status before God.

There are four areas where one might choose to disagree with this statement. First, one may argue that the scriptural offices of pastor and deacon involve the exercise of spiritual authority over others. This is true, but this authority is not inherent in the individuals holding these offices. It is the result of the calling of God. Furthermore, pastors and deacons are responsible to enforce God's spiritual standards, not their own. But even this exercise of authority has its limits. Pastors and deacons are not authorized to be dictators over their congregations, nor are they authorized to force spiritual conformity in others. Peter instructed elders, or pastors, to "shepherd God's flock among you, not overseeing out of compulsion but freely, according to God's will; not for the money but eagerly; not lording it over those entrusted to you, but being examples to the flock" (1 Pet. 5:2–3).

Second, one can argue that if there is no such thing as a spiritually superior person, parents would not have the right to exercise spiritual authority over their children. To an extent this is true. Parents are authorized by God to guide their children spiritually not because they are spiritually superior but because they have been tasked by God to impart his spiritual values to them (Deut. 6:4–8; Prov. 22:6). However, not even a parent can force a child to believe. A parent can coerce compliance and outward conformity to his religious beliefs and practices, but he cannot make the spirit of the child accept these things.

Third, one could argue that the state has authority over men. This authority has been granted by God (Rom. 13:1–7). But there is no evidence that this authority is supposed to extend to spiritual matters. This issue is developed further below when we discuss the difference between Israel and all other political entities.

Fourth, some would argue that a husband exercises spiritual authority over his wife. But this is an incorrect view of spiritual headship. Headship entails responsibility for the physical, emotional, and spiritual well-being of the family, which of course includes the wife, but nowhere in Scripture is it said that the husband is the spiritual superior of the wife. Paul said that in matters relating to God, there is neither Jew nor Greek, slave nor freeman, male nor female (Gal. 3:28). All people, including husbands and wives, enjoy religious liberty. The husband is responsible to see to it that his wife has opportunity for spiritual growth and worship, but he does not have the authority to force her to mature spiritually, to worship, or to believe.

We gain further insight on the doctrine of religious liberty from the fall. In Genesis 2:16–17, God told the man and the woman that they were free to eat from any tree in the garden except for the tree of the knowledge of good and evil. This instruction implies that God had given these first humans significant latitude in their choices. He created them as free moral agents. They were given a will capable of choosing whether to obey God. Their subsequent choice to disobey (Gen. 3:1–7) reveals the reality of this liberty.

One can see in this event a significant freedom in religious matters granted to our original parents. God put them in the garden, surrounded them with all they could need, and then gave them the freedom to choose his way or their own. As we are well aware, they chose their own way. From that moment on, the biblical story depicts God's activity calling men and women back to himself and his plan to redeem them. Yet not once do we find that God violated humanity's freedom to choose between their own sinful ways and God. Granted, he resorted to considerable instruction and punishment (for example, the flood and the forty years of wilderness wandering), but people were still free to choose their spiritual path.

There is yet more to be learned about religious liberty from the fall. Fallen man is incapable of fully interpreting the will of God in all matters for other people, and he is certainly incapable of properly enforcing spiritual standards. Fallen man's propensity for cruelty and merciless retribution, too often in the name of just causes, provides a strong argument for religious liberty. Jeremiah declared, "The heart is more deceitful than all else and is desperately sick" (Jer. 17:9). Cain feared that his sin would be a cause of retribution from anyone who met him, which was evidently more than God required. In response God took the unusual step of providing assurance that men would not require more than he had already exacted (Gen. 4:9–16). James Wood summarizes this principle eloquently. He comments, "The sinful nature of man negates the possibility of the absolutizing of human authority, religious or political, and by limiting all human authority provides an important foundation for religious liberty."[13]

13. James E. Wood Jr., "A Biblical View of Religious Liberty," *The Ecumenical Review* 30 (Jan. 1978): 37.

God's respect for individual choice carries over to the church as well. In the book of Revelation, Jesus chided the church at Laodicea for their severe spiritual failings (3:14–22), declaring them lukewarm (3:16). Yet in spite of the Lord's obvious disappointment with the Laodicians, he still did not call for any external compulsion to force their change. Instead, he called on them to be zealous and repent, and then issued his amazing invitation: "Behold, I stand at the door and knock; if anyone hears My voice and opens the door, I will come in to him" (Rev. 3:20). Even here Jesus' respect for human choice would not allow him to coerce change. He appealed to the believers to make their own decision to change.

God's attitude toward man's freedom of choice highlights an essential aspect of faith. Faith is ultimately an internal matter. Coercion can produce external compliance to a set of behavioral standards, but it cannot produce a change in mind. Brainwashing can produce a desired response, but it does not represent the true opinion of a person. It is an overlay that turns the victim into a mindless drone. Evidently, God did not desire this kind of person, or he would have created humans with the right mind-set toward him and made it impossible for them to hold a contrary opinion. Since God so highly values individual choice, it seems unlikely that he would designate any other individual or institution to exercise power over that which he himself has left inviolable.

Ultimately, religious liberty is about man's conscience. The conscience is the crucial internal guide to moral judgment in the New Testament. H. C. Hahn writes of the conscience: "Conscience appears—to put it graphically—as a court of appeal which is not able to promulgate any statutes (for only God himself can do this) but is able to deliver judgment on the cases before it."[14] Paul spoke of the conscience of the unbelieving Gentiles that was capable of directing them to obey the law written on their hearts (Rom. 2:14–15). He also spoke of the conscience as the judge of his own moral life (Rom. 9:1). Paul trusted that other people's consciences would testify to the truthfulness of his message (2 Cor. 4:2). Hahn concludes, "The conscience can be regarded as the place where the 'mystery of faith' is to be found (1 Tim. 3:9)."[15]

14. H. C. Hahn, "Conscience," in *The New International Dictionary of New Testament Theology* (Grand Rapids: Zondervan, 1975), 1:350.
15. Ibid., 351.

Conscience is the inviolable witness within each person that instructs him about his moral accountability. Johnson asserts that Paul referred to the conscience as the guiding principle in his instructions to other Christians on the question of diversity of practice. The cases involved questions about whether believers could eat meat that had been offered at pagan shrines and whether they could take part in meals at pagan shrines (1 Cor. 8–10). Johnson notes that Paul's answer focuses on the individual's perception of things, not the objective facts of the case. He observes that "proper behavior depended on the circumstances, and the discernment of the circumstances in turn was the business of the individual's conscience." A person either follows its leadings and experiences harmony within himself, or he refuses its guidance and experiences condemnation. The conscience is a realm of moral guidance unique to each person, and Paul taught that it was inviolable. No one is to create a situation in which he offends or interferes with an individual's conscience.[16] Consequently, Johnson concludes that human conscience "provides the fundamental ground for religious liberty."[17]

The centrality of liberty of conscience in matters of faith seems to have first appeared in literary form in a 1612 confession of faith referred to as "Propositions and Conclusions concerning True Christian Religion, containing a Confession of Faith of certain English people, living at Amsterdam." W. L. Lumpkin suggests that the document may have been a modification of a confession written in Dutch by John Smyth, a principal leader in what would become the General Baptist church.[18] This confession states:

> That the magistrate is not by virtue of his office to meddle with religion, or matters of conscience, to force or compel men to this or that form of religion, or doctrine: but to leave Christian religion free, to every man's conscience, and to handle only civil transgressions (Rom.

---

16. Wood comments, "Persons are to be free in matters of conscience and religion, without hindrance or coercion, first and foremost in order that God may be sovereign of their lives and that in turn they may freely respond to that sovereignty and bring about the ordering of their lives according to the will of God." Wood, "A Biblical View of Religious Liberty," 35.
17. Johnson, "Religious Rights," 89.
18. W. L. Lumpkin, *Baptist Confessions of Faith,* rev. ed. (Valley Forge, Pa.: Judson, 1969), 123. Estep speaks with more certainty about this. He says that Smyth "can be considered the author." W. R. Estep, *Religious Liberty: Heritage and Responsibility* (Newton, Kans.: Bethel College, 1988), 37.

> xiii), injuries and wrongs of man against man, in murder, adultery, theft, etc., for Christ only is king and lawgiver of the church and conscience (James iv. 12).[19]

Lumpkin credits the confession as "perhaps the first confession of faith of modern times to demand freedom of conscience and separation of church and state."[20]

Freedom of conscience was a key issue in Roger Williams's arguments for religious liberty. In his 1644 tractate, "The Bloudy Tenent of Persecution," Williams made the matter of conscience a central theme.

> It is the will and command of God that, since the coming of His Son the Lord Jesus, a permission of the most paganish, Jewish, Turkish, or anti-christian consciences and worships be granted to all men in all nations and countries, and they are only to be fought against with that sword which is only, in soul matters, able to conquer, to wit, the sword of God's Spirit, the word of God.

Williams also avowed, "God requires not a uniformity of religion to be enacted and enforced in any civil state; which enforced uniformity, sooner or later, is the greatest occasion of civil war, ravishing of conscience, persecution of Christ Jesus in his servants, and of the hypocrisy and destruction of millions of souls."[21]

In 1773, Isaac Backus offered a similar opinion:

> God alone is Lord of the conscience, and hath left it free from the doctrines and commandments of men, which are, in *any thing* contrary to his word; or *not contained in it;* so that to believe such doctrines, or to obey such commands, out of conscience, is to *betray* true liberty of conscience; and the requiring of an implicit faith, and an absolute blind obedience, is to destroy liberty of conscience and reason also.[22]

19. Lumpkin, *Baptist Confessions,* 140.
20. Ibid., 124.
21. Roger Williams, "The Bloudy Tenent of Persecution for Cause of Conscience," in *Roger Williams,* ed. Richard Groves (Macon, Ga.: Mercer University Press, 2001), 3.
22. Isaac Backus, *An Appeal to the Public for Religious Liberty, Against the Oppressions of the Present Day* (Boston: John Boyle, 1773), 56.

The theological doctrine of man sheds further light on the doctrine of religious liberty. In Paul's great sermon to the Areopagus in Athens, he acknowledged that God created man with a capacity to seek him. He said that God "made from one man, every nation of mankind to live on all the face of the earth . . . that they would seek God, if perhaps they might grope for Him and find Him" (Acts 17:26–27 NASB). Paul asserted that God wanted all men to seek him and find him. It seems reasonable to deduce from this truth that God intended men to have the freedom to search for him.

Unquestionably, this search would result in false formulations of faith, yet Paul intimated that this was just part of the search process. Men had to search out questions of faith in order to come to the end of their own efforts and be prepared to accept the truth when it appeared. Luke Johnson's reflections on this passage led him to conclude that Paul's statement is "remarkably positive toward the legitimacy of Gentile religious longing."[23]

Additional confirmation of the God-given right of religious liberty is available in the doctrine of Christ. Jesus provides a perfect example of God's respect for religious liberty. Throughout his ministry, Jesus respected the right of every person to choose or reject him. He even came in the form of a servant rather than a king (Matt. 20:25–28; Phil. 2:5–8). As a servant he pointed people to God and faith, but he is never depicted as coercing faith. Scripture relates many examples of this attitude, but a prime example is Jesus' lament over the city of Jerusalem. He declared, "O Jerusalem, Jerusalem, the city that kills the prophets and stones those sent to her! How often I wanted to gather your children together, just as a hen gathers her brood under her wings, and you would not have it" (Luke 13:34). Here Jesus acknowledged his desire to see Jerusalem embrace him, yet he did not force them to accept him. This is all the more significant when we recognize that, as God, he had the power to make people do anything. Nevertheless, he chose a very different approach.

He revealed that approach in his parable of the wheat and tares (Matt. 13:24–30). In the parable the wheat symbolized true believers, and the tares symbolize unbelievers. When the servants in the parable asked their master if they should go and uproot the tares, the master replied, "Allow both to grow together until the harvest" (Matt. 13:30).

23. Johnson, "Religious Rights," 87.

In this parable Jesus made clear that he does not want unbelievers to be rooted out for their unbelief. That will happen in God's time.

The doctrine of salvation itself contributes to our understanding of God's design for religious liberty. Salvation is an individual, spiritual event. It is a matter of the will. Scripture shows the apostles preaching, even pleading with people to trust Christ as Savior, but it never shows them violating the right of the individual to choose or reject their message, and ultimately salvation. In fact, the individual nature of salvation requires religious liberty. People must be free to respond to the gospel. It is unlikely that God would have ordained an institution that would have been by design opposed to the freedom of people to make decisions in matters of faith. To have designed humans to seek him and find him, and then to ordain an institution with the power of life and death to restrict them from this search, would be equivalent to creating people with a need for water and then not providing any water to drink.[24]

The doctrine of the church holds additional important keys to developing a biblical understanding of religious liberty. The church is not a governmental entity. It is a spiritual entity. It has not been given the means to exercise control over those outside the faith. Consequently, the church cannot dictate to others on matters of faith. Scripture teaches that God established three institutions—the family, the church, and government. The family is the foundational social structure which nourishes its members physically, emotionally, mentally, and spiritually, to provide a citizenry capable of fulfilling God's design for creation. Civil government is the institution charged with maintaining civil order. According to Paul it is God's minister to reward good behavior and punish evil behavior (Rom. 13:1–5). The church is God's spiritual institution. Its task is to provide a structure for Christian ministry and spiritual maturity.

Each of these institutions has its distinct tasks. While the institutions share some responsibilities, none of them are designed to fulfill the God-given purposes of the other. For example, the family and the church share a common responsibility for the spiritual development of others, but the church is not a substitute for the family. The father is the one responsible for the spiritual development of the family. The church is there to assist him in that task. Similarly, the church is tasked with the

24. J. D. Hughey remarked concerning this that "no earthly power has the right to enforce obedience to God, since his authority over the spirit of man has not been delegated." Hughey, "The Theological Frame of Religious Liberty," 1365.

responsibility to share the gospel throughout the world. In fulfilling this task, she depends on governments to protect the rights of her workers but not to do her work.

This understanding of separation of responsibility has not always been respected. For example, too many fathers today look to the church to be the primary providers of spiritual direction in their families. In the past the church looked to civil government to enforce its vision of Christian comportment in matters of belief and practice. Contrary to the thinking of some people, this marriage of the church and civil government was not restricted to the Roman Catholic Church. Many leaders of the Reformation also used the power of the state to enforce church doctrine. Today a monument stands in Geneva as a testament to Michael Servetus, killed for his heretical views, whose death John Calvin does not appear to have opposed, only the manner in which it was to be carried out.[25]

In thinking about the interdependence of the God-ordained institutions, a question inevitably rises: Does the state possess the legitimate authority, either by its own choice or by consent of the church, to rule over matters pertaining to the church? This, of course, is not an idle question. This was a serious issue well into the late eighteenth century in this country. Baptists found themselves regularly persecuted by the state for their refusals to follow the prescribed church practices, including infant baptism, and for disturbing the peace, i.e., preaching the gospel. Of course, we know that it was a Baptist, John Leland, who led the charge to write an end to these practices into the United States Constitution, through the First Amendment. The question is, was he correct to insist

---

25. David Little tracks the development of the modern conception of separation of church and state in the Reformed tradition. He credits Calvin himself for much of the confusion of later Reformers on the relationship between the two. He notes that, while Calvin stipulated a clear separation between the two on matters of internal faith, he considered false doctrine and impious behavior as a threat to the civil order, for which the civil magistrate was responsible. Consequently, the civil magistrate had a mandate to secure the peace, which included jurisdiction over external faith practices that it considered dangerous to this peace. David Little, "Reformed Faith and Religious Liberty," *Church and Society* (May/June 1986), 9. Perez Zagorin credits Calvin's complicity in the execution of Servetus as the impetus for Sebastian Castellio's anonymously published 1553 work, *Concerning Heretics and Whether They Should Be Persecuted.* He calls it "one of the first great protests in the sixteenth century against the persecution of heresy and a landmark in the struggle for religious toleration." Perez Zagorin, *How the Idea of Religious Toleration Came to the West* (Princeton: Princeton University Press, 2003), 103.

on the separation of the state from the church? Scripture supports this position.

The only possible way someone can argue that the church can rely on civil authorities to enforce its doctrines and to punish error is to apply to the church Old Testament teachings intended for Israel. Obviously, Israel was a theocracy. She had judges, governors, a king, and an army. God had stipulated death for a number of errant beliefs and practices within this community, and the Old Testament acknowledges that the sentence of death was carried out.

If the church is the continuation or replacement for the theocracy of Israel, then it is possible to argue that the church can employ the power of the state to enforce its views. However, there are many evidences that this is not the case. First, Jesus intimated that the church was a new thing, not to be equated with Israel. In Matthew 16:17–19, he said he would build his church on Peter's confession. The church was not a continuation of the old but something entirely new. Second, Jesus discouraged the use of physical force to protect himself. He declared that his kingdom was not of "this world" (John 18:36). Therefore, it was inappropriate to use the powers of this world to its benefit. Third, the church has two offices, pastor and deacon. These offices are spiritual in nature, not civil. There is no army, no king, no civil magistrate within the church structure. Consequently, there is no structure provided in Scripture for the use of physical force to advance the work of the church or to defend it.

It seems clear that there was only one theocracy—Israel. The church is an entirely new organism. Therefore, one cannot apply the religious state model of Israel to the church or to the state. The church and the state are separate entities, addressing different aspects of human life. Each supports the other but is not tasked with doing the other's work. Jesus put it simply: "Render to Caesar the things that are Caesar's; and to God the things that are God's" (Matt. 22:21 NASB; see also Mark 12:17; Luke 20:25).

This central truth was a crucial component in the thinking of John Locke. Locke was strongly opposed to the union of the state and the church. He made the same argument I have made here: the civil magistrate and the church have different tasks, and they are not to be relegated to the other or assumed by the other. In considering the relationship between faith and the state and the bearing of Israel on the subject, Locke commented:

> The laws established [in Israel] concerning the worship of One Invisible Deity were the civil laws of that people and a part of their political government, in which God Himself was the legislator. Now, if any one can show me where there is a commonwealth at this time, constituted upon that foundation, I will acknowledge that the ecclesiastical laws do there unavoidably become a part of the civil, and that the subjects of that government both may and ought to be kept in strict conformity with that church by the civil power. But there is absolutely no such thing under the Gospel as a Christian commonwealth.[26]

Today much of the discussion of religious liberty takes place within the context of the Christian faith because Christians are under extreme pressure to limit their activities in the United States and around the world. But religious liberty does not apply only to Christianity. Religious liberty extends to all people and all faiths or no faiths. Jesus sent his disciples into all the world to make disciples, but their method was to make disciples by teaching others to observe all that he had taught them (Matt. 28:19–20). There is no hint in the Great Commission that Jesus expected his disciples to coerce true faith or to stop people from practicing false religion.

The Vatican "Declaration" agrees. It states, "From the very origins of the Church the disciples of Christ strove to convert men to faith in Christ as the Lord—not, however, by the use of coercion or by devices unworthy of the gospel, but by the power, above all, of the Word of God." The declaration cites both 1 Corinthians 2:3–5 and 1 Thessalonians 2:3–5 in support.[27]

If ever there was an opportunity to force true faith on others, it was during Israel's days as a kingdom, complete with a king and an army. Yet whenever God wanted to get the attention of the surrounding nations, he didn't call on the kings of Israel to send in their armies; he called prophets to go and preach repentance. Jonah is the perfect

26. John Locke, *A Letter Concerning Toleration* (New York: Liberal Arts Press, 1950), 43.
27. "Declaration on Religious Freedom," 1965.

example of this. The Assyrians were a wicked people. They needed to repent. They certainly needed to believe in the true God. Yet, knowing what the stakes were—God's wrath or his mercy—God sent Jonah to preach. The people had to decide based on an appeal.

Some may object that God certainly instructed the Israelites to wipe out all the pagans in Canaan when they took possession of the land. That is true, but we must remember, first of all, that this was the fulfillment of a judgment God had determined long before then (Gen. 15:16). Second, God was establishing a theocracy with Israel. It is entirely within the nature of a theocracy to use the power of the state to eradicate error if it chooses to do so.

In conclusion, there is ample theological support for the doctrine of religious liberty. Two questions remain, however. First, does religious liberty apply only to the freedom of people to believe certain things but not to express them in public or possibly even in private? The Bible does not present any theological model for the right of the state to restrict religious speech or public or private practice. The only instances where the Bible describes state-sanctioned efforts to regulate spiritual life, outside of the theocratic government of Israel, are negative. Jesus was executed under the auspices of the Roman government. The apostles were jailed and otherwise persecuted, even executed under the authority of the state because of their religious practices. The book of Revelation describes a time in the future when people of faith will once again be persecuted under the auspices of the state for their beliefs and practices.

The early church recognized the power the state possessed to punish evil and reward good (Rom. 13:1–5), and the Bible calls on Christians to honor the civil authorities and obey them (1 Pet. 2:13–17). The early church also recognized that the state had the power to punish them for their beliefs and practices, but they did not believe they were bound to obey the government when its dictates violated their spiritual calling. For example, the apostles were brought before the civil authorities and told to stop preaching about Jesus. Rather than accept this requirement, they responded with the famous statement, "We must obey God rather than men" (Acts 5:29).

H. Richard Niebuhr answered the question of the state's ability to interfere in matters of faith. He stated, "Religion, so understood, lies beyond the provenance of the state not because it is a private, inconsequential, or other-worldly matter but because it concerns men's allegiance to a sovereignty and a community more immediate, more inclusive, and more fateful than those of the political commonwealth."[28] A. F. Carillo de Albornoz actually reversed the argument of separation of church and state. He commented:

> Now, it seems that it would be extremely difficult to find in the Christian revelation the precise limits of civil authority concerning man *in virtue of the State's nature.* On the contrary, Christian revelation does show us that man, as he has been created, redeemed and called by God and as God intends to deal with him, is responsible solely to God and that, *therefore,* the State, which is subordinated to God's authority and laws, must respect this human responsibility before God. Consequently, in thinking this way, religious liberty would *not* be ultimately based on the limitation of political authority but, inversely, the latter would flow from the freedoms which God has given man.[29]

A second question is if religious liberty applies also to public expressions, can legitimate limitations be placed on these freedoms by third parties, for example, governments? Writers, dissidents, and scholars have addressed this question numerous times. Carillo de Albornoz noted that the Vatican Declaration usually referred to religious freedom in the singular, but in reality it was proclaiming "many religious freedoms: freedoms exercised by different classes of people—organizations, families, individuals—or involving different activities—preaching, teaching, witnessing, etc."[30] He argues that each of these contexts requires a separate treatment since they can infringe on other social conventions. At times he argues that religious freedoms must give way to other rights within the community.

Philip Wogaman agrees with Carillo's categorization of religious freedoms, but he differs with him on the abridgement of those freedoms when they interfere with other rights. He provides three useful categories of religious freedom and then discusses briefly how the intersection

28. H. Richard Niebuhr, *Radical Monotheism and Western Culture* (New York: Harper & Row, 1960), 70–71.
29. A. F. Carillo de Albornoz, *The Basis of Religious Liberty* (New York: Association Press, 1963), 87.
30. A. F. Carillo de Albornoz, *Religious Liberty* (New York: Sheed & Ward, 1967), 13–14.

of other rights might affect their exercise. "Absolute religious liberty" is the internal freedom to believe and worship as one pleases. "Qualified absolute religious liberty" is the freedom to profess or to express one's faith verbally through social communication. He calls this a qualified liberty because "a case must be made for limiting speech which is not designed as communication of faith, knowledge, or opinion but as malicious slander or incitement to action of an illegal sort." "Qualified religious liberty" is the freedom to act in accordance with one's religious insights and values. He says this kind of liberty "raises problems" when it is made into an absolute. Issues like withholding medication for religious reasons, education of children, and activities that harm other people require that this liberty be restricted in some manner.[31]

These are not only useful distinctions; they are reasonable. As we make claims for religious liberty and fight for them with zeal, we must keep in mind that humans are still fallen, and some will abuse any liberty. This could unfortunately result in the restriction of legitimate religious liberties as authorities attempt to deal with the impact of the illegitimate exercise of religious liberty toward others. That said, however, we must always be mindful of what is at stake when we are dealing with religious liberty. Faith is the principal point of connection between God and man. Through faith, people commune with God, learn his will, and act in the world in response to him. What one government may decide is inappropriate religious behavior because it interferes with the life of the community may be a perfectly legitimate behavior in the eyes of God.

For example, China is currently engaged in a brutal policy of repression of the house church movement. The government believes that these groups pose a real threat to order. To the degree that these house churches encourage freedom of thought, the government has reason to be concerned since the Bible will lead men to desire freedom from tyranny and oppression. Yet in this case we must do all we can to assert the right of these Christians to engage in this legitimate expression of their faith. Whenever anyone claims a legitimate right to abridge the religious liberty of another, it is incumbent upon that one to prove that his interests are greater than the God-given right of those affected to believe and practice their faith according to the dictates of their conscience.

---

31. Philip Wogaman, *Protestant Faith and Religious Liberty* (Nashville: Abingdon, 1967), 182–90.

In conclusion, I reiterate that many men and women have contributed in significant ways to our current understanding of religious liberty, often at the expense of their lives. Many have made their statements about this topic in powerful and instructive ways. But I believe it would be difficult to find a more succinct statement of the Christian doctrine of religious liberty than that found in the Baptist Faith and Message. Article 17 reads:

> God alone is Lord of the conscience, and He has left it free from the doctrines and commandments of men which are contrary to His Word or not contained in it. Church and state should be separate. The state owes to every church protection and full freedom in the pursuit of its spiritual ends. In providing for such freedom no ecclesiastical group or denomination should be favored by the state more than others. Civil government being ordained of God, it is the duty of Christians to render loyal obedience thereto in all things not contrary to the revealed will of God. The church should not resort to the civil power to carry on its work. The gospel of Christ contemplates spiritual means alone for the pursuit of its ends. The state has no right to impose penalties for religious opinions of any kind. The state has no right to impose taxes for the support of any form of religion. A free church in a free state is the Christian ideal, and this implies the right of free and unhindered access to God on the part of all men, and the right to form and propagate opinions in the sphere of religion without interference by the civil power.
>
> *Genesis 1:27; 2:7; Matthew 6:6–7,24; 16:26; 22:21; John 8:36; Acts 4:19–20; Romans 6:1–2; 13:1–7; Galatians 5:1,13; Philippians 3:20; 1 Timothy 2:1–2; James 4:12; 1 Peter 2:12–17; 3:11–17; 4:12–19.*

Chapter 2

Mutually Exclusive or Biblically Harmonious? Religious Liberty and Exclusivity of Salvation in Jesus Christ

Paige Patterson

Is it possible for one to hold to an exclusive view of salvation—i.e., Jesus and Jesus alone can save, and no one can be saved outside of conscious faith in Jesus, the Christ—and still be a proponent of religious liberty? Or is the possibility of religious liberty nullified or imperiled once one takes such an exclusivist position? This chapter attempts to answer that question. To set the stage, I begin with an illustration of a personal experience.

Some years ago I appeared regularly on a nationwide program called *The American Religious Town Hall Meeting*. On this occasion a Roman Catholic priest; a Jewish rabbi; a Methodist bishop; an Episcopalian priest; a Seventh Day Adventist, who was the moderator of the meeting; and I were participants. Usually I found the whole group pitted against me. What frustrated my colleagues endlessly was my insistence that salvation comes only through explicit faith in Jesus Christ.

What really made things interesting on this day occurred when the discussion turned to the question of exclusivism. The Roman Catholic priest looked at me and pointed to the Jewish rabbi and said, "You admit that he is a good man?"

I replied, "Absolutely, I do."

"You admit that he is your friend?"

"Absolutely, he is my friend."

"You admit that he is a faithful shepherd of his flock?"

"Well, I have not had the opportunity to observe that, but I would be shocked if it were any other way."

"But you will say that if he does not come to Christ and accept him as Messiah and as Lord he will go to hell?"

I knew that with the way things were staged I was going to be in trouble no matter what I did. So I replied, "Well, you need to understand that he is hardly the only one on this panel about whom I am concerned." When I said that, the place virtually exploded, and the three-ring circus was underway. After the show, one of the questions the panel continued to ask was, "How can you claim to be an advocate of religious liberty and hold the position that all men outside of Christ are lost?"

This legitimate question is one I intend to answer in two ways. First, I will look at the biblical witness. Admittedly I will be carrying coals to Newcastle since most of those likely to read this book know the Scriptures. Why, then, carry coals to Newcastle? Is it because Newcastle hasn't enough coal? No, but our Southern Baptist "Newcastle" may in recent times have forgotten to stoke the fires found in God's Word with regard to these questions. Therefore, carrying the coals again to Newcastle serves to stoke those fires and get them burning once again concerning this issue of exclusivity and religious liberty. Second, I will present some incidents from the sixteenth-century Anabaptists who prominently held to Christ alone for salvation but who were at the same time the strongest possible advocates of religious liberty.

The Biblical Witness

Jesus and Exclusivism

The biblical witness can be divided into two areas: the witness of Jesus and the witness of the remainder of the New Testament. In the context of the Fourth Gospel, was our Lord an exclusivist? Did he believe that all other religious claims contrary to his own were false, and did he believe that his own position was true and indeed the only way of salvation?

In the meeting of Jesus with the woman of Samaria, she asked serious questions about the appropriate location of worship, juxtaposing the view of the Samaritans over against the view of the Jews. Jesus responded, "Believe Me, woman, an hour is coming when you will worship the Father neither on this mountain nor in Jerusalem" (John 4:21). And then he said, provocatively, "You Samaritans worship what you do not know. We worship what we do know, because salvation is from the Jews" (4:22).

Regardless of the context in which you might express this idea in postmodern society, the understanding conveyed by that simple statement would certainly be a great source of irritation for any inclusivist or pluralist listener. Clearly Jesus was not attempting to follow modern, conventional wisdom because in essence he plainly said, "You are mistaken in what you are believing." And then he continued, "We know what we worship. Salvation is of the Jews."

A discussion occurred between Jesus and the Pharisees, and Jesus responded to their questions:

> "Even if I testify about Myself, My testimony is valid, because I know where I came from and where I'm going. But you don't know where I come from or where I'm going. You judge by human standards. I judge no one. And if I do judge, My judgment is true, because I am not alone, but I and the Father who sent Me [judge together]. Even in your law it is written that the witness of two men is valid. I am the One who testifies about Myself, and the Father who sent Me testifies about Me."
>
> Then they asked Him, "Where is Your Father?"
>
> "You know neither Me nor My Father," Jesus answered. "If you knew Me, you would also know My Father" (John 8:14–19).

That is an exclusive claim, but the Pharisees answered, "Our father is Abraham!" (John 8:39).

> "If you were Abraham's children," Jesus told them, "you would do what Abraham did. But now you are trying to kill Me, a man who has told you the truth that I heard from God. Abraham did not do this! You're doing what your father does."
>
> "We weren't born of sexual immorality," they said. "We have one Father—God."
>
> Jesus said to them, "If God were your Father, you would love Me, because I came from God and I am here. For I didn't come on My own, but He sent Me. Why don't you

> understand what I say? Because you cannot listen to My word. You are of your father the Devil, and you want to carry out your father's desires" (John 8:39–44).

Obviously, Jesus was running no popularity contest, then or now. Indeed, what he was saying is clear. Either you know the Father through Jesus, or you do not know the Father. Either you love God through Jesus, or you do not love God. That was a powerful and exclusive declaration then as now.

The man who was blind from birth got into trouble when he was healed by Jesus. At the end of John 9, when Jesus had heard that the Pharisees had cast the man out of the synagogue, Jesus found him and asked, "Do you believe in the Son of Man?"

> "Who is He, Sir, that I may believe in Him?" he asked.
>
> Jesus answered, "You have seen Him; in fact, He is the One speaking with you."
>
> "I believe, Lord!" he said, and he worshiped Him.
>
> Jesus said, "I came into this world for judgment, in order that those who do not see will see and those who do see will become blind."
>
> Some of the Pharisees who were with Him heard these things and asked Him, "We aren't blind too, are we?"
>
> "If you were blind," Jesus told them, "you wouldn't have sin. But now that you say, 'We see'—your sin remains" (John 9:35–41).

This language is tough. It clearly establishes Jesus as the only way to the Father. The Pharisees' rejection of Jesus was a rejection of the Father.

This brief study is concluded by a look into the Upper Room Discourse recorded in John 14 where Jesus presented most definitively the exclusivity of the faith that he was inaugurating in response to a question from Thomas. Jesus told him, "I am the way, the truth, and the life. No one comes to the Father except through Me. If you know Me, you will also know My Father. From now on you do know Him and have seen Him" (14:6–7).

How did the disciples see the Father? They saw him revealed in Jesus. Now, when Jesus says, "No one comes to the Father except through Me," all who are Hindu and do not repent and place their faith in Christ alone are excluded. The same is true for Muslims, Buddhists, or anybody who is excluded from salvation because he has not explicitly exercised faith in Jesus. Jesus is making an exclusivist statement.

Jesus and Religious Liberty

However, did Jesus also trumpet the cause of religious liberty? If one could be so exclusive in his view of salvation, could he have also been an advocate of religious liberty? Barrett Duke says in his chapter that there is no clear exclusive declaration of religious liberty in the Bible. I concur with that; but I also believe, and know that he would agree, that the concept is implicit on almost every page of Scripture.

> John said to him, "Teacher, we saw someone driving out demons in Your name, and we tried to stop him because he wasn't following us."
>
> "Don't stop him," said Jesus, "because there is no one who will perform a miracle in My name who can soon afterwards speak evil of Me. For whoever is not against us is for us. And whoever gives you a cup of water to drink because of My name, since you belong to the Messiah—I assure you: He will never lose his reward" (Mark 9:38–41).

Conceivably one might say that Jesus was talking here about others who are actually His followers though John did not realize they were Jesus' followers. That may well be the case, but, nevertheless, the attitude of the Lord is that one should not interrupt a person's religious practice in a coercive manner. You may confront him with the truth, but you dare not prevent him from his practice.

The favorite Anabaptist passage for defending religious liberty was Jesus' parable in Matthew 13:24–30:

> "The kingdom of heaven may be compared to a man who sowed good seed in his field. But while people were sleeping, his enemy came, sowed weeds among the wheat, and left. When the plants sprouted and produced grain, then the weeds also appeared. The landowner's slaves came to him and said, 'Master, didn't you sow good seed in your field? Then where did the weeds come from?'

> "'An enemy did this!' he told them.
>
> "'So, do you want us to go and gather them up?' the slaves asked him.
>
> "'No,' he said. 'When you gather up the weeds, you might also uproot the wheat with them. Let both grow together until the harvest. At harvest time I'll tell the reapers: Gather the weeds first and tie them in bundles to burn them, but store the wheat in my barn'" (Matt. 13:24–30).

The Anabaptists never tired of pointing out that Jesus said to let the weeds and wheat grow together. Our business is not to remove that which was sown by the enemy by coercion. One may, however, warn them of an impending judgment. A day is coming when there is going to be a call for the reapers to come, and those reapers will take the weeds and burn them in fervent heat, but the wheat will be gathered into the Master's barn. Again, Jesus was apparently taking a position against coercion in matters of religious conscience. Discernment is the responsibility of the church, but judgment belongs only to God.

Another text that supports the New Testament idea of religious liberty is John 18:10–11. The soldiers and officers from the chief priests and Pharisees came to arrest Jesus, and Simon Peter was typically overreactive. Forgetting that he was outnumbered, he drew his sword and cut off Malchus's ear, though that was doubtless not the object for which he was aiming. Jesus restored the severed ear and said to Peter in verse 11, "Sheathe your sword! Am I not to drink the cup the Father has given Me?" Jesus argued against coercion in matters of religion and forbade Peter's use of coercive means. Jesus consistently resisted the use of force.

Someone might raise a question regarding Jesus' cleansing of the temple (Matt. 21; John 2). The passage is a difficult one for those who advocate pacifism because obviously not only did Jesus make a whip, but he also evidently connected with it. In fact, since I believe Jesus to have been perfect God, I believe he connected perfectly. In sharp distinction to Simon Peter, he had excellent aim. He undoubtedly landed blows, and surely one of the reasons the money changers left with such alacrity was in order to avoid future blows. Therefore, what about Jesus' action in light of the argument for religious liberty?

In the temple Jesus defended his Father's house as a house of prayer for all nations. He did not forbid them from practicing their nefarious trades. He simply said that they were not to do it in his Father's house. Therefore, Jesus did not violate any principle of religious liberty because again, as Peter later made clear, when Jesus was reviled, he did not revile in return. He made no effort to reply. He certainly could have, but he chose not to because he did not exercise coercion in religious matters but rather accepted the sweet providences of God.

The New Testament and Exclusivism

With regard to the rest of the New Testament, the doctrine of the exclusivity of Christ is well represented. Perhaps the clearest statement is found in Peter's address to the Sanhedrin, "There is salvation in no one else, for there is no other name under heaven given to people by which we must be saved" (Acts 4:12). When one looks at this passage in conjunction with John 14:6, there is not just a soteriological question but also a Christological question. If Jesus were deceived or deceiving in this claim, he is unworthy of our worship. If, on the other hand, he is Lord, then we must affirm what he affirms. Was Jesus lying, or was he telling the truth? Peter believed Jesus was telling the truth to the degree that he was willing to say so before the religious officials. If you are really a follower of Jesus Christ, you no longer have an option. You are a religious exclusivist. By definition you have decided that Jesus is the only way of salvation.

Elsewhere we have the account of what happened on Mars Hill: "While Paul was waiting for them in Athens, his spirit was troubled within him when he saw that the city was full of idols. So he reasoned in the synagogue with the Jews and with those who worshiped God, and in the marketplace every day with those who happened to be there" (Acts 17:16–17). "Reasoned" (Gk. *dielegeto*) will appear in several other contexts. If one is following Jesus, that is what he will do also. All believers have an evangelistic mandate and imperative to follow Jesus—i.e., the Great Commission. Therefore, daily we should be reasoning with people about Christ.

Picking up again in Acts 17, the Epicureans and the Stoic philosophers encountered Paul.

> Some said, "What is this pseudo-intellectual trying to say?"

> Others replied, "He seems to be a preacher of foreign deities"—because he was telling the good news about Jesus and the resurrection.
>
> They took him and brought him to the Areopagus, and said, "May we learn about this new teaching you're speaking of? For what you say sounds strange to us, and we want to know what these ideas mean." Now all the Athenians and the foreigners residing there spent their time on nothing else but telling or hearing something new.
>
> Then Paul stood in the middle of the Areopagus and said: "Men of Athens! I see that you are extremely religious [Gk. *deisidaimonesterous*] in every respect." For as I was passing through and observing the objects of your worship, I even found an altar on which was inscribed: TO AN UNKNOWN GOD. Therefore, what you worship in ignorance, this I proclaim to you. The God who made the world and everything in it—He is Lord of heaven and earth and does not live in shrines made by hands. Neither is He served by human hands, as though He needed anything, since He Himself gives everyone life and breath and all things" (Acts 17:18–25).

Finally, Paul concluded:

> "Being God's offspring, then, we shouldn't think that the divine nature is like gold or silver or stone, an image fashioned by human art and imagination.
>
> "Therefore, having overlooked the times of ignorance, God now commands all people everywhere to repent, because He has set a day on which He is going to judge the world in righteousness by the Man He has appointed. He has provided proof of this to everyone by raising Him from the dead" (Acts 17:29–31).

There were diverse reactions to this event, but at least two trusted the Lord and followed him that day. Paul's claim was an exclusivistic claim, but you will note, however, that there is no hint of any coercive effort on his part. He was reasoning (Gk. *dialegomai*) with them.

In Galatians 1:6–9, Paul says:

> I am amazed that you are so quickly turning away from Him who called you by the grace of Christ [and are turning] to a different gospel—not that there is another [gospel], but there are some who are troubling you and want to change the gospel of Christ. But even if we or an angel from heaven should preach to you a gospel other than what we have preached to you, a curse be on him! As we have said before, I now say again: if anyone preaches to you a gospel contrary to what you received, a curse be on him!

What friendship award did Paul seek? What a statement of the exclusive nature of the gospel! I do believe Paul here used a deliberate play on words. I know that to take words like *different* or *other* in verse 6 and *another* in verse 7 and say one word always means this and another word always means that is dangerous. Clearly that is not the case. But here I think Paul made an intentional selection when he said, "Who has turned from the grace of Christ to a *heteron* gospel." This is *another* gospel of a different kind which in fact is not an *allo* (same kind) gospel. Paul said that if someone preaches anything else other than the true gospel, let him be accursed.

The same phenomenon is observable in the book of Hebrews. In the great chapter on the atonement, Hebrews 9, the author concluded that according to the law, almost all things are purified with the blood, and without the shedding of blood (clearly the blood of Christ, in light of the context of the rest of the chapter) there is no remission (Heb. 9:22). That is exclusivism.

The New Testament and Religious Liberty

Does the rest of the New Testament also speak of religious liberty or lack of coercion in the gospel other than that of appealing to people? What you find in the New Testament is not a direct statement but rather a discovery of the constant language of appeal.

In 2 Corinthians 5:20, we read, "Therefore, we are ambassadors for Christ; certain that God is appealing through us, we plead on Christ's behalf, 'Be reconciled to God.'" Paul said, "We plead (Gk. *parakalountos,* lit. 'calling beside'). We call you to our side in Christ's behalf and ask you to be reconciled to God." No coercion here! We plead. We beg you in Christ's stead to be reconciled to God.

Acts 20:21 records that the disciples, especially the apostle Paul, were "testifying" (Gk. *diamarturomenos*), to both the Jews and the Greeks of repentance toward God through the Lord Jesus Christ. "Testify" is the language of personal experience, not of coercion.

"Then Paul, as his custom was, went in to them, and for three Sabbaths reasoned [Gk. *dielexato,* the same word again] with them from the Scriptures" (Acts 17:2 NKJV). He opened the Scriptures to them. In Acts 18:4, the same word is used again: "He reasoned [Gk. *dielegeto*] in the synagogue every Sabbath, and persuaded [Gk. *epeithen*] both Jews and Greeks" (NKJV).

In Acts 19:8–9, we read, "And he went into the synagogue and spoke boldly for three months, reasoning [Gk. *dialegomenos*] and persuading [Gk. *peithōn*] concerning the things of the kingdom of God. But when some were hardened and did not believe, but spoke evil of the Way before the multitude, he departed from them and withdrew the disciples, reasoning daily in the school of Tyrannus" (NKJV). He did not force them but simply withdrew when they would not hear.

There is still a different word in 1 Peter 3:15: "But set apart the Messiah as Lord in your hearts, and always be ready to give a defense [Gk. *apologian,* lit. an "apology"] to anyone who asks you for a reason for the hope that is in you." You cannot have coercion with meekness and fear. Those two words are never a part of coercion. In fact, "defense" suggests the exact opposite. The word *apologia* is anglicized as "apology," having evolved in an odd way into being used today as a way of expressing regret.

For example, if I were in a weaving way as I preached and I accidentally stepped on someone's toe, his intense agony would probably yield some verbal objection. I would say, "I am sorry." But how do we get "I am sorry" out of a word that really means a defense? I would seldom say, "I am sorry. I was clumsy." I would probably say, "I am so sorry. You see, I was moving around and did not notice where your foot was. I did not realize I was moving that way." All of this explanation is how we got the word *apology* in English. Originally, the word referred to a defense or an organized presentation and defense of one's position: "To everyone who asks you for a reason for the hope that is in you with meekness in fear."

Acts 28:23 combines three different words, some of which we have already observed in other texts. "After arranging a day with him [Paul], many came to him at his lodging. From dawn to dusk he expounded [Gk. *exetitheto,* lit. 'placing out before them, exposing in the sense of explaining'] and witnessed [Gk. *diamarturomenos,* with the preposition *dia* enhancing the sense of the word, meaning that he witnessed through the thing with them; he walked through the whole thing with them (cf. Acts 20:21)] about the kingdom of God. He persuaded [Gk. *peithōn*] them concerning Jesus from both the Law of Moses and the Prophets."

In light of this text and others, the Bible does present a case for the proposition that there is only one way to be saved. And yet, never did New Testament witnesses resort to coercion, and always they attempted to persuade the wills and the hearts of those who listened. I believe the testimony of Scripture rests.

The Historical Witness

What about the historical witness? While one could invoke the story of English Baptists, American Baptists, and others, for the purpose of this chapter to focus alone on the Anabaptists of the Radical Reformation is sufficient. The name *Anabaptist* was used by the opponents of the Radical Reformation as a descriptive term because of the radical's insistence on believer's baptism. Since almost all had been "baptized" as infants, from the perspective of both the Roman Catholics and the Magisterial Reformers, this act of believer's baptism constituted "rebaptism" or *anabaptism.* However, the name notwithstanding, the essence of Anabaptism was the idea of a regenerate church witnessed by believer's baptism as a public profession of faith and the living of one's life with self-discipline so as to remain a holy and sanctified body.

My favorite Anabaptist theologian, Balthasar Hubmaier, was a remarkable individual. He was the only Anabaptist ever to attain a terminal degree. Hubmaier had a doctorate from the University of Ingolstadt under one of the keenest theological debaters of the era, John Eck. And Eck, who interacted prominently with Luther in the Leipzig Disputation, was not only adroit in debate, but also he made the mistake of teaching Balthasar Hubmaier everything he knew about debate. Once Hubmaier read his Greek New Testament, he came to conversion through Christ and he became an Anabaptist. And so he began to preach an exclusive Christ—Christ as the only way to salvation.

For example, in his book *On the Christian Baptism of Believers* in 1525, Hubmaier said, "Therefore, it is not sufficient to point one to Christ, he must actually call upon Him and hear and believe [the gospel] for the remission of sins."[1] That is exclusivism. The same exclusivism is observable in the hymn Hubmaier wrote.

> Rejoice, rejoice, ye Christians all and break forth into singing!
> Since far and wide on every side the word of God is ringing,
> And well we know no human foe our souls from Christ can sever,
> For to the base, and men of grace, God's word stands sure for ever.
> And, Peter, Jude, and James all three do follow in this teaching;
> Repentance and confession they through Christ our Lord are preaching.
> In him men must put all their trust, or they shall see God never.
> The wolf may tear, the lion, the bear—God's word stands sure for ever.

For our purposes, I want to highlight that one line, "In him men must put all their trust or they shall see God never." Hubmaier was an exclusivist preaching Christ as the only way of salvation. Then he concluded:

> Ah, man, blind man, now hear the word, make sure your state and calling;
> Believe the Scripture is the power, by which we're kept from falling.
> Your valued lore at once give o'er, renounce your vain endeavor;
> This shows the way, no longer stray, God's word stands sure for ever.

1. Balthasar Hubmaier, "On the Christian Baptism of Believers," in *Anabaptist Beginnings (1523–1533)*, ed. William R. Estep (Nieuwkoop: B. De Graff, 1976), 77.

O Jesus Christ, thou Son of God, Let us not lack thy favor,
For what shall be our just reward, if the salt shall lose its savor?
With angry flame to efface thy name in vain shall men endeavor;
Not for a day, the same for aye, God's word stands sure for ever.[2]

Hubmaier had perceived the Scriptures correctly. Based on the epistemological truthfulness of God's Word, it is known that Jesus is the only way of salvation.

Hubmaier could be rough in argumentation. His argumentation made use of logic, exegesis of Scripture, irony, and even "gentle" sarcasm. Would he then be an opponent of absolute religious freedom? The following is from a book he wrote in 1524 entitled *Concerning Heretics and Those Who Burn Them.*[3] A series of articles developed Hubmaier's logical position.

Article 1 states, "Heretics are those who deceitfully undermine the Holy Scriptures, the first of whom was the Devil, when he spoke to Eve. You shall not surely die." The second article states, "The same are also heretics who conceal the Scriptures and interpret them other than the Holy Spirit demands, such as, those that everywhere proclaim a wife as a benefice; ruling for pastoring; stones for the rock; Rome for the Church, and compelling us to believe this prattle."

However, article 3 says, "One should overcome such people with holy artifice, not with wrangling but softly, although the Holy Scriptures also contain wrath." Our approach should not be one of coercion but of holy artifice. Hubmaier continued in the fifth article, "If they will not learn with strong proofs or evangelical reasons then leave them alone, and permit them to rage and be furious, that those who are now filthy will become more filthy still." There is no coercion there at all. It is an articulate statement in favor of religious liberty.

The sixteenth article says, "But a Turk or heretic will not be convinced by our act either with sword or yet by fire but alone with patience

2. Balthasar Hubmaier, "God's Word Stands Sure Forever," in *Anabaptist Beginnings (1523–1533),* 169–72.
3. Balthasar Hubmaier, "Concerning Heretics and Those Who Burn Them," in *Anabaptist Beginnings (1523–1533),* 47–53.

and witness and so we, with those who are patient, await the judgment of God."

The twenty-second article says, "Therefore, it is well and good that the secular authority puts to death the criminals who do physical harm to the defenseless (Rom. 13). But no one may injure the atheist who wishes nothing for himself other than to forsake the gospel." We are not to coerce even the atheist. We are to help him see the truth, but we are not to coerce him.

The twenty-ninth article states, "Since it is such a disgrace to kill a heretic, how much greater the offense to burn to ashes the faithful preachers of the Word of God without a conviction or arraignment by the truth."

Article 36 reads, "Now it is apparent to everyone, even the blind, that the law which demands the burning of heretics is an invention of the Devil."

Balthasar Hubmaier was not alone. The other Anabaptists also vigorously held to religious liberty even though they held to the absolute necessity of Christ as the only way of salvation. Conrad Grebel and others sent a letter in 1524 to Thomas Müntzer, who was beginning to advocate a much more determinedly coercive form of the faith. Grebel wrote, making clear that he favored religious toleration:

> Press forward with the Word and create a Christian church with the help of Christ and His Rule as we find it instituted in Matthew 18 and practiced in the epistles. *Apply it with earnestness and common prayer and fasting, in line with faith and love, and without law and compulsion.* Then God will bring you and your lambs to full soundness, and the singing and tablets will be abolished. There is more than enough wisdom and counsel in the Scripture, how all classes and all men shall be taught, governed, instructed, and made God-fearing. Whoever will not repent and believe, but resists the Word and moving of God, and so persists [in sin], after Christ and His Word and Rule have been preached to him, and he has been admonished in the company of the three witnesses and the congregation, *such a man, we declare, on the basis of God's Word, shall not be killed, but regarded as a heathen and a publican, and let alone.* One should

> also not protect the gospel and its adherents with the sword, nor themselves. We learn from our brother that this is also what you believe and hold to. True believing Christians are sheep among wolves, sheep for the slaughter. They must be baptized in anxiety, distress, affliction, persecution, suffering, and death. They must pass through the probation of fire, and reach the Fatherland of eternal rest, not by slaying their bodily [enemies] but by mortifying their spiritual enemies. They employ neither worldly sword nor war, since with them killing is absolutely renounced.[4]

In the 1520s, when Felix Manz was on trial, there were several different hearings at which he appeared, and Harold Bender notes that "the Zurich court records show that twice . . . [Manz] admitted that he taught that those of other faiths are to be left undisturbed in their practice."[5] That is absolute religious liberty.

Hans Denck, the Hebraist of the Anabaptists, said:

> But with those who may not hear me and still will not remain silent regarding matters which are in dispute, I cannot have much fellowship. For I do not perceive in such the spirit of Christ, but a perverted one that would drag me from my faith by force and compel me to do his will. . . . Then he should know that in the matters of faith all should be left free and uncoerced. . . . Concerning another who has subjected me to persecution and through the same kind of fear, ostracized me, but my heart has not separated itself from him and, above all, from no God-fearing man.[6]

Whatever the case and however stinging may have been the attempts to suppress the Anabaptist idea of religious liberty, the Anabaptist legacy was released in the sixteenth century like a tiger from its cage.

---

4. "Letters to Thomas Müntzer from the Swiss Brethren, Conrad Grebel and Others, Zurich, September 5, 1524," in *Anabaptist Beginnings (1523–1533)*, 35.
5. Harold S. Bender, *The Anabaptists and Religious Liberty in the Sixteenth Century* (Philadelphia: Fortress, 1970), 7. See also Bender, *Conrad Grebel, c. 1498–1526: The Leader of the Swiss Brethren* (Scottdale, Pa.: Herald, 1950), 158–59.
6. "Hans Denck's Recantation, 1527," in *Anabaptist Beginnings (1523–1533)*, 135.

The biblical ideas discovered by these courageous men and women will never be caged again. If we ever begin to faint in the way beneath the satanically induced onslaught of the state or state-sponsored ecclesiastical religion, then let us be invigorated afresh by the superlative examples of these Anabaptists who taught us how to advocate both the exclusivity of Jesus Christ and absolute religious liberty while debating, standing, and dying for our Lord.

Conclusions

As a result of the study of the Word of God and a brief look at the march of the free church through the ages, I will present my conclusions. To sound perfectly biblical, I need to have seven, and they follow:

First, exclusivism in religion carries two potential dangers: (1) The passions generated by the confidence that one is correct in his devotion and conviction lead to condescension and ultimately to coercion of others. This is evident in Islam. (2) The strategy employed to communicate those views can be such that the evangelist appears tyrannical or threatening. Either would be unfortunate. Our method of presentation is important along with the content of the gospel message itself. If someone refuses Christ because of the offense of the gospel, his rejection needs to be because of the offense of the gospel and not the offense of the evangelist.

Second, exclusivism in religion does not necessarily lend itself to either of these unfortunate possibilities. Exclusivism may be maintained in nonthreatening ways.

Third, Christians embracing the exclusivity of Christ as the only saving and accurate expression of the true and living God are properly the most effective advocates of absolute religious liberty. Why would that be the case?

- Because of their quiet confidence that truth will eventually triumph, which gives them the assurance and the ability to continue on without coercion.
- God himself is the only ultimate and adequate judge.
- The free marketplace of ideas favors the truth of Christ and will inevitably result in many people embracing that truth.

- The powerful presence of the Holy Spirit witnessing to the truth of Christ presented with both passion and compassion provides the most effective weapon in the appeal to the mind, heart, and will of man.

Fourth, religious liberty, properly understood, is not just the right of an individual to remain in the faith context of his birth, but he also has the right to consider any and all perspectives and, if informed by conscience, the prerogative to change his position and worship.

Fifth, for freedom of religion to exist in more than theory or name, a free marketplace of ideas must be guaranteed by civil governments and authorities. Individuals must be guaranteed the right to hear, contemplate, and accept or reject the truth claims and values of any religion as long as the public airing of these views does not endanger the physical well-being of anyone.

Sixth, to become a consistent advocate of freedom for all, the government of the United States must be constantly exhorted to formulate foreign as well as domestic policy with a view toward establishing religious liberty around the globe. The words *constantly* and *exhorted* have been carefully chosen. Congress as a whole does not understand this concept. Unfortunately, the vast majority of senators and congressmen, and even most members of the Supreme Court, think that religious liberty means basically the right to continue in whatever context you were born. They do not tend to understand what a free marketplace of ideas is all about and the fact that pressure needs to be put on other governments to grant freedom.

Seventh, Baptists and other evangelicals who embrace the concept of religious liberty—especially those who insist on the exclusivity of Christ in salvation—must develop greater courage and determination in the advocacy of this idea.

In 1415, when Jerome of Prague was about to be burned at the stake, his tormenters asked if he had any final words. He was a preacher. What would you expect him to do? Jerome was not about to miss this opportunity, so he launched into a sermon about the sufficiency of Christ and how people could come to the Lord and be saved, totally oblivious to what was about to happen to him. In the midst of his sermon, the executioner grew weary of listening and thought he would get on with the execution. So he slipped around behind him with the torch and was about to ignite the flames.

Jerome caught sight of him out of the corner of his eye and put a comma right there in his sermon. He stopped and said, "Don't light the fire behind me. If I feared it, I would not have come here. Light it in front of me where all can see."[7] He was a man of genuine courage. May God help us be courageous advocates of absolute religious liberty, defined as the free marketplace of ideas. We never have to fear such liberty because with the truthfulness of Scripture and the witness of the Holy Spirit of God empowering that message, truth will always ultimately carry the day. May God help us to do so until he returns.

7. For this account of Jerome of Prague's death, see William Gilpin, *The Lives of John Wicliff, and of the Most Eminent of His Disciples: Lord Cobham, John Huss, Jerome of Prague, and Zisca* (np: John Mein, 1814), 214.

Chapter 3

The Defense of Religious Liberty by the Anabaptists and the English Baptists

Thomas White

The Baptist defense of religious liberty did not begin in a vacuum, nor did it begin in America. Years before the first Europeans set foot on American soil, the foundation for religious liberty had been laid by the Anabaptists and the English Baptists. These predecessors of modern Baptists fought vehemently for religious liberty, and discussion of this topic would not be complete without acknowledging those who paved the way with martyrdom or imprisonment. Thus, this chapter will discuss and summarize the defense of religious liberty as presented by the Anabaptists and the English Baptists.[1]

A lack of religious toleration cost many Anabaptists their lives. From 1520 to 1560 approximately three thousand legally sanctioned executions for heresy occurred. About two-thirds of those executed belonged to the Anabaptist movement.[2] Two of the earliest works arguing for complete religious liberty were *On Heretics and Those Who Burn Them* written by Balthasar Hubmaier and *Concerning Heretics: Whether They Are to Be Persecuted and How They Are to Be Treated* by Sebastian Castellio.[3] Strong support for religious liberty continued through the

1. Although the movement known as Anabaptism had a polygenesis beginning with diverse groups, the term *Anabaptist* in this chapter will describe primarily the group which arose in 1521 in Germany who baptized over again "as a due performance of what has been ineffectually performed previously." Found in J. A. Simpson and E. S. C. Weiner, *The Oxford English Dictionary,* 2nd ed. (Oxford: Clarendon Press, 1989), 1:425. This chapter does not intend to answer the issue of when Baptists originated; however, this chapter will give the Anabaptists due recognition for supporting the Baptist distinctive of religious liberty.
2. William Monter, "Heresy Executions in Reformation Europe, 1520–1565," *Tolerance and Intolerance in the European Reformation,* ed. Ole Peter Grell and Bob Scribner (Cambridge: Cambridge University Press, 1996), 49.
3. Balthasar Hubmaier, "On Heretics and Those Who Burn Them," in *Balthasar Hubmaier: Theologian of Anabaptism,* trans. and ed. H. Wayne Pipkin and John H. Yoder (Scottdale, Pa.:

Anabaptist movement which included the Waterland Mennonite Church. This church influenced John Smyth's beliefs about religious liberty and thus impacted the English Baptists. The English Baptists under Thomas Helwys and others fought for religious liberty in England, partially achieving their goal. This story of their defense of religious liberty will make up the content of this essay.

To trace the defense of religious liberty, this chapter will examine the most important written works of the Anabaptists and the English Baptists on the topic of religious liberty. The arguments presented by various members of these groups contain several areas of agreement. These areas of agreement continue to form the foundation for the Baptist defense of religious liberty. This chapter will demonstrate the use of six common beliefs supporting complete religious liberty. Those areas of agreement are: (1) that under God's ultimate authority there exist two separate kingdoms—the worldly and the spiritual,[4] (2) that civil government has no authority over the soul, (3) that spiritual discipline should be handled by the church, (4) that voluntary faith cannot be coerced, (5) that killing a heretic ends any evangelistic opportunity for that person, and (6) that complete religious liberty should be extended to all groups—even heretics.

In order to systematically prove this position, this chapter will discuss the Anabaptist position as represented in Hubmaier, Castellio, and others before tracing the Waterlander influence on John Smyth resulting in his defense of religious liberty, progressing to Thomas Helwys, and other English Baptists' defenses of religious liberty, concluding with Roger Williams. From the beginning it becomes obvious that the writers discussed in this chapter felt it necessary to speak prophetically to the government.

Herald, 1989). Hubmaier wrote his work in 1524. Sebastian Castellio, *Concerning Heretics: Whether They Are to Be Persecuted and How They Are to Be Treated,* trans. Roland Bainton (New Jersey: Columbia University Press, 1935). Castellio wrote his work after the death of Michael Servetus, who died October 23, 1553. This work was published in 1554.

4. One may object that two kingdoms do not exist but that God controls all. The belief in two kingdoms recognized God's ultimate authority over both kingdoms but interpreted the parable of the wheat and the tares in Matthew 13 as stating that sinners and saints would coexist until Christ's return. As a result, God in Romans 13 established the state to rule over the unregenerate (worldly kingdom) and the church to enforce the laws of Christ through church discipline on the regenerate. Christ alone rules the spiritual kingdom. Further evidence is found in John 18:36, where Jesus told Pilate that his kingdom was not of this world.

The Anabaptist Defense of Religious Liberty

The various groups of people referred to as Anabaptists held to varying opinions on whether a Christian could participate in the state; however, the vast majority disagreed with a coercive state establishing religion.[5] The main area of departure came from their unique understanding of the church. Timothy George claimed, "Menno and the Anabaptists denied the legitimacy of the *corpus christianum,* whereby church and society formed an organic unity and religion was undergirded by the coercive power of the state. This attitude was truly revolutionary in the 16th century and led to violent reprisals against the nonconforming Anabaptists."[6]

Harold Bender wrote:

> Here the Anabaptists and the Reformers parted. For the latter, the state was to be the *Defensor fidei,* with the power and duty to maintain religious and ecclesiastical uniformity and suppress dissent. The Anabaptists broke completely with the state-church system with its *corpus christianum,* which the Reformers retained. Hence the Anabaptist concept of religious liberty and religious pluralism, advanced far beyond its time, was in direct clash with both the Catholic and Protestant concept.[7]

Finally, William Estep said, "It was clear that while the Anabaptists rejected the sacral society of medieval creation, they did not reject the state but rather redefined its role according to their understanding of the church."[8] The focus on the church as separate from the worldly kingdom controlled by the state quintessentially prepared the way for achieving complete religious liberty while challenging the hegemony of the Catholic Church.

5. For more information on the Anabaptists, see George Huntston Williams, *The Radical Reformation,* 3rd ed. (Kirksville, Mo.: Truman State University Press, 2000).
6. Timothy George, *Theology of the Reformers* (Nashville: Broadman, 1988), 286.
7. Harold S. Bender and Henry Smith, eds., "Anabaptist-Mennonite Attitude Toward the State," *The Mennonite Encyclopedia* (Scottdale, Pa.: Mennonite Publishing House, 1955), 612.
8. William R. Estep, *Revolution within the Revolution: The First Amendment in Historical Context, 1612–1789* (Grand Rapids: Eerdmans, 1990), 27.

Balthasar Hubmaier

Perhaps Balthasar Hubmaier presented the clearest and most formally educated Anabaptist voice on the issue of religious liberty. He served as the cathedral preacher at Regensburg and with John Eck on the faculty of the University of Ingolstadt. Sometime around September 1524, Hubmaier fled Waldshut for refuge in Schaffhausen. Hubmaier remained in the monastery there for about two months, writing *On Heretics.* On March 10, 1528, Hubmaier experienced firsthand the rejection of his arguments when he was burned to death for heresy in Vienna. His wife Elizabeth Hugline was drowned for the same reason three days later.[9]

Hubmaier did not believe the Bible supported state-sanctioned persecution of heretics. In *On Heretics and Those Who Burn Them,* he stated in article 6, "The law which condemns heretics to [execution by] fire is based upon Zion in blood and Jerusalem in wickedness."[10] He continued in articles 21 and 22, "Every Christian has a sword [to use] against the godless, namely the [sword of the] Word of God (Eph. 6:17ff), but not a sword against the evildoers. . . . It is fitting that secular authority puts to death the wicked (Rom. 13:4) who cause bodily harm to the defenseless. But the unbeliever should be harmed by no one should he not be willing to change and should he forsake the gospel."[11]

Hubmaier believed that one should correct true heretics and then leave the heretics alone so that in due time perhaps they might change their minds. To execute heretics sealed their fate instead of praying for their redemption. In article 13 he stated, "It follows now that the inquisitors are the greatest heretics of all, because counter to the teaching and example of Jesus they condemn heretics to fire; and before it is time they pull up the wheat together with the tares."[12] Additionally, he supported complete religious liberty for all by stating, "But a Turk or a heretic cannot be overcome by our doing, neither by sword nor by fire, but alone with patience and supplication, whereby we patiently await divine judgment."[13]

Hubmaier felt that an open marketplace of ideas would provide the opportunity to solve disagreements, and he criticized the state for not

9. Estep, *Revolution within the Revolution,* 31.
10. Hubmaier, "On Heretics and Those Who Burn Them," 60.
11. Ibid., 63.
12. Ibid., 62.
13. Ibid.

hearing and properly correcting the accused. He stated, "If to burn heretics is such a great evil, how much greater will be the evil, to burn to ashes the genuine proclaimers of the Word of God, without having convinced them, without having debated the truth with them."[14] Thus, Hubmaier defended religious liberty by supporting two kingdoms in which the state has no authority over the soul and by extending religious liberty to all, including heretics, acknowledging that in due time they could change their minds to make the necessary voluntary decision to follow Christ.

Sebastian Castellio

Sebastian Castellio was a layman for most of his life. At times he identified with John Calvin, and at others he criticized Anabaptists who denied the right of Christians to serve as magistrates.[15] However, his criticism of the October 23, 1553, execution of Michael Servetus, which included a defense of religious liberty, resulted in his identification as an Anabaptist. Castellio wrote under the names Martin Bellius, Basil Montfort, and George Kleinberg.[16] While writing *Concerning Heretics* under the name Martin Bellius, he founded the movement known as Bellianism which denoted advocates of religious liberty including David Joris and Bernardino Ochino.[17]

In *Concerning Heretics,* Castellio specifically addressed the persecution and death of Michael Servetus. He stated concerning the persecution of Christians by Christians, "We rather degenerate into Turks and Jews than convert them into Christians. Who would wish to be a Christian, when he saw that those who confessed the name of Christ were destroyed by Christians themselves with fire, water, and the sword without mercy and more cruelly treated than brigands and murderers?"[18]

---

14. Ibid., 64.
15. For more information on Sebastian Castellio, see Roland Bainton, *The Travail of Religious Liberty* (New York: Harper & Brothers, 1951), 97–124; Roland Bainton et al., *Castellioniana: Quatre études sur Sébastien Castellion et l'idée de la tolérance* (Leiden: Brill, 1951); Ferdinand Buisson, *Sebástien Castellion: Sa vie et son oeuvre (1515–63): étude sur les origines du protestantisme liberal françis,* 2 vols (Paris: Hachette, 1892); and Williams, *The Radical Reformation,* 959–62.
16. Bainton, *The Travail of Religious Liberty,* 108.
17. For more information on David Joris, see Bainton, *The Travail of Religious Liberty,* 125–48. David Joris was a Hollander and an Anabaptist. For information on Bernardino Ochino, see Bainton, *The Travail of Religious Liberty,* 149–76.
18. Castellio, *Concerning Heretics,* 133. A brigand was a person who lived by plundering, a bandit.

Castellio began his argument by stating that current rulers should follow the example of Christ. He wrote, "When I consider the life and teaching of Christ who, though innocent Himself, yet always pardoned the guilty and told us to pardon until seventy times seven, I do not see how we can retain the name of Christian if we do not imitate His clemency and mercy."[19] The primary argument of Castellio came by dividing the world into two separate kingdoms, both ultimately established by God. The civil authorities possess authority over the kingdom of the world but not over the kingdom of Christ. He stated:

> First of all we must observe that the children of Adam fall into two groups, the one in the kingdom of God under Christ, the other in the kingdom of the world under the magistrate. . . . Civil government has laws which extend only to bodies and goods on earth. God, who alone has jurisdiction and authority over the soul, will not suffer it to be subject to mundane laws. When civil government undertakes to legislate for souls, then it encroaches upon the province of God and merely perverts and corrupts souls.[20]

When addressing the work of Martin Luther, Castellio used stronger language: "Yet, consummate fools though they be, they must confess that they have no authority over souls. No man can kill the soul or make it alive, lead it to heaven or to hell. Christ makes this plain in the tenth chapter of Matthew."[21] He added, "The heart they cannot compel, though they burst themselves in the attempt."[22]

He pointed out two great dangers about the term *heretic*. First, the person being held as a heretic was not really a heretic.[23] Second, the real heretic would be punished in a manner more severe than that required by Christian discipline.[24] Castellio gave as the common definition of a heretic those "with whom we disagree."[25] He then sought to redefine heretic as one who has ignored proper church discipline and correction.

---

19. Ibid., 125.
20. Ibid., 141–42.
21. Ibid., 143. Matthew 10:28, "Fear not them which kill the body, but are not able to kill the soul: but rather fear him which is able to destroy both soul and body in hell" (KJV).
22. Castellio, *Concerning Heretics,* 145.
23. Ibid., 126.
24. Ibid.
25. Ibid., 129.

He concluded that religions of all beliefs had various actions which were considered wrong and worthy of punishment; however, such consensus could not be found among religious beliefs. He concluded, "Let not the Jews or Turks condemn the Christians, nor let the Christians condemn the Jews or Turks, but rather teach and win them by true religion and justice, and let us, who are Christians, not condemn one another, but, if we are wiser than they, let us also be better and more merciful."[26]

Other Anabaptist Defenses of Religious Liberty

Some, such as Dirk Philips, argued that true Christians should expect persecution but should not themselves persecute. He wrote, "Thus, the true Christian must be persecuted here for the sake of the truth and of righteousness, but they persecute no one because of their faith."[27] Philips believed religious persecution jeopardizes a true church's status, stating, "They can never more exist or be considered a congregation of the Lord who persecute others on account of their faith. For, first of all, God the heavenly Father has thus given all judgment to Christ Jesus, that he should be a judge over the souls and consciences of people."[28] The congregation possessed no authority to forcefully compel unbelievers. He continued:

> Here [Matt. 13:29ff] is revealed that no congregation of the Lord may have domination over the consciences of people with an external sword, nor compel the unbeliever to faith with violence, nor kill the false prophets with sword and fire. But they must judge and exclude with the Lord's Word all who are within the congregation and found to be evil. Anything more than this that happens is neither Christian, evangelical, nor apostolic. And if someone wants to say that the authorities have not received the sword in vain, Rom. 13:1[ff], and that God through Moses has commanded to kill the false prophets, Deut. [15], to that I answer briefly: The authority has not received the sword from God to judge over spiritual matters (for these must be judged by the spiri-

---

26. Ibid., 133.
27. Dirk Philips, "The Congregation of God," in *The Writings of Dirk Philips: 1504–1568*, trans. and ed. Cornelius J. Dyck, William E. Keeny, and Alvin J. Beachy (Scottdale, Pa.: Herald, 1992), 374.
28. Ibid.

> tual only spiritually), 1 Cor. 2:13, but to keep its subjects in good order and to keep peace, protect the pious, and punish the evil.[29]

Thus, Philips upheld the belief in two separate kingdoms established by God with different purposes.

Hans Denck stated, "For he must know that in matters of faith everything must be free and uncoerced."[30] He said of those who persecuted others, "For I do not notice the mind of Christ in them but a perverted spirit that seeks to coerce me from my faith with violence and to convert me to another regardless of whether it is right or not."[31] Denck consistently applied this freedom to all. He stated that "be he Turk or heathen, believing what he will—through and in his land, not submitting to a magistrate in matters of faith. Is there anything more to be desired? . . . That is to say, no one shall deprive another—whether heathen or Jew or Christian—but rather allow everyone to move in all territories in the name of his God."[32]

One final document, the Schleitheim Confession of 1527, demonstrated again the support of two kingdoms and religious freedom. In article 6, the confession stated, "The sword is ordained of God outside the perfection of Christ. It punishes and puts to death the wicked, and guards and protects the good."[33] The articles continued, "In the perfection of Christ, however, only the ban is used for a warning and for the excommunication of the one who has sinned, without putting the flesh to death,—simply the warning and the command to sin no more."[34] This confession rigorously defended religious liberty by clearly acknowledging two kingdoms, with the magistrate governing one and the church the other.

Conclusion

Roland Bainton concluded, "The best things on religious liberty were said in the sixteenth century but not practiced until the nineteenth."[35]

29. Ibid., 375.
30. Hans Denck, "Recantation," in *Anabaptism in Outline,* ed. Walter Klaassen (Scottdale, Pa.: Herald, 1981), 305.
31. Ibid.
32. Hans Denck, "Commentary on Micah," in *Anabaptism in Outline,* ed. Walter Klaassen (Scottdale, Pa.: Herald, 1981), 292.
33. William Lumpkin, *Baptist Confessions of Faith* (Valley Forge, Pa.: Judson, 1969), 27.
34. Ibid.
35. Bainton, *The Travail of Religious Liberty,* 253.

The Anabaptists' views were ahead of their time and not accepted during the heights of the movement in the sixteenth century. However, the truth of their arguments paved the road to the eventual acceptance of religious liberty. Current Baptists must remember the shed blood of the Anabaptists and forever appreciate their dedication to establishing religious freedom.

The Development of Religious Liberty in England

The English Baptist movement began in the winter of 1609 when John Smyth took water from a basin and poured it over his head in the name of the Father, the Son, and the Holy Ghost, by self-baptizing and then baptizing the entire congregation at Amsterdam.[36] Smyth and others who withdrew from the Anglican Church argued for religious liberty.[37] A brief survey of a few major figures in this movement will now occupy our attention.

John Smyth

Smyth failed to serve as a solid leader for any one movement. Continuously developing, Smyth's theology changed like leaves in the fall, moving from Anglican to Puritan to Separatist to Baptist and almost becoming an Anabaptist. His move from Baptist to seeking membership with the Waterland Mennonite Church occurred because he began to doubt his self-baptism. Smyth doubted the validity of his baptism when someone brought to his attention that not even Christ baptized himself. In addition to changing views on his self-baptism and other theological beliefs, Smyth's thinking shifted on the issue of religious liberty.[38] This chapter will now examine John Smyth's shifting views on religious liberty.

Early on, Smyth believed the state should coerce all men to worship God. He stated that "the Magistrates should cause all men to worship the true God, or else punish them with imprisonment, confiscation of

36. For more information on John Smyth, see Walter H. Burgess, *John Smyth the Se-Baptist, Thomas Helwys, and the First Baptist Church in England* (London: James Clarke, 1911), and Jason Lee, *The Theology of John Smyth* (Macon, Ga.: Mercer University Press, 2003).
37. For a complete discussion of English Baptist literature on religious liberty, see Leon McBeth, *English Baptist Literature on Religious Liberty to 1689* (New York: Arno, 1980).
38. For more information on the shifting theology of John Smyth, see Lee, *The Theology of John Smyth.*

goods, or death as the qualitie of the cause requireth."[39] Even though Smyth himself was threatened by King James, he continued to support the role of the magistrate. In his first publication as a Separatist, he encouraged princes to erect churches and command their subjects to enter them.[40]

By 1609, Smyth began to doubt this view of the role of government because of Anabaptist influence. Timothy George stated, "Baptist historians have sometimes gone to great lengths to prove that Smyth's theological development was free from Anabaptist influence. Whatever may be said about his acceptance of believer's baptism and his break with Calvinistic theology, this case can hardly be made with reference to his view of church and state."[41] As already alluded, Smyth doubted his self-baptism and sought membership with the Waterland Mennonite Church. John Smyth and forty-two members of his congregation signed the confession written by Hans de Ries known as the Waterlander Confession of Faith.[42]

This confession, which Smyth defended, stated, "Worldly authority or magistry is a necessary ordinance of God, appointed and established for the reservation of the common estate. . . . This office of the worldly authority the Lord Jesus hath not ordained in his spiritual kingdom, the church of the New Testament, nor adjoined to the offices of his church."[43]

Shortly after Smyth's death in August 1612, a book containing one hundred propositions which Smyth had written was published. In articles 83–86, Smyth addressed the role of the magistrate. He affirmed it as part of the "permissive ordinance of God for the good of mankind" but also cautioned that a Christian magistrate must not kill, punish,

39. John Smyth, *The Works of John Smyth,* ed. W. T. Whitley (Cambridge: Cambridge University Press, 1936), 1:166.

40. Ibid., 252.

41. Timothy George, "Between Pacifism and Coercion: The English Baptist Doctrine of Religious Toleration," *Mennonite Quarterly Review* 58 (January 1984): 34–35. McBeth also alludes to this connection between Smyth and the Dutch Mennonites as being one source of the Baptist position. He does not limit it to this source but includes it as a "primary known factor" along with the English Bible. See McBeth, *English Baptist Literature on Religious Liberty to 1689,* 282–83.

42. For more information, see Cornelius J. Dyck, "The First Waterlander Confession of Faith," *Mennonite Quarterly Review* 36 (1962): 5–13; and idem, "A Short Confession of Faith by Hans de Ries," *Mennonite Quarterly Review* 38 (1964): 5–19.

43. Lumpkin, *Baptist Confessions of Faith,* 111. For Smyth's defense of the Waterland Confession, see John Smyth, "Defence of Ries' Confession," in *The Works of John Smyth* (Cambridge: Cambridge University Press, 1915), 685–709.

imprison, or banish his enemies but love them, practically accepting the Mennonite position.[44] However, the most important article was 84. McBeth commented of this article, "Article eighty-four is the clearest Baptist statement up to this time on religious liberty. It is properly regarded as the first major landmark among Baptists, and indeed among English speaking peoples, of the doctrine of absolute religious liberty."[45] Smyth wrote:

> That the magistrate is not by virtue of his office to meddle with religion, or matters of conscience, to force or compel men to this or that form of religion, or doctrine: but to leave Christian religion free, to every man's conscience, and to handle only civil transgressions (Rom. xiii), injuries and wrongs of man against man, in murder, adultery, theft, etc., for Christ only is the king, and lawgiver of the church and conscience (James iv. 12).[46]

This position put forth by Smyth came at the end of his life when theoretically his thought should be mature. In addition, he did not simply affirm the work of another but with pen in hand formulated a succinct statement arguing for religious liberty. Although Smyth may have been the first of the English Baptists to argue for religious liberty, he would not be the last.

Thomas Helwys

Thomas Helwys, born into a notable family in England, became a loyal follower of Smyth, even allowing Smyth to stay in his home during a lengthy illness.[47] In fact, Helwys was the leading advocate of the exile to Amsterdam which brought the group in contact with the Waterland Mennonite Church. Because Helwys did not doubt the validity of his baptism, this partially led to his disagreement with Smyth's efforts to join with the Waterland Mennonites. Furthermore, Helwys decided that fleeing to avoid persecution was not right, so he and others

---

44. Lumpkin, *Baptist Confessions of Faith,* 139–40.
45. McBeth, *English Baptist Literature on Religious Liberty to 1689,* 26.
46. Lumpkin, *Baptist Confessions of Faith,* 140.
47. For a discussion of Helwys family history, see Walter H. Burgess, "The Helwys Family, with Pedigree," *Transactions of the Baptist Historical Society* 3 (1912–13): 18–30; W. T. Whitley, *Thomas Helwys of Gray's Inn and Broxtowe Hall, Nottingham* (London: Kingsgate, n.d.).

returned to England, establishing what has generally been regarded as the first Baptist church on English soil.[48] As a matter of survival as well as belief, Helwys pleaded with the king for religious liberty.

In 1612, Helwys submitted his appeal for complete religious liberty in the form of *A Short Declaration of the Mistery of Iniquity.*[49] McBeth and Robinson commented that Helwys likely wrote and published the book in Holland, distributing it immediately upon his return to England.[50] Unlike advocates of religious tolerance, Helwys's work supported complete religious liberty. Robinson wrote, "Helwys clearly was ready to give the liberty for which he asked to all those opponents, even the Roman Catholics—a fact which shows us how much ahead of his times he was."[51]

Helwys summarized his work in the flyleaf:

> Hear O King, and despise not the counsel of your poor, and let their complaints come before you. The King is a mortal man, and not God therefore hath no power over immortal souls of his subjects, to make laws and ordinances for them, and to set spiritual Lords over them. If the Kings have authority to make spiritual Lords and laws, then he is an immortal God and not mortal man. O King be not seduced by deceivers to sin so against God whom you should obey, nor against your poor subjects who should and will obey you in all things with body life and goods, or let their lives be taken from the earth. God save the King.[52]

The basic beliefs of Helwys mirror those already presented. Two kingdoms exist, and the magistrate must exercise power only in the kingdom of the world while the church of Christ must exercise authority in spiritual matters. Helwys wrote, "None ought to be punished either with death or bonds

48. For more information, consult E. A. Payne, *Thomas Helwys and the First Baptist Church in England* (London: Baptist Union of England and Ireland, 1962); George, "English Baptists and Religious Toleration," 37.
49. This author could not find publication data on this work, except for the date. In 1935, the Kingsgate Press published a facsimile copy with an introduction by H. Wheeler Robinson.
50. McBeth, *English Baptist Literature on Religious Liberty to 1689,* 29. H. Wheeler Robinson, "Introduction," in Thomas Helwys, *The Mystery of Iniquity* (London: Kingsgate Press, 1935), ix.
51. Robinson, "Introduction," xiv.
52. Helwys, from the flyleaf of *The Mystery of Iniquity,* cited in McBeth, *English Baptist Literature on Religious Liberty to 1689,* 31.

for transgressing against the spiritual ordinances of the New Testament, and that such offences ought to be punished only with spiritual sword and censures."[53]

Helwys believed that the magistrate held no power in the spiritual kingdom but simply functioned as a layman. He commented, "Far be it from the King to take from Christ Jesus any one part of that power and honor which belongs to Christ in his kingdom."[54] In addition to supporting the view of two separate kingdoms, Helwys also consistently supported complete religious liberty. Liberty should be extended to those of all faiths. He stated, "Let them be heretics, Turks, Jews, or whatsoever it appertains not to the earthly power to punish them in the least measure."[55]

Helwys, like the Anabaptists before him, felt that spiritual decisions were personal decisions which must be made through faith and that no amount of force could coerce a sincere decision. He believed that men should "choose their religion themselves seeing they only must stand themselves before the judgment seat of God to answer for themselves."[56] He added that since the secular kingdom held no power to create genuine decisions, any attempt to use such force marked a lack of faith in the power of the spiritual kingdom. Thus, people of faith should never resort to coercion with force.

Despite much common ground, Helwys differed with the Waterland Anabaptists by allowing for war and admitting magistrates to church membership. He wrote, "Our lord the king hath power to take our sons and daughters to do all his service of war, and of peace, yea all his servile service whatsoever."[57] In allowing for Christian magistrates, Hewlys possessed similarities with Hubmaier while Smyth and the Schleitheim Confession both opposed this position. Helwys furthered the case for religious liberty by holding to two separate kingdoms, supporting complete religious liberty for all groups, and denying the effectiveness of coercion in producing genuine spiritual decisions.

Other English Baptist Defenses of Religious Liberty

Leonard Busher. Little is known about Leonard Busher other than the fact that he contributed to the fight for religious freedom with his

53. Helwys, "The principal matters handled in the Booke," no pagination.
54. Helwys, *The Mystery of Iniquity,* 49.
55. Ibid., 69.
56. Ibid., 46.
57. Ibid., 39–40.

publication titled *Religion's Peace: A Plea for Liberty of Conscience,* published in 1614.[58] Some believe this work was the earliest publication exclusively dedicated to the subject of religious liberty.[59]

Busher furthered arguments alluded to in earlier writings by focusing on evangelism to produce genuine spiritual decisions. He wrote:

> Also, if the believing should persecute the unbelieving to death, who should remain alive? Then none but the believing should live in the world, and the unbelieving should die in their unbelief, and so perish for ever. The Lord will not that the believing should live to the destruction of the unbelieving, but unto their conversion, edification, and salvation. And by persecuting of princes and people to death, because they will not hear and believe, is no gaining of souls unto God, but unto the devil.[60]

In addition to advancing the argument for evangelism, he continued previously used arguments. He held that new birth in Christ could only be achieved through the word and Spirit of God and held to two kingdoms, specifically mentioning the "kingdom of Christ" and the "kingdom of antichrist."[61] McBeth wrote of Busher's defense of religious liberty, "Perhaps Busher's most significant contribution is his attempt to justify religious liberty on the basis of spiritual necessity and abstract right. Liberty is no civil favor to be granted or withheld by the whim of the king; it is a God-given right of man and is essential because of the very nature of Christianity."[62]

John Murton. John Murton and his two works supporting religious liberty deserve mention. In 1615 and 1620 two documents were anonymously printed which apparently had the same author. Evidence since

58. McBeth notes that "for years no copy of the original publication was thought to exist. There is, however, a copy in the Huntington Library Collection. The book was republished, with some changes, in 1646." See McBeth, *English Baptist Literature on Religious Liberty to 1689,* 39. This paper has used the edition of Edward Bean Underhill, ed., *Tracts on Liberty of Conscience and Persecution* (London: Haddon, 1846).

59. Underhill calls it the "earliest treatise known to be extant on this great theme." See Underhill, *Tracts on Liberty of Conscience and Persecution,* 6. Earlier works addressed more than just religious liberty.

60. Leonard Busher, "Religions Peace: A Plea for Liberty of Conscience," in *Tracts on Liberty of Conscience and Persecution,* 21.

61. Busher, "Religions Peace: A Plea for Liberty of Conscience," 16–17.

62. McBeth, *English Baptist Literature on Religious Liberty to 1689,* 47.

that time has indicated that John Murton was the author.[63] In Murton's work, titled "The Epistle," one can clearly see the idea of two separate kingdoms. He wrote:

> We do unfeignedly acknowledge the authority of earthly magistrates, God's blessed ordinance, and that all earthly authority and command appertains unto them; let them command what they will, we must obey, either to do or suffer upon pain of God's displeasure, besides their punishment: but all men must let God alone with his right, which is to be lord and lawgiver to the soul, and not command obedience for God where he commandeth none.[64]

Additionally, he commented that "earthly authority belongeth to earthly kings; but spiritual authority belongeth to the one spiritual King who is KING OF KINGS."[65] Murton also argued that true conscious faith could not be coerced, devoting an entire section to defending this belief.[66]

The First London Confession. H. Leon McBeth commented in the work which resulted from his dissertation, "In volume, quality, and measurable influence, the 1640's must be accounted the great decade in English Baptist literature on religious liberty."[67] Among those documents was the First London Confession of 1644. The First London Confession, signed by Baptist leaders such as William Kiffin, John Spilsbury, and Samuel Richardson, established a clear position in articles 48–52. In these articles the confession stated: (1) that the civil magistrate is an ordinance of God, (2) that believers should obey the laws of the king and parliament in secular matters, (3) that there are two kingdoms (one of God and one of caesar), and (4) that man must obey God in spiritual matters.[68] This document represents the agreement of the Particular Baptists with what previous General Baptists and Anabaptists had been saying.

---

63. Ibid.
64. John Murton, "The Epistle," in *Tracts on Liberty of Conscience and Persecution,* 100.
65. John Murton, "Persecution for Religion Judged and Condemned," in *Tracts on Liberty of Conscience and Persecution,* 134.
66. John Murton, "A Humble Supplication to the King's Majesty," in *Tracts on Liberty of Conscience and Persecution,* 225–31.
67. McBeth, *English Baptist Literature on Religious Liberty to 1689,* 275–76.
68. Lumpkin, *Baptist Confessions of Faith,* 169–71.

Roger Williams's views as presented in *The Bloudy Tenent* were influenced by the previously discussed work of Murton. He began with twelve statements which summarize the work. Among those twelve Williams argued along the same lines as those before him. He stated that "civil states" are "not judges, governors, or defenders of the spiritual, or Christian, state and worship."[69] With this statement Williams supported the view of two kingdoms—one secular and one spiritual. He also supported complete religious liberty when he wrote, "It is the will and command of God that, since the coming of his Son the Lord Jesus, a permission of the most paganish, Jewish, Turkish, or anti-Christian consciences and worships be granted to all men in all nations and countries, and they are only to be fought against with that sword which is only, in soul matters, able to conquer, to wit, the sword of God's Spirit, the word of God."[70] Williams took these beliefs to the American continent and influenced the establishment of American religious liberty.

Unfortunately, this current discussion is bound by page limitations, and many worthwhile authors cannot be discussed in detail. Solace can be taken in the fact that many of these works repeat what has already been stated; however, the scholar interested in further research should consult the following authors: Edward Barber, Christopher Blackwood, Thomas Collier, William Dell, Richard Laurence, Samuel Richardson, John Tombes, John Clarke, Henry Denne, and John Sturgion, to name a few.

Roger Williams. Roger Williams spent most of his life in colonial America, and the discussion of his defense of religious liberty primarily belongs in a discussion of American development. However, Williams's activity also played an integral part in English Baptist history which warrants his mention in this essay. He grew up in London in the midst of an Anglican tradition before graduating from Cambridge in 1627. In 1631, Williams made the journey to Boston. He returned to England in 1643 to obtain a charter for Providence, Rhode Island, and while in England, he wrote *The Bloudy Tenent of Persecution for Cause of Conscience.*[71] He returned the next year to Providence.

69. Williams, *The Bloudy Tenent,* 1.
70. Ibid.
71. Roger Williams, *The Bloudy Tenent of Persecution for Cause of Conscience* (London, 1644; reprint, Macon, Ga.: Mercer University Press, 2001).

Conclusion

From this historical discussion six statements summarize the defense of religious liberty. First, God established two separate kingdoms with one governing the worldly and the other the spiritual. Second, the civil government has authority in worldly matters but not over spiritual ones. Third, the church should handle spiritual discipline. Fourth, none can influence the soul to accept or reject Christ by force. Conversion must occur by a voluntary decision of the individual in order to have validity. Fifth, killing a person for improper spiritual beliefs does not allow him due time to accept the proper beliefs, and ignores Christ's teaching of the parable of the wheat and the tares in Matthew 13. Sixth, complete religious liberty must extend to all people, including heretics.

A blanket statement suggesting that all Baptists had consistently advocated religious liberty as discussed in this chapter might be an overstatement;[72] however, the majority of published authors have consistently supported religious liberty. McBeth wrote concerning the English Baptists, "That Baptists alone in seventeenth-century England consistently advocated complete religious liberty is to their credit."[73] Additionally, through publishing works on religious liberty, these authors believed it necessary to speak prophetically to the government. While Baptists must place their faith wholly and only in Christ and not in secular authorities, Baptists must also continue to speak prophetically to the government. This is religious freedom.

72. For instance, consider the Muenster Anabaptists and the English Fifth Monarchists.
73. McBeth, *English Baptist Literature on Religious Liberty to 1689,* 278.

★★★★★★★★★★★★★★★★★★★★★★★★★★★★★★

Chapter 4

Political Theology at the Foundation of the Southern Baptist Convention

Malcolm B. Yarnell III

Since it is rare for a Southern Baptist to present a paper on "political theology," an apology is necessary. Indeed, this may be one of the first Southern Baptist papers to treat political theology as a viable discipline. Twentieth-century Southern Baptists advocated the American doctrine of political liberalism known as "the separation of church and state." The term *political theology* seems an oxymoron to the modern mind. The Enlightenment advocated the separation of politics and theology, and Southern Baptist scholars for the most part furthered that program as part and parcel of the separation of church and state.

Unfortunately, this encouraged many to prematurely yield the public square to the secular priesthood of liberal journalists, solipsist politicians, and academic ideologues. Religion, for atheistic humanist and Baptist Christian alike, became a merely private matter and any religio-political discourse brought dire proclamations against the betrayal of the Baptist tradition. Indeed, Bill Moyers detected a conspiracy—wherein a certain retired judge from Houston figured prominently—which would lead to both "theocracy," the rule of the state by the church, and "civil religion," the rule of the church by the state. Moyers's contradictory thesis seems not to have been challenged.[1]

According to Oliver O'Donovan, "Theology must be political if it is to be evangelical. Rule out the political questions and you cut short the proclamation of God's saving power; you leave people enslaved where they ought to be set free from sin—their own sin and others."[2] Although

1. Bill Moyers, "Foreword," to William R. Estep, *Revolution within the Revolution: The First Amendment in Historical Context, 1612–1789* (Grand Rapids: Eerdmans, 1990).
2. Oliver O'Donovan, *The Desire of the Nations: Rediscovering the Roots of Political Theory* (New York: Cambridge University Press, 1996), 3.

we may tweak some of O'Donovan's assertions, his basic thesis is correct. It is time for Southern Baptists to reexamine the benefits and dangers, and the avenues and limits, of the theological basis of politics. If theology is not concerned with politics, a branch of ethics, then we surrender politics, and eventually ethics, to the enemies of the kingdom of God. Indeed, to confess with integrity that "Jesus is Lord" entails the construction of not only personal soteriology but also a communal ecclesiology and a political theology. Perhaps this chapter will prompt other Southern Baptists to construct carefully a political theology.

Two Southern Baptist Traditions of Political Theology

In spite of contrary ideological biases, there are two traditions in the Southern Baptist conversation concerning church and state. They may be referred to as the "major tradition" and the "minor tradition," or perhaps the "Virginia tradition" and the "South Carolina tradition." The Virginia tradition is identified with the rhetoric of John Leland, the agitation of the Danbury Baptist Association, and the subsequent official promulgation of the separation doctrine by the federal judiciary. The Virginia tradition is upheld by numerous ideologues, Baptist and secular, theological and juridical.

In sum, the Virginia narrative rehearses the advocacy of the separation of church and state in English Baptist life, claims Roger Williams established Rhode Island with "complete religious liberty," and exults in an 1802 letter by a heretical politician.[3] Thomas Jefferson's letter took on more than quaint historical interest in 1878 when, in the case of a polygamist Mormon, Justice Waite used Robert Baylor Semple's *A History of the Rise and Progress of the Baptists in Virginia* to interpret the First Amendment in terms of "a wall of separation between the church and state."[4] It became a serious matter, however, when in 1947,

3. Joseph Martin Dawson, *Baptists and the American Republic* (Nashville: Broadman, 1956); Robert A. Baker, "Baptist Heritage and Religious Liberty," in *Christianity and Religious Liberty: Messages from the Eighth Annual Christian Life Workshop* (Fort Worth: Texas Baptist Christian Life Commission, 1964), 8–19; Estep, *Revolution within the Revolution*; Bill J. Leonard, *Baptists in America* (New York: Columbia University Press, 2005), 157–61.
4. Philip Hamburger, *Separation of Church and State* (Cambridge: Harvard University Press, 2002), 260.

in the case of *Everson v. Board of Education,* Justice Black elevated separation to the status of a constitutional right.[5]

The Virginia tradition has institutional advocates, not only from the juridical perspective in the Supreme Court of the United States and in Americans United for the Separation of Church and State, but in Baptist life with the J. M. Dawson Institute of Church and State Studies at Baylor University and its *Journal of Church and State.*[6]

The Virginia tradition has not lacked its theological and juridical critics, however. As early as 1937, Baptist scholars discovered inconsistencies in the story. For instance, the English Baptist confessions advocated religious liberty but left separation unstated. English Baptist treatises trumpeted liberty of conscience, the antithesis of persecution, but they also proposed parliamentary laws that placed boundaries around religious discourse.[7] Williams's Rhode Island granted citizenship only to Christians, discriminated against both blacks and Roman Catholics, and used state funds to construct the First Baptist Church sanctuary. "A degree of religious toleration existed from the beginning but there was no complete separation of church and state." Fortunately for the Virginia tradition, it has been concluded that at least Virginia Baptists deserve a "merit award" for "religious liberty."[8]

Baptist concerns aside, from the juridical perspective, historians and legal scholars have begun to cast doubt on the original intent of the founding fathers of America. It has been argued that the judicial doctrine of separation may legally protect the lone ranger while it restricts the freedoms of churchgoers. Indeed, there is some doubt as to whether Jefferson really intended the establishment clause to be understood in the modern metaphorical sense of a wall of separation between church

5. Ibid., 454–78.
6. The current editor's interests concerning the separation doctrine seem more juridical than theological. Cf. Derek Davis, "A Commentary on the Supreme Court's 'Equal Treatment' Doctrine as the New Constitutional Paradigm for Protecting Religious Liberty," *Journal of Church and State* 46 (2004): 724–32.
7. Leonard Busher wanted an open marketplace of religious discussion, but discussions were to be limited by the authority of Scripture and were to refrain from "reproach or slander." While king and parliament should refrain from interfering with the church, they were to enforce the Bible's moral law. Busher, *Religions Peace* (Amsterdam: 1614; reprint, London: 1646), 22, 31. "Busher was not entirely a utopian dreamer: he believed that freedom of conscience would need some hedges round it if it were to work." Barrie White, "Early Baptist Arguments for Religious Freedom: Their Overlooked Agenda," *Baptist History and Heritage* 24 (1989): 7.
8. Conrad Henry Moehlman, "The Baptist View of the State," *Church History* 6 (1937): 24–49.

and state. In other words, the metaphor may be carrying more intellectual and juridical weight than warranted. Questions of original intent have driven cultural and legal scholars to reexamine the context and import of Jefferson's famous statement.[9] Of course, from a theological perspective, Jefferson's intent is germane only insofar as he faithfully reflected broadly based Baptist beliefs.

Alongside the Virginia tradition stands the South Carolina tradition. Besides the obvious geographical difference, the traditions differ in their class orientations and relationship to government. Virginia Baptists were of the "lower" and "middling" sorts, being vividly described by a contemporary as "hare-lipped, blear-eyed, hump-backed, bow-legged, clump-footed; barely any of them looked like other people. But they were all strong for plunging."[10] Moreover, Virginia Baptists in the eighteenth century fought a trenchant establishment foe in the aristocratic Church of England. Through persecution they became convinced the state should never address religion. Upon returning to Connecticut from Virginia, John Leland vigorously wrote, "Let every man speak freely without fear, maintain the principles that he believes, worship according to his own faith, either one God, three Gods, no God, or twenty Gods; and let government protect him in so doing, i.e., see that he meets with no personal abuse, or loss of property, for his religious opinions."[11]

The Virginia tradition bequeathed Baptists the doctrine of separation of church and state as a negative statement of political theology. The separation of church and state seeks to guarantee that no church be established by government or in any way privileged over any other church or religion.

The South Carolina tradition offers Baptists a more positive statement of political theology. South Carolina Baptists arose from the first

9. Hamburger, *Separation of Church and State,* 479–92; Daniel L. Dreisbach, "'Sowing Useful Truths and Principles': The Danbury Baptists, Thomas Jefferson, and the 'Wall of Separation,'" *Journal of Church and State* 39 (1997): 455–501; James H. Hutson, "Thomas Jefferson's Letter to the Danbury Baptists: A Controversy Rejoined," *The William and Mary Quarterly* 56 (1999): 775–90; "A Letter of Concern from the Scholars Listed Below," Press Release, Americans United for Separation of Church and State, 29 July 1998; Daniel L. Dreisbach, *Thomas Jefferson and the Wall of Separation Between Church and State* (New York: New York University Press, 2002).

10. Frank Lambert, *The Founding Fathers and the Place of Religion in America* (Princeton, N.J.: Princeton University Press, 2003), 151; Contemporary quoted in Moehlman, "Baptist View of the State," 41.

11. *The Rights of Conscience Inalienable, and, Therefore, Religious Opinions Not Cognizable by Law* (1791), in *The Writings of the Late Elder John Leland* (New York: G. W. Wood, 1845), 184.

wave of British immigrants to what became the wealthiest American city in the eighteenth century, Charles Town or Charleston. These Baptists owned massive tracts of land and slaves, kept houses in the city and plantations in the country, advocated classical learning, and participated in colonial government. Their earliest members included aristocrats like Lady Elizabeth Axtell Blake.[12] Lady Blake was the wife of a governor of South Carolina, Landgrave Joseph Blake, and the descendant of a regicide.[13]

In order to discern the South Carolina tradition, evaluations will be made of the political theology advocated by three of its earliest and most prominent pastors: William Screven, Oliver Hart, and Richard Furman. Their pastorates at First Baptist Church of Charleston stretch from 1696 to 1825. These three theologians represent no mere historical sideline. Screven was the first Baptist pastor in the south; Hart established the first Baptist association in the south, and Furman founded the first national convention of Baptists and the first state convention.

The Political Theology of William Screven

Dissenters, including Presbyterians, Baptists, Quakers and Huguenots, came to South Carolina with the promise of religious liberty. In 1663, shortly after "the era of the great persecution" began in England, Charles II granted a charter that guaranteed both religious liberty and limited self-government for those who would immigrate to Carolina.[14] In the advertisements published in 1664 and 1666 to entice settlers, religious liberty was prominent. "There is full and free Liberty of Conscience granted to all, so that no man is to be molested or called in question for matters of Religious Concern; but every one to be obedient to the Civil Government, worshiping God after their own way."[15]

12. Robert A. Baker and Paul J. Craven Jr., *Adventure in Faith: The First 300 Years of First Baptist Church, Charleston, South Carolina* (Nashville: Broadman, 1982), 24–26.

13. M. Eugene Sirmans, "Politics in Colonial South Carolina: The Failure of Proprietary Reform, 1682–1694," *The William and Mary Quarterly* 23 (1966): 36. Concerning the South Carolina aristocracy composed of landgraves and cassiques, see ibid., 37n.

14. B. R. White, *The English Baptists of the Seventeenth Century* (Didcot: Baptist Historical Society, 1996), 95–133. The grant was reissued in 1665. Samuel Wilson, *An Account of the Province of Carolina in America. Together with an Abstract of the Patent* (London: 1682), 22, 25 [arts. 7, 19].

15. *A Brief Description of the Province of Carolina on the Coasts of Floreda* (London, 1666), 6. Cf. William Hilton, *A Relation of a Discovery lately made on the Coast of Florida . . . Together with Proposals made by the Commissioners of the Lords Proprietors, to all such*

In 1669, The Fundamental Constitutions, drawn up by John Locke, Enlightenment philosopher and proponent of toleration, defined the structure of colonial self-governance and the extent of religious liberty. While restricting citizenship to theists and allowing the colonial parliament to grant public maintenance to the Church of England, covenanted churches were allowed to form, set their own terms of communion, and expect protection from disturbance or molestation.[16]

Revised in 1682, The Fundamental Constitutions retained their guarantees of religious liberty, furthering them in one important way: Dissenters could not be taxed to support the established church.[17] One of the Lords Proprietor, John Archdale, was active in both South Carolina and Maine as colonial governor. He was governor of Maine in 1691 and 1695, returning to Carolina each time. A moderate Quaker, Archdale was earlier driven from Maine by the New England authorities. A certain Baptist from Maine followed Archdale upon his final return to Carolina.[18]

William Screven, the Baptist from Maine, was the first Baptist pastor to settle among these dissenters. Originally from Somerton in western England, Screven signed the 1656 Somerset Confession drawn up by Thomas Collier. Collier has been described by his most recent biographer as a "political preacher" who conceived authority as deriving from "the Agreement of the people." Collier engaged the religious politics of both Levelers and Fifth Monarchists. Although a Particular Baptist messenger, Collier mitigated against hard-line Calvinism. In the mid-1650s, Screven surfaced as a disciple of Collier, helping Collier organize western Baptists.[19]

Screven next appeared in the governmental records of Maine and the church minutes of the Baptist church in Boston, Massachusetts. In 1676, he was named constable for lower Kittery, Maine, and served

---

persons as shall become the first Setlers on the Rivers, Harbors, and Creeks there (London, 1664), 34 [art. 18].

16. John Locke, *The Fundamental Constitutions of Carolina* (n.p: n.d.), 20–23 [arts. 95–106].

17. Sirmans, "Politics in Colonial South Carolina," 34–35.

18. Peter H. Wood, s.v. "Archdale, John (1642–1717)," *Oxford Dictionary of National Biography* (Oxford University Press, 2004).

19. Baker and Craven, *Adventure in Faith,* 33–40; Stephen Wright, s.v. "Collier, Thomas (*d.* 1691)," *Oxford Dictionary of National Biography* (Oxford: Oxford University Press, 2004). Collier's openness toward General Baptists may explain how Screven at first countenanced the fellowship of General Baptists with his own church.

on the grand jury in 1678 and 1679. Also in 1679, he signed a petition asking the king to grant "liberty to tender consciences" against the theocracy of Massachusetts. In 1682, he was licensed by the Boston church and soon constituted a Baptist church at Kittery by covenant.[20] He was called before the colonial courts because "Infant Baptisms hee sayd was an ordinance of the Devil." After sentencing by three successive courts, he avoided punishment by agreeing to leave the province. However, he changed his mind, ignored the courts, grew the Kittery church, and raised a prosperous family. After the temporary weakening of the Massachusetts theocracy in 1684, he occupied several important civil offices.

Over a decade later Screven immigrated to South Carolina along with several of his church members, purchasing a vast tract of land called Somerton. Screven's public weight, manifested in his ability to ignore the judgments of numerous courts, prompted Robert A. Baker, a meticulous historian, to conclude that "he and his church were not driven from Maine by Puritan persecution." Apparently, economic incentive and greater political influence compelled the move.[21]

Screven did not leave a corpus of extant writings, except for the occasional letter, covenant, or confession. However, from his life and in these fragments, the rudiments of a political theology are discernable. In terms reminiscent of revolutionary English Baptist thought, he identified Jesus Christ as "the Lord . . . the King of saints."[22] He believed that "the ministry of civil justice is an ordinance of God, and that it is the duty of the saints to be subject thereunto not only for fear, but for conscience sake, and that for such, prayers and supplications are to be made by the saints."[23] His disobedience toward the Massachusetts magistrates is best explained by his belief that royal authority was superior to colonial authority.

20. In line with the Collier tradition, the Kittery covenant affirmed the authority of Word and Spirit. They covenanted to keep the ordinances that are "revealed to us in his sacred word of ye ould & new Testament and according to ye grace of God & light att present through his grace given us, or here after he shall please to discover & make knowne to us thro his Holy Spirit to ye same blessed word." Quoted in Baker and Craven, *Adventure in Faith,* 60–61.

21. Robert A. Baker, "The Contributions of South Carolina Baptists to the Rise and Development of the Southern Baptist Convention," *Baptist History and Heritage* 17 (1982): 3.

22. Screven to Thomas Skinner, 13 September 1682, quoted in Baker and Craven, *Adventure in Faith,* 58.

23. *A Confession of the Faith of Several Churches of Christ in the County of Somerset, and of some Churches in the Counties neer adjacent* (London: 1656), art. 44, in William L. Lumpkin, ed., *Baptist Confessions of Faith,* rev. ed. (Valley Forge: Judson, 1969), 215.

A scrupulous man who was motivated by the desire to obey "all [Christ's] most holy & blessed Commandm.tts Ordinances Institutions or Appointments," Screven detected no conflict between holding ecclesiastical and civil offices simultaneously. Like many in his time, he believed God intimately directs the affairs of men: his ministry, even his health, were subject to being "cast" about "by providence."[24] In a series of letters to the Boston church in 1708, Screven reaffirmed his belief in Providence and surmised that God was punishing theocratic Boston with sickness for committing "the sin of persecution."[25]

Interestingly, two 1711 letters to the Euhaw church, closely affiliated with Screven's Charleston church, were sent from the South Moulton church in Devonshire, in response to the Euhaw church's query concerning slavery. The Devonshire and Somersetshire churches associated with one another in the days of Screven's English residence. The South Moulton church and the Western association of churches approved the institution of slavery since it was legalized "by the Majestrate." Screven seems to have countenanced the institution.[26]

The above information is available in the modern literature; however, an important letter which Screven authored has not been recognized. Moreover, a seminal struggle for religious liberty in South Carolina has been misunderstood if not misrepresented.[27] In 1704, a rogue governor and rump session of South Carolina's parliament tried to weaken their political opponents, many but not all of whom were dissenters, by establishing the Church of England. The two acts accomplishing this, adopted amidst scenes of acrimony and violence, were the Establishment Act and the Preservation Act.

---

24. Kittery Church Covenant; Baptist Church of Boston minutes, 11 January 1682; Screven to Skinner, 13 September 1682; quoted in Baker and Craven, *Adventure in Faith,* 53, 59, 60.

25. Screven to Baptist Church of Boston, 2 June 1707; Screven to Ellis Callender, 10 February 1708; Screven to Ellis Callender, 6 August 1708; quoted in Baker and Craven, *Adventure in Faith,* 86–90.

26. William G. McLoughlin and Winthrop D. Jordan, "Baptists Face the Barbarities of Slavery in 1710," *The Journal of Southern History* 29 (1962): 495–501. B. R. White, ed., *Association Records of the Particular Baptists of England, Wales and Ireland to 1660: Part 2. The West Country and Ireland* (London: Baptist Historical Society, 1973), 53. See also the Western association's negative position in 1655 and 1656 on government maintenance of Baptist ministers. Ibid., 62–66, 74–75. These associational meetings had representatives, including William Screven, from Somerton.

27. Joe M. King, whose research is otherwise helpful, naively claims that the Establishment Act, which was "first passed in 1704, was again adopted in 1706." King, *A History of South Carolina Baptists* (Columbia, S.C.: South Carolina Baptist Convention, 1964), 137.

The Establishment Act constituted six Berkeley county parishes, funded their buildings through voluntary gifts first and then the public treasury, made parochial charges payable by all inhabitants, and established a commission to govern the Anglican clergy. The Preservation Act, mirroring the occasional acts then seeking passage through England's Parliament, excluded from the colonial assembly those who would not receive the sacrament from or swear to the Church of England.

This created a firestorm of protest in both South Carolina and London. In 1705, Daniel Defoe wrote a treatise on behalf of the dissenters for presentation primarily to the House of Commons. Defoe identified "Party-Tyranny" with "High-Church-Tyranny" and asked the House of Commons to "defend the English Subjects from all manner of Invasions of their Liberty."[28] Petitions and petitioners arrived in quick succession from South Carolina.

In 1706, a small book, *The Case of Protestant Dissenters,* presented the dissenters' logic and relevant documents, not to the House of Commons, but to the House of Lords. The anonymous writer warned that dissenters, who are "above two Thirds of the Inhabitants of Carolina, as well as the most sober, orderly, and the richest, that is, the most Landed and Trading Men in the Province," have been unconstitutionally persecuted. If their religious liberty is not protected, then civil liberty will also be lost, not only in the colony but in England.[29]

In a brilliant move, the dissenters rejected the thesis of Defoe that establishment represented the views of the high church party in the Church of England. The dissenters appealed to the travails of the Charleston Anglican priest, Edward Marston, a nonjuror, as proof of the subversive nature of the South Carolina acts. They heightened the emotional appeal with accounts of dissenting nobles, such as Landgrave Thomas Smith, whose family included Baptists, being accosted in the streets by government rabble, an account of an Anglican minister being whipped by a government leader, and an account of the rape and murder of a pregnant woman. They also printed a letter from Lady Elizabeth Blake

28. "An Act for the Establishment of Religious Worship in this Province according to the Church of England," in *The Case of Protestant Dissenters in Carolina, Shewing How a Law to prevent Occasional Conformity There, has ended in the Total Subversion of the Constitution in Church and State* (London: 1706), Addenda, 44–55; "An Act for the more effectual Preservation of the Government of this Province," in ibid., Addenda, 38–41; Daniel Defoe, *Party-Tyranny or, An Occasional Bill in Miniature; As now Practiced in Carolina* (1705), in Alexander S. Salley, Jr., ed., *Narratives of Early Carolina 1650–1708* (New York: Scribner, 1911), 224.
29. *Case of Protestant Dissenters,* 4, 16–17.

concerning the tyranny of governance "by arbitrary power" as opposed to constitutional power.[30]

The dissenters also presented an affidavit signed by the leading Presbyterian minister, Archibald Stobo, and the Baptist minister, William Screven. Screven, whose name is listed first, reviewed a recent sermon on the fifth commandment by Marston, the high church minister in Charleston. Screven concurred with Marston's assertion that a minister did not owe an accounting to the government for his actions, even if he received a government stipend. He also agreed that Marston was due a maintenance "by divine right" and that a minister is superior to the government, "his Authority being from Christ." "We (ministers of the gospel) do not arrogate too much to our selves, nor take too much upon us, when we affirm, That we are superior to the People, and have an Authority over them in Things Spiritual, and appertaining to God."[31]

Although the lead proprietor, against the protests of the dissenting aristocracy, approved the new laws and defended them in print, the dissenters carried the day.[32] The House of Lords, upon reviewing the case, resolved that the Act of Establishment was "not warranted by the charter granted to the Proprietors" and that the Act of Preservation "is founded on falsity in matter of fact, is repugnant to the laws of England, contrary to the charter of the Proprietors, is an encouragement to atheism and irreligion, destructive to trade, and tends to the depopulation and ruin of the Province." In their address to Queen Anne, the House of Lords asked her to deliver South Carolina "from the arbitrary oppressions under which it now lies" since "the powers given by the crown have been abused by some of your subjects."

Queen Anne vowed to protect her Carolinian subjects "in their just rights," nullified the acts, and considered revoking the proprietary charter. The defeat of the conformists was complete. Even the Society for the Propagation of the Gospel in Foreign Parts, an Anglican missionary society formed to counter the influence of American dissenters, passed a resolution against the Act of Establishment. A Presbyterian historian

30. Ibid., Addenda, 42–44.

31. Bishop Ezekiel Hopkins's works are subsequently cited as authoritative in the matter. Ibid., Addenda, 55–56.

32. *An Account of the Fair and Impartial Proceedings of the Lords Proprietors, Governour and Council of the Colony of South Carolina* (1706). A petition by Joseph Boone and others entitled *The Case of the Church of England in Carolina* is referenced, but the document is not extant.

affirmed that "wise and religious men of all denominations" aided in breaking the colonial government.[33]

Subsequently, Blake's 1697 Act for Granting Liberty of Conscience was recognized as authoritative. The Acts of Preservation and Establishment and similar acts were "Repealed, Annulled, Revoked and forever made void." A new Act of Establishment was adopted in 1706 but under a severely chastened form. The Church of England was indeed established and its parish system received parliamentary definition, but the dissenting churches, though not established, were nevertheless protected. Moreover, the colony moved toward voluntary maintenance of the churches. An act from the sixth year of George II, which discussed the construction of St. George's parish church, mandated that the minister's stipend was to be funded by pew rents and by the expected gift of "any person or persons" of a glebe.[34] The charter's grant of religious liberty was again recognized by the colony in 1712.

By 1720, Baptists were celebrating marriage ceremonies in spite of Anglican complaints. By 1744, the Anglican clergy reluctantly affirmed the rights of such dissenters to "full Liberty of Conscience." When the General Baptists and Particular Baptists argued over the ownership of the Charleston church property in 1745, all parties appealed to the colonial assembly. The assembly judiciously rendered a split decision, seeking to satisfy the influential members of the First Baptist Church of Charleston. The only possible case of persecution after the 1704 debacle occurred shortly before 1772, when a Baptist preacher named Joseph Cates was publicly whipped. However, Cates was being punished for immorality—certainly not a *cause celebre* for religious liberty.

Moreover, at this time a visiting Anglican minister complained that dissenters dominated the colonial government and nobility. By 1790, although the parishes were still established, the limited ministerial maintenances which had been provided for a few of the original parishes in the 1706 revision were simply absented from the public laws. The 1712 blue law requiring attendance at some religious assembly on Sunday and the 1722 poor law requiring parochial maintenance of

33. Alexander Hewat, *An Historical Account of the Rise and Progress of the Colonies of South Carolina and Georgia* (London: 1779), 161–78. Cf. John Oldmixon, *The British Empire in America, Containing the History of the Discovery, Settlement, Progress and State of the British Colonies on the Continent and Islands of America* (London: 1741), 1:473–91.
34. Nicholas Trott, ed., *The Laws of the Province of South Carolina in Two Parts* (Charles-Town, 1736), 1:105–6, 127–44; 2:63.

public welfare remained but occasioned no comment. The oath of all public officers required the swearer to "maintain and defend the laws of God, the Protestant religion, and the liberties of America."[35] No South Carolina Baptist appears to have objected.

Eighteenth-century Baptists in South Carolina, under the leadership of Screven, who died at an advanced age in 1713, rose to the top of society and prospered within the colonial government. When their religious liberty was threatened, they formed alliances with Presbyterians, Quakers, and even nonjuror Anglicans to maintain a tolerable environment.

The Political Theology of Oliver Hart

After Screven's death the Charleston church entered a period of internecine struggle. The core of the church, composed of Particular Baptists, sought to fulfill Screven's desire that their next pastor subscribe to the Second London Confession. However, the Calvinist party vied both with a Unitarian-Arminian party and with a moderating party led by their next pastor, Thomas Simmons. The parties split into separate fellowships, but the Arminian and moderate fellowships declined and ultimately disappeared. The only pastoral ministry came from Isaac Chanler of the nearby Ashley River church, and when he died in December 1749, the Baptists of the area despaired. Providentially, however, Oliver Hart, a Baptist minister from the Philadelphia Association, having heard of the needs in Charleston, arrived by ship on the same day as Chanler's funeral. Discerning divine mercy, the Charleston church immediately called Hart as their pastor.[36]

Hart was shaped religiously not only by the Particular or Regular Baptist ethos of the Philadelphia Association but also by the revivalistic fervor of the Great Awakening. Hart was especially affected by George Whitefield's preaching and later invited him to speak in his church. One of his own preacher boys, Nicholas Bedgegood, managed Whitefield's Savannah orphanage. Whitefield's preaching, it is widely believed, by violating parish boundaries, created a democratic impulse that fostered

35. In 1730, the charter of the proprietors was revoked and the colony received royal protection. John Faucheraud Grimke, ed., *The Public Laws of the State of South-Carolina* (Philadelphia: 1790), 11–14, 17–21, 100, 117–18, 203, 297; Baker and Craven, *Adventure in Faith,* 107–21; Grimke, *Public Laws,* xxxv; King, *History of South Carolina Baptists,* 137–38.

36. Loulie Latimer Owens, "Oliver Hart, 1723–1795: A Brief Biography," *Baptist History and Heritage* 1 (1966): 21–25.

the American Revolution.[37] Hart may have supported the egalitarian impulses set loose by the Great Awakening, but he also maintained a traditional view of "ranks and orders."

In stark contrast with the disparaging picture of Virginia Baptists, the South Carolinian pastor was described thus by Richard Furman: "In his person he was somewhat tall, well proportioned, and of a graceful appearance; of an active, vigorous constitution, before it had been impaired by close application to his studies, and by his abundant labours; his countenance was open and manly, his voice clear, harmonious and commanding; the powers of his mind were strong and capacious, and enriched by a fund of useful knowledge; his taste was elegant and refined." As a result, Hart was highly respected by the wider Charleston community. Basil Manly noted that, having been robbed of 30 pounds in currency, the townspeople, not including Baptists, reimbursed Hart with 730 pounds. Manly rehearsed how Hart left the Charleston church with a phenomenal endowment of 14,700 pounds.

The cultured Hart developed irenic relations not only with Regular Baptists, General Baptists, Welsh Baptists, and Separate Baptists but also with Independents, Methodists, Presbyterians, and Anglicans. Hart was comfortable with wealthy citizens of all denominations in this premiere southern city. Being "elegant and refined" was obviously a prerequisite for the leading Baptist pastor in the high culture of late colonial Charleston.[38]

Hart's influence reaped political as well as social and financial rewards for the Baptists. He organized the first association of Baptist churches in the southern United States in 1751. This association furnished the exemplar for all future southern associations and state conventions and gave southern Baptists a comprehensive model of denominational cooperation. The Charleston Association's powers were carefully restricted to that of "a Council of Advice," but this did not prevent the association from promoting missions, ministerial education,

37. Nancy Ruttenburg, "George Whitefield, Spectacular Conversion, and the Rise of Democratic Personality," *American Literary History* 5 (1993): 429–58; Nathan O. Hatch, *The Democratization of American Christianity* (New Haven: Yale University Press, 1989), 56–57; Lambert, *The Founding Fathers and the Place of Religion in America,* 127–49.

38. Richard Furman, *Rewards of Grace Conferred on Christ's Faithful People: A Sermon, Occasioned by the Decease of the Rev. Oliver Hart, A.M.* (Charleston: 1796); Basil Manly, *Mercy and Judgment: A Discourse, Containing Some Fragments of the History of the Baptist Church in Charleston, S. C.* (Charleston: 1837), 34n, 45–46; Baker and Craven, *Adventure in Faith,* 133–35.

the adoption of a confession, the adoption of an official ecclesiology, and most importantly for our purposes, the advocacy of religious liberty. In 1775, the association sought contributions for Massachusetts Baptists in their struggle for effective religious liberty. In 1777, the association encouraged Baptist churches to incorporate themselves with the government. In 1779, the association delegated authority to Hart and two other leading ministers to "treat with government on behalf of the churches" and monitor the ministers in the area.[39]

In 1776 and 1777, Hart joined the leading Independent minister, William Tennent, to promote a multidenominational petition for a constitution that established all Protestant churches and provided full religious and civil liberty for all Protestants. A bill for the new constitution was published by the General Assembly of South Carolina on February 3, 1777. Two days later the Charleston Association issued a circular letter composed largely by Hart. Hart said the bill provided "universal religious liberty in this State" and included "reasonable and easy" terms which should be adopted by all the churches.

The bill detailed five beliefs that an established church must affirm in order to be "incorporated, and esteemed as a Church of the established religion of this state." All Christian denominations were deemed equal; the clergy were given basic instructions on piety and performance; voluntary giving was recognized as the only means of support; and clergy were placed on the same level as laity, except that they were barred from government office.

A week later, in a private letter to Richard Furman, Hart opined that Baptists should look to the state to grant "all our Privileges, civil and religious." His only fear was that some of the Separate Baptists might not "unite together in one band" in order to have more influence on the state. One Virginia ideologue deemed this constitution "a definite limitation on liberty of conscience," but Hart, the leading Baptist in eighteenth-century South Carolina, was rather enthusiastic.[40]

39. King, *History of South Carolina Baptists,* 62–68; Baker and Craven, *Adventure in Faith,* 149–54.

40. "*First,* That there is one eternal God, and a future state of rewards and punishments. *Second,* That God is to be publickly worshiped. *Third,* the Christian Religion is the true religion. *Fourth,* That the Holy Scriptures of the Old and New Testament, are divinely inspired, and are the rule of faith and practice. *Fifth,* That it is lawful, and the duty of every man being thereunto called by those that govern, to bear witness to the truth." *A Bill for Establishing the Constitution of the State of South Carolina* (Charlestown: 1777), 14, 19–23. Hart to Furman, 12 February 1777. Baker and Craven, *Adventure in Faith,* 167–71.The primary source ma-

Hart was a fervent advocate of the American Revolution. His cousin, John Hart, signed the Declaration of Independence for New Jersey. Hart himself scouted British military activities in New York, and upon his return to Charleston, was deputed by the Council of Safety for a special task. Along with Tennent and William-Henry Drayton, subsequently president of the South Carolina Congress, Hart traveled to "the back country" to represent the revolutionary cause and counter the influence of Tories and pacifists upon the Separate Baptists. Hart's commission referred to him as a "lover of constitutional liberty." For his largely successful services, he was publicly recognized by the provincial congress in November 1775.

Unfortunately, the British troops also recognized Hart's contributions, and when they occupied Charleston, the Baptist properties were used to store salt beef and forage. Hart fled the city to the home of his daughter, who had married Captain Thomas Screven. He subsequently fled northward from the advancing British troops, ending his days as pastor of a New Jersey church.[41]

Hart advocated the political theology of the South Carolina tradition not only in deed but also in print. His diaries and letters are filled with references to the guidance of divine Providence over the affairs of individual men and of nations, in war and in peace. In the same paragraph he could refer both to the constitutional deliberations of men and to their utter dependence on God. "After all, nothing can save us but the Interposition of the great Governor of the Universe; in Him may we place all our Confidence and may He mercifully condescend to help a sinful People." Hart not only correlated divine Providence with constitutionality, he also correlated the emergence of civil liberty with religious liberty. The "perfect form of Government" is that in which "the best of Rulers [are] chosen by ourselves." In the context of the expected establishment of civil liberty, religion, "encouraged and promoted, shall spread far and wide."[42]

In 1767, he led the Charleston Association to adopt the Philadelphia Confession of Faith, an expansion of the Second London Confession. The Charleston Confession defined divine Providence as God bounding,

---

terials printed by Baker for this period are helpful, but his commentary reflects the Virginia tradition.

41. *Extracts from the Journals of the Provincial Congress of South-Carolina* (Charlestown: 1776), 164; Manly, *Mercy and Judgment,* 44; Owens, "Oliver Hart," 31–33; King, *History of South Carolina Baptists,* 91–95, 139–40.

42. Oliver Hart to Joseph Hart, 5 July 1778; Oliver Hart to Joseph Hart, 16 February 1779; quoted in Baker and Craven, *Adventure in Faith,* 170–73.

governing, and ordering creation "in a manifold dispensation." As the "first Cause," God uses "Means" or "second Causes, either necessarily, freely, or contingently," thereby preserving his holiness while advancing his will. Providence delivers judgment on the wicked and both mercy and judgment upon the elect "for their good." Christian liberty is spiritual in nature: "Freedom from the Guilt of Sin." Liberty of conscience means, "God alone is Lord of the Conscience, and hath left it free from the Doctrines and Commandments of Men which are in any Thing contrary to his Word, or not contained in it." As for the civil magistrate, God has ordained them to be "under him, over the People, for his own Glory, and the publick Good."[43]

In a fascinating sermon published by the Philadelphia Association, Hart envisioned the perfect religio-political society. The text was Haggai 2:4, and the central figures were "the King of Saints," followed by first, "a prince," second, "an high priest," and last, "the people." The ordering is not merely textual but theological. Repeatedly, Hart cited "the several ranks and orders of men in the christian church." First, he considered "the civil magistrate," whose office "is by no means incompatible with true piety and church-membership." Indeed, pious magistrates, like King David or King Solomon or Constantine the Great, are "nursing fathers" who believe the work of the church is "their main concern." The work of the civil magistrate is to "protect and defend" the church, "attend" worship as an example to others, "contribute chearfully and liberally," and revere ministers of the church as "ambassadors of Christ."

However, magistrates also have limits with regard to the church. In general, they "have no power in, or over the church, by virtue of civil office." Specifically, "1. They have not authority to enact laws to bind the consciences of men," since "Christ is the sole Lord of conscience." "2. They have no coercive power to compel men to be of this, that, or the other religion; or to worship God in any way, contrary to their own free and voluntary consent." "3. Neither have magistrates any right to impose taxes on church members, or any others, for the support of religion."

Hart next sketched the responsibilities of pastors and deacons and, finally, ordinary church members. His social ordering is reminiscent of

43. *A Confession of Faith Put forth by the Elders and Brethren of many Congregations of Christians (Baptized upon Profession of their Faith) in London and the Country. Adopted by the Baptist Association met at Philadelphia, Sept. 25, 1742,* 6th ed. (Philadelphia: 1743), 26–30, 75–77, 86–87.

the medieval great chain of being. The "Lord of Hosts" exceeds angels who exceed rulers who exceed other men. Although he would not allow any man to "arrogate the title of Head of the church, or vicar of Christ," Hart called rulers, "the vicegerents of Almighty God!"[44]

What was the influence of Oliver Hart? The leading Southern Baptists of the next generation were extensive in their praise. Numerous ministers in the south and a few in the north were ordained and/or educated by this pastor. Edmund Botsford called him "my honored Father." Basil Manly gave him the greatest compliment a Baptist could receive: "While his great end in life was the glory of God, he viewed the salvation of sinners as a principal means of promoting it." Richard Furman honored the life and ministry of "that venerable and excellent man of God" with a printed sermon. Furman noted the careful interconnections and distinctions of the relationship between politics and religion as taught by Hart.

On the one hand, Hart sought "to preserve his *political liberty,* with which he found his *religious [liberty]* intimately connected." He loved liberty and pursued the rights of his country "against the encroachments of arbitrary power." "Yet he did not mix politics with the gospel, nor desert the duties of his station to pursue them; but attending to each in its proper place, he gave weight to his political sentiments, by the propriety and uprightness of his conduct; and the influence of it was felt by many." Furman concluded with this lament, "The loss of such a father demands a tear on *your* part, but on *his [part],* you have reason to rejoice."[45]

Where William Screven brought South Carolina Baptists governmental influence, Oliver Hart taught Baptists how politics and religion might be "intimately connected" without being improperly mixed, on both the national and local levels.

The Political Theology of Richard Furman

After Oliver Hart's departure, the church looked to the Charleston Association to provide ministerial leadership. They offered the pulpit to Richard Furman, who was then pastor at High Hills of Santee, but

44. Oliver Hart, *An Humble Attempt to Repair the Christian Temple* (Philadelphia: 1795), 3–5, 7–12, 40, 45.

45. Manly, *Mercy and Judgment,* 34; Furman, *Rewards of Grace,* 7, 22, 26–27; Baker and Craven, *Adventure in Faith,* 183; Owens, "Oliver Hart," 28–29.

he declined. Later, however, Furman surmounted the difficulties of the move "by the clear convictions of duty in his own mind, and he accepted the call." Manly reckoned that Furman's pastorate represents "the most important period of the church's history."[46] Furman's political theology had three major aspects. First, he considered all human events to be the outworking of divine Providence. Second, divine approval of human authority is granted only through a constitution based upon human consent. Third, God has providentially ordained the structures of society, and it is a human duty to live within those structures.

First, in his sermon commemorating the life of George Washington, Furman asserted that God "speaks to man in afflicting dispensations" and exercises "special interposition in favor of the just and innocent." God is "the great Arbiter of heaven and earth," who directs "all events, both of the moral and natural world," with regard to individuals and to nations. Although some have tried, it is "impiety, folly, and madness" to oppose Providence. Rather, "let us learn sincere and humble resignation" to him. With Washington, Furman believed the armies of the Revolution succeeded under "the divine auspices" or "the patronage of Heaven." Indeed, "genuine and enlarged liberty, both civil and religious, brought about by the revolution, and . . . constitutionally established" are due to "God's moral government." Therefore, the new nation can be called "our American Israel." Our "sacred duty" is to preserve those "rights and privileges" which accompany constitutional liberty.

However, every nation is subject to judgment, and "the grand schemes of Providence" will be revealed only at the end of time. Although Furman warned against mistaking the human instrument for the divine provider, he lauded the virtues of Washington. These virtues included the classic virtue of justice, the Christian virtue of piety, and the Machiavellian virtue of magnanimity. Of course, the president's greatest virtue was his piety. Although Washington may not have been as public with his faith as desired, Furman believed he was "acquainted with the sublime doctrines of christianity, and their gracious, experimental influence on the heart."[47]

46. In 1787, the church petitioned the state legislature to grant the church property entirely to the Calvinist group which had incorporated. The petition was granted by the state, and the city, moreover, withdrew its claims to part of the property after Furman spoke to them. Furman then led his church to formally "frame constitutional rules and by-laws" ensuring congregational governance. Manly, *Mercy and Judgment,* 52–54.

47. Furman envisioned a dynamic interplay between divine sovereignty and human responsibility. Although he extolled the surety of Providence, he also demanded human action. "What exertions should we not make, to obtain an interest in the justifying righteousness, atoning

The second aspect of Furman's political theology states that the only legitimate authority is constitutional. General Richard Richardson printed and distributed a 1775 address by young Furman advancing the revolutionary cause. In the address Furman defended the actions of the American Congress in opposing the unlawful authority of king and parliament. If a person does not object to another man's exercise of unlawful authority, "I then submit to his unlimited power over me; and by my own consent, he has a right to lay upon me, what he pleases." Inaction itself results, therefore, in the grant of authority.

In a unique reading of Romans 13, Furman subjected the king to the constitution. The "peace and happiness of the people" is guaranteed by the principles of the British "Constitution," which is a "mixt monarchy, where the King and People make laws. The people do this by their representatives, whom they choose." Representative law then becomes binding upon the people. However, by ignoring colonial representation, the British had "broken the principles of the constitution, by taking away the power of our Assemblies." In order to preserve the constitution, the American colonies opposed London's Parliament. Such rebellion is not rejection of the King's "lawful authority," for "what the King does, contrary to the constitution, is not the power, that is of God, spoken of in Scripture, and therefore ought not to be obeyed."

In other words, legitimate authority is divinely granted by the people through a constitution. Since America only seeks to preserve constitutional liberty, any who oppose her may incur "divine displeasure." Moreover, by submitting to the British, Americans will "bind yourselves, unde[r] the sway of Arbitrary power." In the end God will judge rightly all human actions, but in the meanwhile those who support the British "conspire against the liberty of Conscience, and would extinguish that precious jewel out of the constitution."[48]

Furman's regard for constitutionality, based on popular consent and resulting in legitimate authority, reappeared throughout his writings

---

blood, and living intercession of the adorable Redeemer, who is the resurrection and the life; and to be found faithful in his service." Furman, *Humble Submission to Divine Sovereignty the Due of a Bereaved Nation: A Sermon Occasioned by the Death of His Excellency General George Washington* (Charleston: 1800), *passim.* Cf. Henry Holcombe, *A Sermon Occasioned by the Death of Lieutenant-General George Washington, Late President of the United States of America* (Savannah: 1800).

48. Furman, *An Address to the Residents Between the Broad and Saluda Rivers Concerning the American War for Independence* (November 1775), printed in James A. Rogers, *Richard Furman: Life and Legacy* (Macon: Mercer University Press, 2001), 268–73.

and drove both his civil and his ecclesiastical politics. From 1784 to 1790, Furman tried to convince the Charleston Association to incorporate itself so that it might receive and disburse educational funds. Other associational leaders at first cautiously supported the idea. However, it soon became apparent there was substantial opposition. Prominent pastors such as Edmund Botsford and Evan Pugh worried the advisory character of the association might be lost. Subsequently, Furman convinced the pastors to support the incorporation of a General Committee affiliated with the association but with no authority over the independent churches. Jesse Mercer, the future leader of Georgia Baptists, was the first beneficiary of Furman's efforts.[49]

In 1790, Furman was elected to represent Charleston at the Constitutional Convention of South Carolina. The 1778 constitution, of which Hart had been an active proponent, was considered a temporary measure. When the convention assembled in May, Furman was asked to "perform divine services in the Convention Chamber," a request he fulfilled and for which he received accolades. However, when the convention discussions began, an objection was raised against the presence of Furman and four other Baptist ministers and one Anglican priest among the delegates. The 1778 constitution had explicitly denied civil offices to the clergy.

But Furman argued that ministers were indeed qualified to serve in such roles, especially when elected by the people. As Johnson reports, "He repudiated the principle of disenfranchising a class of citizens on the ground of their consecration to holy office." His opponent disagreed, expressing concern that clerical influence might be too great. Furman's opponent prevailed, and ministers were barred from holding state offices. Hart's victories in securing incorporation and "free exercise" for the churches were affirmed, but the language of establishment was dropped. Moreover, liberty of conscience was retained, but this liberty was not to "be so construed as to excuse acts of licentiousness, or justify practices inconsistent with the peace or safety of this state." Charles Pinckney presided over the 1790 convention.[50]

---

49. Rogers, *Richard Furman,* 118–23.

50. *A Bill for Establishing the Constitution,* 14; *The Constitutions of the Sixteen States which Compose the Confederated Republic of America, According to the Latest Amendments* (Newburg: 1800), 219, 222, 224; William B. Johnson, "Biographical Sketch of Dr. Richard Furman," *Annals of the American Baptist Pulpit* (New York: 1860), 163; Zaqueu Moreira de Oliveira, "Richard Furman, Father of the Southern Baptist Convention," in William R. Estep,

Furman believed the church could use state resources and should influence civil government. In his early days as a preacher, he attempted to preach in the Camden courthouse. The sheriff barred him from doing so, and some bystanders became irate, but Furman quietly drew the people to an open field. Impressed with his demeanor and delivery, "the most respectable persons" made certain he could preach from the courthouse in the future. During the war he was such a proponent of the revolution that Lord Cornwallis offered a large reward for "so notorious [a] rebel." In the 1800 presidential race, it will be recalled that the infidel Thomas Jefferson was the Republican candidate for religious liberty while John Adams and his running mate, Charles Pinckney, ran on the Federalist platform of religious orthodoxy. Furman and Pinckney had a longstanding relationship, and Furman publicly supported Pinckney's own subsequent candidacy for the presidency. Thus, the Danbury Baptists under Leland and the Charleston Baptists under Furman found themselves political opposites.

In 1801 Furman led his association to petition the South Carolina House of Representatives to allow slaves a measure of religious liberty. In 1804 Furman preached before two civil societies concerning the death of Alexander Hamilton in a duel. "The address began as a sermon, continued as a eulogy, and concluded as an attack against dueling, with a call to abolish it by law." Again, Furman led the Charleston Association to petition the legislature to abolish dueling. Upon his return from an 1814 convention, Furman traveled through Washington, D.C. After a conversation with James Monroe, he was invited to preach before the president, foreign ambassadors, and numerous other dignitaries. He boldly proclaimed from Acts 22:16 their need to "arise and be baptized." In 1822, he addressed the governor of South Carolina concerning the issue of slavery on behalf of the Baptist Convention of South Carolina. Simultaneously, the convention sought a government-led "Day of Humiliation, Prayer, and Thanksgiving."[51]

ed., *The Lord's Free People in a Free Land: Essays in Baptist History in Honor of Robert A. Baker* (Fort Worth: Faculty of the School of Theology, 1976), 92; Rogers, *Richard Furman,* 69–70.

51. De Oliveira, "Richard Furman," 92; Rogers, *Richard Furman,* 71–72, 163–64, 210–11; Furman *et ux* to South Carolina, Records of the General Assembly, 1801; Lambert, *Founding Fathers and the Place of Religion in America,* 274–85; James Pickett Wesberry, *Baptists in South Carolina Before the War Between the States* (Columbia: Bryan, 1966), 46, 60–63.

Furman's constitutionalism also influenced the development of ecclesiastical polity. In 1814, Furman was elected the first president of the newly formed "General Missionary Convention of the Baptist Denomination in the United States of America for Foreign Missions," popularly known as the Triennial Convention. Furman and his protégé, Johnson, were elected to a fifteen-member constitutional committee during the first session of the convention. After an 1813 meeting with Luther Rice, the premier proponent of American Baptist missions, Johnson had prepared a constitution for the event. However, the committee began to debate and was reduced to five members. Furman was retained, but Johnson was dropped.

The constitutional debate concerned whether the new convention would follow the multidimensional, church-based associational model or the single-task, broader-membership society model. Furman advocated the associational model but temporarily acquiesced to the convention's adoption of a society model. The convention organized only for the foreign mission, but Furman expected the convention to address eventually the home mission and "deeply regretted" that more attention was not paid to ministerial education.[52]

A greater disappointment occurred, however, when Luther Rice and the Board of Foreign Missions tried to enact Furman's plans for a national seminary without proper planning and without constitutional authority. Concerned with this "hasty" and unauthorized procedure, Furman led the Charleston Association to object publicly. Ultimately, Furman's wisdom was vindicated, and Rice suffered severe criticism for his financial missteps with Columbian College. In 1821, Furman developed the constitutional principles of the first state convention of Baptists, that of South Carolina. In 1822, he and Johnson dominated the convention committee which drafted the new constitution. Furman, Johnson, and Manly successfully defended the polity of the new state convention with its comprehensive embrace of missions, education, and other endeavors against its Baptist detractors. Created under divine

52. Address concerning the formation of the Triennial Convention, in *Proceedings of the Baptist Convention for Missionary Purposes* (Philadelphia: 1814), 38–43; cited in H. Leon McBeth, ed., *A Sourcebook for Baptist Heritage* (Nashville: Broadman, 1990), 209–10. Rogers, *Richard Furman,* 148–61; Robert Andrew Baker, *Relations Between Northern and Southern Baptists* ([n.p.]: 1948), 12–14; W. W. Barnes, *The Southern Baptist Convention, 1845–1953* (Nashville: Broadman, 1954), 1–11.

Providence, this constitution formed the basis for that of the Southern Baptist Convention.[53]

The third aspect in Furman's political theology concerns social order and personal duty. Furman believed that Providence compelled the definition of freedom in terms of constitutional power. Providence then required men to fulfill their duties according to their social order. In an 1802 sermon entitled *America's Deliverance and Duty,* Furman rehearsed his doctrines of Providence and of constitutionalism, and began developing his doctrine of duty. The sermon enlarged two truths: "the American revolution was effected by the special agency of God," and certain "duties and obligations are incumbent on our citizens, in consequence of his kind interposition."

The duties of the American citizenry include expressing gratitude to God, securing and improving his blessings, and relying on his Providence in the future. The best means of securing the nation is "a strict attention to religion." This did not mean the establishment of a national religion by civil authority but personal attention to religion by the people. If the people reject Christ, then they will incur divine wrath and endanger the American Revolution. Religion leads to virtue which leads to "real happiness" in the individual and in the body politic. In order to prevent national sin, Furman provided a litany of cures, including strict adherence to the constitution, respecting constitutional authorities, electing only virtuous leaders, and maintaining the love of liberty.[54]

In a circular letter, "On Religious and Civil Duties," Furman rehearsed a similar list of duties required of those who have received "civil and religious liberty." He also reviewed parental responsibilities in educating children and servants. This is a matter to which "much attention, therefore, should be bestowed." Furman believed that Scripture clearly taught the "station and duties of servants." Since Providence "has placed them in that situation," servants must learn to obey "as to the Lord." Likewise, masters are obligated "to rule their servants with justice and moderation; to afford them a reasonable portion of the com-

53. De Oliveira, "Furman Rogers," 94–95; Rogers, *Richard Furman,* 179–96, 231–43, 305–8; Hortense Woodson, *Giant in the Land: A Biography of William Bullein Johnson, First President of the Southern Baptist Convention* (Nashville: Broadman, 1950), 45–49.

54. Richard Furman, *America's Deliverance and Duty: A Sermon Preached at the Baptist Church* (Charleston: 1802), in *Life and Works of Dr. Richard Furman, D.D.* (Harrisonburg, Va.: Sprinkle Publications, 2004), 389–408. Thanks to Tom Nettles for his assistance in acquiring this text. See also Thomas J. Nettles, "Richard Furman," in Timothy George and David S. Dockery, eds., *Baptist Theologians* (Nashville: Broadman, 1995), 140–64.

forts, as well as necessaries of life; and to regard with seriousness their religious interests, as of persons who are placed by the Divine government under their care and direction."[55]

It is with that unique institution, slavery, that Furman's political theology becomes troubling. Furman himself was ambivalent about the institution. Southern evangelicals went through several phases concerning slavery. Until approximately 1800, many criticized slavery. Between 1800 and 1820, they began to cooperate with it. Finally, between 1820 and 1845, they began to defend it.[56] Furman reflects this same transition. Early in the nineteenth century, Furman said slavery was "undoubtedly an evil." In 1821, Manly said it was introduced "from motives of avarice" and considered it "repugnant to the spirit of our republican institutions."[57] But after the Denmark Vesey uprising in the summer of 1822, South Carolina Baptists reevaluated their position.

In a December 1822 communication to the governor of South Carolina, Furman's concept of order solidified. Citizens were reminded of "the government of the Deity," that he dispensed both "mercies" and the "chastening rod." Furman defended slavery from the Old and New Testaments, simultaneously affirming that slaves are men. "In things purely spiritual, they appear to have enjoyed equal privileges; but their relationship, as masters and slaves, were not dissolved." Indeed, the apostles enjoined obedience on the part of slaves. Although Christians live under the Golden Rule, "this rule is never to be urged against the order of things, which the Divine government has established."

Moreover, slavery need not be cruel and unjust. For example, Furman himself treated his slaves as if he were their "father." The Africans, moreover, were enslaved under constitutional principles, "by their own consent." By this, he meant they had become enslaved through their own customs of war with other Africans. Freedom is not a permanent right "when that right is forfeited, or has been lost" in this way. (With this coercive definition of consent, Furman's otherwise attractive system loses its coherence.) Furman was interested in their salvation and saw slavery

55. Furman, "On Religious and Civil Duties" (1800), in *Life and Works of Dr. Richard Furman*, 545–49.
56. Marty G. Bell, "The Beginnings of the Southern Baptist Convention, 1845," *Baptist History and Heritage* 30 (1995): 18–19.
57. Loulie Latimer Owens, *Saints of Clay: The Shaping of South Carolina Baptists* (Columbia: Bryan, 1971), 70–71.

as the means by which Africans were introduced to Christianity.[58] This leading Baptist pastor and patriarch ruled many blacks in his church and his family. Not only was he called "Father" by child and slave, he was titled "Our Beloved Father" by his peers and has been named "Father of the Southern Baptist Convention."[59]

Political Theology at the Foundation of the Southern Baptist Convention

Finally, summarily considered is the political theology of two founding leaders of the Southern Baptist Convention, both of whom represent the South Carolina tradition: Basil Manly Sr., a successor of Furman and leader of Alabama Baptists, and William B. Johnson, a coworker of Furman and leader of South Carolina Baptists. These men considered themselves heirs of the South Carolina tradition. Johnson wrote a biography of Furman, and Manly detailed the contributions of Screven, Hart, and Furman in his monumental history of the Charleston church. Manly and Johnson, among many others, absolutely revered Richard Furman.

Basil Manly Sr. worked alongside Furman in associational endeavors until the latter's death. He was afterward called to serve as pastor of the First Baptist Church of Charleston. In his history of this church, *Judgment and Mercy,* Manly reiterated Furman's doctrines of divine Providence and duty. In Psalm 101, David sang of God's mercy and judgment, which Manly took to be "very important principles of government." Mercy is God's "benevolence to sinners"; judgment concerns the "mysterious and afflictive" acts of the sovereign God. The dialectic of divine mercy and judgment provides a theology of history not only for churches but for states. Church history is the record "of those mysterious, but wise dispensations of Providence, in which mercy and judgment are blended."

Rehearsing history encourages Christians to fulfill their "duty" and adjust their course "to the methods of his mercy and judgment." History helps Baptists fulfill their duty by furnishing direction, imposing restraints, supplying powerful motive, and promoting perseverance.

58. Furman, *Exposition of the Views of the Baptists Relative to the Coloured Population of the United States* (Charleston: 1822), in Rogers, *Richard Furman,* 274–86.
59. De Oliveira, "Richard Furman," 87, 95.

Manly apparently believed history was scaling new heights with "a call in providence for our churches . . . to send the gospel among the heathen" through the Baptist convention.[60]

Manly left the Charleston church to become a university president, plantation owner, and the leading figure among Alabama Baptists. Having been led to Christ by a slave, he encouraged his slaves to become Christians. He also encouraged them to submit to the design of Providence in establishing the social order into which they were providentially born. He helped found the Southern Baptist Convention in Augusta, Georgia, in 1845 after being publicly abused by a northern abolitionist. He could "agree to disagree" with the moderate northerner Francis Wayland and "by love to serve one another." But he believed the abolitionist movement intractably violated Baptist principles, forcing an undesirable separation. He authored the Alabama resolutions which prompted the Acting Board of the Triennial Convention to deny convention authority. The Convention had repeatedly resolved that slavery should not be addressed, but the Acting Board finally admitted it would "never be a party to any arrangement which would imply approbation of slavery."[61]

Manly later assisted in the foundation of the Southern Baptist Theological Seminary. On February 18, 1861, he attended the inauguration of Jefferson Davis as president of the Confederate States of America, consecrating Davis to his office. Manly supported the Confederate war effort wholeheartedly, even authoring patriotic tracts.[62]

William Bullein Johnson's local ministry encompassed Georgia and South Carolina and both ecclesiastical and educational institutions, but his greatest impact was on the national stage. He was trained as a lawyer and had an organizational outlook. It has been said that Furman's "mantle fell squarely upon him." In 1809, he organized the First Baptist Church of Columbia, South Carolina. In 1813, he led the Savannah Baptist Society for Foreign Missions to adopt a constitution in which

60. Manly, *Mercy and Judgment,* 3–7, 59. Manly developed a series of twenty-one "Sermons on Duty." Cf. "Notes of a Sermon Delivered by Rev. Basil Manly, D.D. at Pleasant Grove Church, Fayette Co., Ala., April 8th, 1849," in Thomas J. Nettles, *Southern Baptist Sermons on Sovereignty and Responsibility* (Harrisonburg, Va.: Sprinkle, 1984), 7–32.

61. G. Thomas Halbrooks, "Francis Wayland: Influential Mediator in the Baptist Controversy Over Slavery," *Baptist History and Heritage* 13 (1978): 21–35.

62. A. James Fuller, *Chaplain to the Confederacy: Basil Manly and Baptist Life in the Old South* (Baton Rouge: Louisiana State University Press, 2000), 1, 292–97; Basil Manly, *The Young Deserter* (ca. 1861–1865; North Carolina Collection, University of North Carolina at Chapel Hill).

the famous terminology of "elicit, combine and direct" first appeared. Although a proponent of church independence, he also believed church union could occur without endangering freedom, to the point of even advocating the administration of baptism and the Lord's Supper at associational and convention meetings. He believed that churches could make a "judicious concentration" of their energies in "one sacred effort" to bring in the kingdom of God through missions and education.

Johnson provided the proforma constitutions for the Triennial, South Carolina, and Southern Baptist Conventions. He served each convention as president and was the first president of the Southern Baptist Convention. Johnson perpetuated Furman's doctrine of constitutionalism in these conventions.[63] Although it has been chic to bash Southern Baptists for breaking with northern Baptists over the failed doctrine of slavery, scholars have recently come to question such a simple answer. Although the cultural issue was indeed slavery, the critical issue was based on polity, specifically the north's flagrant violation of constitutional principles.[64]

The South Carolina tradition of political theology, which reached its apex in Richard Furman, impacted far more than Johnson and Furman. Further soundings could be made into the lives and writings of Jesse Mercer of Georgia, Richard Fuller of South Carolina, James P. Boyce of South Carolina, Basil Manly Jr. of Alabama, Jeremiah B. Jeter of Virginia, and James B. Taylor of Virginia—all of whom were early Southern Baptist Convention leaders. Each of these leading churchmen give evidence of the South Carolina understanding of political theology through the lens of Providence, constitutionality, and social order. It would be difficult to exaggerate the importance of the South Carolina tradition to Southern Baptist foundations. Robert A. Baker, a leading Southern Baptist church historian of yesteryear, cited approvingly the statement by W. W. Barnes, another leading Southern Baptist church

63. Wesberry, *Baptists in South Carolina Before the War Between the States,* 63–66; William B. Willis, "William Bullein Johnson," *Baptist History and Heritage* 1 (1965): 24–26; James M. Morton Jr., "Leadership of W. B. Johnson in the Formation of the Southern Baptist Convention," *Baptist History and Heritage* 5 (1970): 3–12, 55; Joe M. King, "William Bullein Johnson," *Baptist History and Heritage* 6 (1971): 76–79; Gregory A. Wills, *The First Baptist Church of Columbia, South Carolina, 1809 to 2002* (Nashville: Fields Publishing, 2003), 1–21, 26–37.

64. Bell, "The Beginnings of the Southern Baptist Convention," 16–24; H. Leon McBeth, "The Broken Unity of 1845: A Reassessment," *Baptist History and Heritage* 24 (1989): 24–31, 48.

historian, that the First Baptist Church of Charleston is "holy ground" for Southern Baptists.[65]

Traditions and Iconography

Which is the major tradition, and which is the minor tradition in Southern Baptist political theology? Is the Virginia tradition a myth and the South Carolina tradition the reality? Is Southern Baptist political theology best characterized by a wall of separation or by an intimate yet unmixed connection between church and state? Perhaps the answer depends on the particular historian or ideologue being asked. Iconography speaks volumes about historiography and ideology, two troublesome disciplines due to their subtly deceptive interdependence. Of "The Ten Most Influential Baptists" identified by the Baptist History & Heritage Society, the first three icons represent the Virginia tradition, but the South Carolina tradition is not represented whatsoever. Of the twenty-one Southern Baptists represented on the portico frieze of the central rotunda at Southwestern Baptist Theological Seminary, four directly represent the South Carolina tradition, and the Virginia tradition is not represented whatsoever. The only icon in both places signifies E. Y. Mullins.[66]

In the case of political theology, the icon of Mullins represents the correct position: we need both traditions. Southern Baptists must maintain the separation of church and state; however, they must also speak prophetically to individuals, social institutions, and the state, and they should expect protection from the state when doing so.

65. Baker, "The Contributions of South Carolina Baptists to the Rise and Development of the Southern Baptist Convention," 2–9, 19. Cf. J. Glen Clayton, "South Carolina Shapers of Southern Baptists," *Baptist History and Heritage* 17 (1982): 10–19.
66. Pamela R. Durso, "The Ten Most Influential Baptists," http://www.baptisthistory.org/contissues/durso.htm, accessed 30 August 2005; W. W. Barnes, "Biographical Sketches of the Twenty One Southern Baptists Represented on the Portico Frieze" (Fleming Library Paper, Southwestern Baptist Theological Seminary, March 1950).

Chapter 5

The Role of Religious Liberty in the Founding and Development of America

Richard D. Land

There is perhaps no more important subject for us to discuss as Christians in America in the first decade of the twenty-first century than religious liberty. In order to gain a clearer understanding of who we are as a people, we need to revisit the role of religious liberty in the founding and development of America. If we are going to examine the role of religious liberty in the founding and development of America, we have to talk about Baptists' role in weaving the principle of religious liberty into America's founding documents.

This notion of religious liberty is critical to the uniqueness of our nation. The English author G. K. Chesterton said that America is "a nation with the soul of a church."[1] You cannot understand America unless you understand that America has been, is, and certainly gives every indication that it will continue to be a religious country.

As an indication of that fact, I cite a recent poll from the Pew Global Attitudes Project. This poll found that 59 percent of Americans believe that religion is very important in their lives.[2] In a separate study the Pew Center revealed nearly 87 percent of Americans believe in God and think he is important.[3]

The Global Attitudes poll found that 30 percent of Canadians believe religion is important in their lives. In Great Britain, only 33 percent of the respondents agreed with the statement. Not surprisingly, only 11 percent of French citizens view religion as having an impact on their

1. *The Collected Works of G. K. Chesterton* (San Francisco: Ignatius, 1990), 21:41–45.
2. The Pew Global Attitudes Project, "Among Wealthy Nations . . . U.S. Stands Alone in its Embrace of Religion," Pew Research Center for the People and the Press (2002).
3. Pew Research Center for the People and the Press, "The 2004 Political Landscape" (2003).

daily lives. Yet in Poland, 36 percent of those polled believe religion is very important in their lives. In Mexico, 57 percent agreed with the assertion. Over 90 percent of Nigerians say religion is very important in their lives.[4] In their view of religion and its role in their lives, it appears that Americans have less in common with Canada and Western Europe and more in common with the rest of the world.

Findings like this drive the modernists and the postmodernists crazy because one of the central tenets of modernity is that as a society develops, its populace, becoming more educated and more affluent, ceases to be as religious. America is a pulsating, living, vibrant *denial* of that central tenet of modernity. Americans have been, and continue to be, a religious people. In a climate of religious freedom that was insisted upon by our Baptist forebears, religion has flourished in America.

Religious liberty is perhaps the unique Baptist contribution to the Reformation. Baptists believe salvation is by grace alone through faith alone, but then so did Luther and all of the Reformers. Baptists believe in the absolute veracity and authority of Holy Scripture, but then of course so did the Congregationalists, Lutherans, Calvinists, and even the Anglican reformers. However, if you consider that there was a right wing to the Reformation and a center and a left wing to the Reformation, Baptists anchored the left wing of the Reformation primarily because they jettisoned church-state union in favor of religious freedom and soul liberty.

I am a Baby Boomer. I was in elementary school in the mid 1950s. During that time, when I was in the first or second grade, the government began issuing identification tags, dog tags, to all of us to wear around our necks. They were made of aluminum. I assume that was so they could identify your cinders that were left after a nuclear attack on the United States by the Soviet Union.

This little aluminum name tag had your name, your address, and an indication of your religious affiliation stamped upon it. Parents had to decide between "Catholic," "Protestant," and "Jewish" as an identifier of their child's faith. Those were the only three choices in that less pluralistic and simpler time in American life. My mother, having been raised on *The Trail of Blood,* said that we were not any of those three selections. "We're not Protestant, we're not Catholic, and we're not Jewish. We're Baptist," I remember her saying. She went down to see

4. Pew Research Center, "Among Wealthy Nations."

the school principal and unsuccessfully argued for my younger brother and me having a *B* on our name tag rather than the *P* for Protestant or the *C* for Catholic or the *J* for Jewish.

Now my mother was historically inaccurate. We are Protestants. If you read *The Trail of Blood* carefully, you will probably agree with me that we do not really want to claim some of those individuals who are on that so-called family tree. Baptists are Protestants, but we are completed Protestants. The impulse of the Protestant Reformation was to get back to the primitive pattern of the New Testament. For various reasons all of the other groups fell off along the way while Baptists persevered. Baptists made it all the way back to the primitive New Testament pattern of local congregations of believers immersed after having professed their faith in Jesus Christ as Lord and Savior.

Luther and Calvin, for all of their greatness, could not jettison the idea that you cannot have a church separate from the state. They were wedded to the idea of the union of church and state. Luther could not do it, Calvin could not do it, and Zwingli could not do it. The Puritan reformers could not do it. They just could not go back and imagine what it was like before the Constantinian synthesis of church and state.

Both the Anabaptists on the continent and the English Baptists in Great Britain were able to envision the two entities separate. They understood that the nature of the church was a visible, gathered body of baptized believers and that the parish church concept was not biblical, not square with New Testament teachings. The Baptists wanted a visible church of gathered saints in a state that did not coerce religious activity but that allowed religious freedom.

This became the cause uniquely identified with Baptists, both in the Old World and the New World. The first Baptists who came to America came here fleeing religious persecution. Yet oddly enough, Baptists in America faced persecution anew from other religious groups who themselves had come here to secure the right to worship freely but declined to extend to their neighbors these same freedoms.

When the Puritans came to America, they came to establish a "City on a Hill," the New Jerusalem to light the way for the Old World.[5] They did

5. John Winthrop, "A Model of Christian Charity," in *Life and Letters of John Winthrop*, ed. Robert C. Winthrop (1867), 19. This essay was written aboard the *Arbella* during the voyage to Massachusetts, 1630.

not share the Baptists' vision for religious freedom. They were Puritans. They wanted to further "purify" the Church of England from what they saw as the "vestiges of popery" and make of the Church of England a really good Presbyterian church. They held to a pure Presbyterian understanding of how the church should be operated—supported by the state with the power of the state behind it. In fact, that is what broke the back of the Puritan revolution in England.

When the king in Great Britain tried to force an Anglican establishment on the people of Britain, who were increasingly out of step with that understanding of how the Christian faith should be expressed, the Puritans went on a seventy- to eighty-year campaign to "purify" the Church of England. That is the source of the name *Puritan*.

As the government pushed more and more in a high-church direction under the Stuart king Charles I and under the odious archbishop of Canterbury, William Laud, the festering resentment among the people finally turned to revolt. The antics of the king drove the commoners into political sympathy with Puritanism as the Anglicans further embraced the royalty. In the first English civil war, the forces of Puritanism won a victory over the government and set about putting in place a Puritan religious establishment.

While the parliament had sanctioned the establishment of a Presbyterian state church, many in Cromwell's army demurred. As history reveals to us, this led to the second civil war at the end of which Oliver Cromwell and his new model army of "religious men" triumphed. The monarchy was dissolved as Charles I was tried and executed. The Puritans first established a republic (1649–1653) and then a protectorate under Cromwell (1653–1660), in what is often referred to as the interregnum ("between reigns"), during which Cromwell allowed a great deal of toleration of religious practice. But here was the problem: Cromwell's army was about half Presbyterian and about half Baptist. The Presbyterians in Cromwell's army wanted a Presbyterian state church paid for by tax money with Presbyterian parish ministers and with no bishops but with presbyteries governing a state Presbyterian church.

The Baptists (and most of the Congregationalists) in Cromwell's army did not want a state church. The Baptists said they would not support a state church. They had debates about it; they had association meetings about it. They concluded that they would not revolt against Cromwell's government if a state church was established, and they would pay their taxes in accordance with biblical instruction, rendering unto Caesar that which was Caesar's. However, they, under no circumstances, would take any money from the state. The Presbyterians told the Baptists that a Baptist minister could be a pastor of a parish church, but the Baptists made clear that if any Baptist took a position in the state church he would immediately be disfellowshipped. There were about a dozen who did and, true to their promises, the Baptists promptly disfellowshipped them.

The Baptists prospered under the protectorate, having secured the chief thing for which they had contended—the freedom to worship as they pleased. Therefore, while they opposed the state church, they would not revolt against the state because of it but would disfellowship any Baptist who participated in the state church.

Immediately after the restoration of the monarchy under Charles II, from 1660 to 1672 in particular, there was severe religious persecution in Great Britain. John Bunyan was imprisoned during those twelve bitter years. It was difficult to be a nonconformist, or someone who declined to conform to the practices of the revived Church of England. Yet the number of Baptists had grown during the interregnum (1649–1660) in Great Britain. Baptists were a small, persecuted minority when the Puritan revolution began, but by 1660 there were about fifty thousand Baptists in Britain. Virtually everywhere the Puritan army went they left a Baptist church in their wake. The Baptist chaplains in Cromwell's army would preach in the communities in which they were stationed. As people were converted to Christ, according to the Baptist practice, they would be immersed. These regenerate individuals would then form a Baptist church in that area. You could almost trace the march of the Puritan army by the Baptist churches that were left in its wake throughout the countryside.

When the government clamped down on nonconformists, beginning in 1660, and Baptists were persecuted severely, many of the Baptists left Great Britain and went to America where they encountered their old Puritan adversaries.

When those Puritans who gave up on Britain came to America, their desire was to build a New Jerusalem to show the Old World how it should be done. In transit to the New World in 1630, John Winthrop said, "For we must consider that we shall be as a city upon a hill. The eyes of all people are upon us."[6] They came for religious freedom for themselves, not religious freedom for anyone else. In the new land, the Puritans severely persecuted Baptists and Quakers, targeting anyone who disagreed with them.

Indeed, Roger Williams, who became a Baptist after he arrived in New England, disagreed with Puritan orthodoxy and presented a bill of indictment against the clergy. The state threatened to put him in chains and send him back to England. This turn of events prompted him to write two polemics against the Puritan establishment of New England, *The Bloody Tenet of Persecution,* followed by *The Bloody Tenet of Persecution Made Yet More Bloody.*

Roger Williams's bill of indictment said the Church of England was not a true church and that citizens should not patronize it. As the Church of England was not a true church, he further asserted that citizens should not pay taxes to support the Church of England in Massachusetts. Furthermore, the indictment read, the Church of England's ministers were not true ministers, and the people should pay them no heed as they were not ministers of the gospel. Williams said the Massachusetts Bay Colony was established on land the Puritans did not own. The Puritans argued that ownership of the land was conveyed by patent from the king. Roger Williams, the supposed champion of separation of church and state, was up to his colonial eyebrows in the most vexing moral issue that was faced by the colonists in the seventeenth century—their shameful treatment of Native Americans. It is not surprising that Williams's publication roiled the Puritan establishment. Roger Williams clearly did not understand separation of church and state as being a separation of religious convictions and religiously informed morality from public policy.

Religious liberty has been an important element in the founding and development of America because Americans are a profoundly religious people. Religion has been inseparable from American politics as long as Americans have been engaged in politics. Yet every generation seems to think that religion intermingling with politics is something new.

In the 2000 and 2004 election cycles, some pundits warned that religion was playing an unprecedented role in the process, a role they said was not good for America. In 1980, I attended a Religious Roundtable

6. Ibid.

meeting in Dallas, Texas, at which Ronald Reagan told us, "You cannot endorse me, but I endorse you."

In 1960 John F. Kennedy came to a convention of Baptist ministers in Houston, Texas, to assure them that he, a Roman Catholic, would not do the pope's bidding if he were elected president. He promised his Catholicism would not interfere with his performance and his duties as president. This was a rather shameful episode in our country's history, in which a man felt compelled to promise he would segregate his faith from his role as president.

I was fourteen years old at the time, and I remember my pastor coming back from that meeting and making a report to the church. He assured us that he was grateful that Senator Kennedy made clear that his Catholicism would not interfere with his performance and his role as president of the United States if elected. He emphasized that the wall of separation between church and state was intact, and everybody in the church applauded. We should have been ashamed of ourselves to ask someone to set his religious faith aside in order to run for president of the United States.

We should not require elected officials to put aside their religious faith or to act in a schizophrenic manner, demanding their religious beliefs have no impact on the way they perform their job, unless they are judges who are required to interpret the law as it is, rather than as they would like it to be.

In the 2000 campaign for president, Connecticut Senator Joseph Lieberman was absolutely right when he said a person could not understand Joseph Lieberman as a candidate for vice president of the United States without understanding the fact that he is an observant Jew. His faith would have impacted how he governed, and voters needed to know that before they cast their ballots. I applauded Senator Lieberman's proclamation of his faith and said, at the time, that it took a hard line anticommunist President Nixon to go to Red China; it took a Democratic president, Bill Clinton, to sign welfare reform; and it might take a vice-presidential candidate who was an observant Jew to make it "kosher" once again to speak about one's faith in public life.

If you go back to the 1950s, you discover that President Dwight Eisenhower "assured the whole nation that belief in God was the first principle of Americanism."[7] Or you can go back to Theodore Roosevelt,

7. Stephen L. Carter, *God's Name in Vain* (New York: Basic Books, 2000), 11.

who said that the president should go to church regularly to set an example for the nation.[8]

President William McKinley sought to prove that he was a better Protestant than his opponent William Jennings Bryan was and fought a holy war against Catholic Spain (the Spanish-American War) to prove it.[9]

In his Second Inaugural Address, Abraham Lincoln suggested the Civil War was, in effect, a war in which both sides believed God was on their side. Lincoln was humble enough to state that perhaps neither side was completely right. I would encourage every American to read carefully President Lincoln's Second Inaugural Address, in which he said, "Both read the same Bible and pray to the same God, and each invokes His aid against the other. It may seem strange that any men should dare to ask a just God's assistance in wringing their bread from the sweat of other men's faces, but let us judge not, that we be not judged. The prayers of both could not be answered. That of neither has been answered fully. The Almighty has His own purposes."

He continued:

> If we shall suppose that American slavery is one of those offenses which, in the providence of God, must needs come, but which, having continued through His appointed time, He now wills to remove, and that He gives to both North and South this terrible war as the woe due to those by whom the offense came, shall we discern therein any departure from those divine attributes which the believers in a living God always ascribe to Him? Fondly do we hope, fervently do we pray, that this mighty scourge of war may speedily pass away. Yet, if God wills that it continue until all the wealth piled by the bondsman's two hundred and fifty years of unrequited toil shall be sunk, and until every drop of blood drawn with the lash shall be paid by another drawn with the sword, as was said three thousand years ago, so still it must be said the judgments of the Lord are true and righteous altogether. With malice

8. Ibid.
9. Ibid.

toward none, with charity for all, with firmness in the right as God gives us to see the right.[10]

President Lincoln's speech is one piece of evidence among many that the greatest single tragedy in American history, so far, was the assassination of Abraham Lincoln. How different post-Civil War history would have been had Lincoln lived!

In searching for the appropriate commingling of faith and politics, we can even go all the way back to Thomas Jefferson, who spent a significant part of his 1800 campaign for president—an election campaign that was far dirtier and nastier than any other campaign in American history, including 2004—denying charges that he was an atheist.[11]

Current controversies about the role of religion in America and religious liberty and separation of church and state are nothing new for America. Only our failure of memory makes them seem peculiar. We need to understand and appreciate the historical relationship between religion and politics in American history in order to understand the need to accommodate religiously informed moral values in the nation's public policy debate.

In America we have long separated the institutional church from the institutional state. This is a sensible and proper idea. We have never separated religion from politics, and we are not likely to start anytime soon.

Indeed, one example of this in our history illustrates the point. In 1854 a group of three thousand New England clergymen signed a petition, which they sent to the United States Senate, petitioning against passage of the Kansas-Nebraska Act of 1854, which would have expanded slavery into the Nebraska territory.

The proslavery senators were apoplectic at the fact that three thousand preachers would dare to interfere in the political life of the nation. Illinois Senator Stephen Douglas, perhaps known best for his debates with Abe Lincoln, said, "We find a large body of preachers, perhaps three thousand, following the lead of a circular which was issued by the Abolitionist confederates in this body, calculated to deceive and mislead the public, have here come forward, with atrocious falsehood and atrocious calumny

10. *Inaugural Addresses of the Presidents of the United States* (Washington, D.C.: U.S. Government Printing Office, 1989).
11. Carter, *God's Name in Vain,* 12.

against this Senate, desecrated the pulpit, and prostituted the sacred desk to the miserable and corrupting influence of party politics."[12]

That sounds a little bit like commentators on MSNBC criticizing evangelical preachers in 2004. Douglas went on to say that these "political preachers ought to be rebuked, and required to confine themselves to their vocation."[13] Not to be outdone, Senator James Mason of Virginia argued that the action of the clergymen was an absolute abomination, saying, "I understand this petition to come from a class who have put aside their character as citizens. It comes from a class who style themselves in the petition, ministers of the gospel and not citizens. . . . Sir, ministers of the Gospel are unknown to this government, and God forbid the day should ever come when they shall be known to it."[14] In other words, Mason was arguing that if you're a minister of the gospel you have forfeited your right of citizenship to speak on the moral and public policy issues of the day.

Senator Sam Houston, at that time a senator from the state of Texas, before he was elected governor, responded to the attacks on the petitioners, saying, "I do not think there is anything very derogatory to our institutions in the ministers of the Gospel expressing their opinions. They have a right to do it. No man can be a minister without first being a man. He has political rights; he also has the rights of a missionary of the Savior, and he is not disenfranchised by his vocation."

Senator Houston went on to say:

> Certain political restrictions may be laid upon him; he may be disqualified from serving in the legislatures of the State, but that does not discharge him from political and civil obligations to his country. He has a right to contribute, as far as he thinks necessary, to the sustentation of institutions. He has a right to interpose his voice as one of its citizens against the adoption of any measure which he believes will injure the nation.[15]

---

12. Ibid., 93–94, quoting Senator Stephen Douglas, statement in the Senate, March 14, 1854, reprinted in *Right of Petition: New England Clergyman* (Washington, D.C.: Buell and Blanchard, 1854), 3.
13. Ibid., 94.
14. Ibid.
15. Ibid., 94–95.

Of course, it needs to be understood that Houston was a staunch Unionist.

This controversy illustrates a point. Proslavery senators calling for a clear separation between those representing the church and the affairs of the state argued that the petition should not even be received or considered but torn up and thrown away. In the end the preachers, not the senators, won the day. They prevailed because they refused to shut up, even when told to do so by members of the esteemed United States Senate. By insisting on the relevance of God's Word in a broken world and by persuading enough of their fellow citizens of the justice of their cause and that the nation was willing to fight a war over it, the preachers understood a simple fact about America that their Senate opponents did not: Most Americans want to talk about God and allow the "salt" and the "light" of the gospel to season public policy. As Americans, we have always done it, we are not about to stop, even when people tell us to shut up. That is one of the consequences, one of the mandatory requirements, of religious liberty.

I am a great believer in what is often called the separation of church and state, as correctly understood. When you do not have separation of the reach of the state from the affairs of the church, the state always corrupts, subverts, and seduces the church. The idea of separating church and state has been completely twisted and distorted beyond all recognition during the last half of the twentieth and the first part of the twenty-first century.

Thomas Jefferson's mention of the concept termed separation of church and state was cited in a 1947 Supreme Court decision, *Everson v. the Board of Education,* in which the court determined that the state of New Jersey's reimbursement of public bus fare to the parents of parochial school students was a type of establishment of religion that was at odds with the First Amendment. The term was lifted from a letter Jefferson wrote to the Baptist ministers of Danbury, Connecticut, who wrote him with complaints about the established church in Connecticut.

Nine of the original thirteen states in the United States of America had tax-supported, established state churches. These state churches discriminated against and persecuted Baptists and other dissenters to varying degrees. In Connecticut and Massachusetts, there were Congregational established state churches. In the South the churches were Episcopal.

In one ten-year period over five hundred Baptist preachers were thrown in jail in Virginia by state authorities for "disturbing the peace." While that may not be the worst definition of preaching I have ever heard, that is not what was meant by the charge. These men were guilty of preaching without a license from the state. The Baptist preachers said, "We don't need a license from the state; we secured our license from God." They refused to accept toleration; they demanded full religious liberty.

John Leland, a famous Baptist preacher, evangelist, and friend of U. S. presidents, planned to campaign against ratification of the Constitution. The Baptists living in Virginia, North Carolina, Massachusetts, and Connecticut were fearful there would be a federal establishment of religion that would deny them their religious freedom in the same manner the state governments with their established state churches were attempting to deny them their religious freedom.

The Baptists, despite being persecuted (some would say because of it), held the balance of power in these states. If the Baptists in Virginia did not vote for the Constitution, it would not be ratified in Virginia. As history reveals to us, Virginia was not just another state; Virginia was the dominant state in early federal America.

Virginia was the biggest state, it was the most populous state, it was the wealthiest state, and it was the most influential state. Washington was a Virginian. Jefferson was a Virginian. Madison was a Virginian. Monroe was a Virginian. Four of our first five presidents hailed from Virginia. If Virginia didn't ratify the Constitution, there was not going to be a Constitution.

Therefore, James Madison met with John Leland in Orange County, Virginia, and they cut a political deal. Leland agreed to withdraw as an antiratification candidate for the Constitutional Convention and to work to convince Baptists in the state to vote for the Constitution, with the understanding that Madison would introduce an amendment to the new Constitution in the first Congress. The amendment would read, "Congress shall make no law affecting an establishment of religion, nor interfering with the free exercise thereof," what we know now as the First Amendment. Both Leland and Madison were true to their word, and that is precisely what happened.

It says, "Congress shall make no law affecting an establishment of religion." It did not do away with the state-established churches. You may wonder: why is there not a Mormon state church in Utah or a Catholic state church in Louisiana? The answer: the Fourteenth Amendment to the Constitution that was ratified in 1867, which every southern state had to ratify as one of the requirements for getting back into the Union, has been interpreted by the Supreme Court to say that whatever the federal government has forbidden itself from doing in the first ten amendments, state and local governments are prohibited from doing as well. From that point forward a state church could not be established because of the Constitution's restriction on the federal government establishing a church.

The First Amendment guarantees the government "shall make no law respecting an establishment of religion, or prohibiting the free exercise thereof."[16] It was not until 1832 that Massachusetts and Connecticut finally got rid of their cold, dead, established state churches.

When Jefferson wrote his oft-misinterpreted letter to the Baptists of Danbury, Connecticut, they still were suffering persecution and discrimination under a state church. Seeking to apply principles laid out in a letter to Baptists who were suffering under a state church to the federal government is ludicrous, even if the Supreme Court did do it. Jefferson never intended for the concept of the separation of church and state to be what the Supreme Court has tried to say he intended.

This historical account is instructive. Leland previously had relocated from Virginia in 1791, back to his native Massachusetts, where he became more involved in politics than I believe a Baptist preacher ought to be. He was so involved that when Thomas Jefferson won the incredibly bitter election of 1800 and the Democrats of western Massachusetts wanted to send a token of their regard and esteem for Jefferson, they sent Leland as the spokesperson. Jefferson received Leland at ten o'clock in the morning on the first Friday of January 1802. Leland arrived at the White House accompanied by a wagon holding a several-hundred-pound cheese.

The president personally came outside to receive the gift, and Leland took the opportunity to praise him publicly. Leland told the president the cheese was a token of the regard of the Democrats of western Massachusetts, and he assured the president that no Federalist cows had contributed any milk to this cheese, only Democrat cows. Leland then praised the president as God's great gift to mankind, praying for his

16. U.S. Constitution, First Amendment.

leadership and his wisdom. As it was a gift, Leland left the cheese with Jefferson. The cheese was taken into the White House. While Jefferson had lunch soon after, it is not recorded whether cheese was on the menu. After lunch Jefferson took the quill and parchment and penned his letter to the Baptist churches of Danbury, Connecticut, writing, "There is to be a wall of separation between the church and the state."[17]

On the same Friday that a Baptist preacher showed up with an enormous cheese, prayed for the president, and the president thanked him for the prayer, the president later that day wrote his well-known letter to the Baptist preachers of Danbury. Two days later, on Sunday morning, Thomas Jefferson attended a Christian worship service in the House of Representatives. With about half the members of Congress in attendance, as well as the president of the United States, John Leland, a Baptist evangelist, preached a revival sermon from the speaker's rostrum of the House of Representatives.

One account from an Episcopal congressman said Leland preached like an untutored frontier preacher. Yet, no matter his style of delivery, he was afforded the opportunity to preach in what was apparently a regularly scheduled worship service, with Jefferson (who was evidently not a regular attendee) sitting on the front row. Clearly Thomas Jefferson did not intend for a wall of separation between church and state to mean the segregation of religious expression from public life in public places, including the House of Representatives.[18]

The real origin of separation of church and state in America is the wall that Roger Williams talked about in the seventeenth century. He talked about it quite a bit. He said there needed to be a wall of separation between the garden of the church and the wilderness of society in order to protect the garden. Williams and his fellow Baptists in colonial America understood just how damaging it was when the wilderness of the state and the wilderness of the society came in and corrupted the garden of the church. The wall of separation was there to protect the church from the state, not to protect the state from the church. The latter assertion would have been considered incomprehensible nonsense by our founding fathers.[19]

---

17. Jefferson to Nehemiah Dodge, Ephraim Robbins, and Stephen S. Nelson, 1 January 1802. Manuscript Division, Library of Congress.
18. Richard Land, *Real Homeland Security* (Nashville: Broadman & Holman, 2004), 208–10.
19. Carter, *God's Name in Vain,* 75–79.

Williams said the responsibility of the gardeners is to seek to domesticate and make more of the wilderness a garden. It's called the Great Commission. It's called being "salt" and "light." All of the restrictions in the First Amendment are on the government—not Christians, not churches, and not people of faith.

The most dangerous threat to religious liberty in America is not people of religious faith being involved in public policy by bringing their religious convictions to bear on the moral issues of the day. The most dangerous threat to religious liberty is secular fundamentalists who want to ghettoize religious faith, marginalize it, trivialize it, and make the wall of separation a prison wall that keeps religion inside a box. Such thinking will only succeed in a representative democracy like the United States if people of faith allow themselves to be bamboozled, brainwashed, emasculated, sterilized, and kept in a cage.

My experience is that people of religious faith in this country are far smarter and far more courageous than that.

Chapter 6

Natural Law and Religious Liberty

Craig Mitchell

It has been said that if India is the most religious nation in the world and Sweden is the most irreligious, then America is a nation of Indians run by Swedes. Unfortunately, there is an element of truth here that is all too poignant. Many politicians and judges in our country apparently take a position of hostility toward religion in general and Christianity in particular. It should be clear from this chapter that this is not the proper position.

Even more amazing is that there are Christians who, proud of their contributions to religious liberty, seem to think that religious liberty means that we are free from religion rather than free to practice it in public life. For instance, Barry Lynn of Americans United for Separation of Church and State seems to be at war with believers who simply want to live out their faith in the public square. What is the cause of this confusion? Possibly it is because many old-line Christians really do not understand the idea of religious liberty in particular, let alone rights in general. This may be because they have not considered the place of natural law as it relates to religious liberty.

This chapter will show how natural law affects our understanding of the First Amendment. This can be demonstrated, first, by explaining what a right is and then by explaining natural law and how it relates to rights. Finally, with this understanding, I will explore what is meant by freedom of religion and what religious freedom includes, as well as what it does not.

Natural Rights

What is a right? Where do rights come from? Does the source of rights make a difference? What is a human right? Is it any different from a natural right? As strange as it may seem, some people do not even believe in the existence of rights. For example, Alasdair MacIntyre compares the belief in rights to the belief in witches and unicorns.[1] Perhaps MacIntyre holds this position because he subscribes to "Ordinary Language Analysis (Philosophy)." This position rejects the concept of metaphysics and teleology. Consequently, it also rejects the idea of natural law as well as natural rights. MacIntyre's acceptance of Hume's fact/value dichotomy is made even more problematic when one considers that W. V. O. Quine destroyed this dichotomy in his famous article "The Two Dogmas of Empiricism."[2]

Like MacIntyre, Jeremy Bentham rejected the idea of rights. Mark Tebbit summarizes Bentham's views by writing, "As a thoroughgoing empiricist, Bentham regarded all rights, including those codified in law, as at best 'fictitious entities' and at worst imaginary conjurings."[3] Bentham's reasons for rejecting rights is that they come only with the sacrifice of liberty. He wrote, "The law cannot create rights except by creating corresponding obligations. It cannot create rights and obligations without creating offenses. It cannot command or forbid without restraining the liberty of individuals."[4]

In contrast to Bentham and MacIntyre, Leif Wenar asserts that rights do exist and that they have an analytical framework. By applying the ideas of the American jurist W. N. Hohfeld, Wenar argues that all assertions of rights can be understood in terms of four basic elements.[5] These elements are privileges, claims, powers, and immunities.[6] According to Wenar, the right to phi involves the privilege to phi or not. A claim means that for me to have the right to phi also means that a second party (sometimes the state) has an obligation.[7]

Concerning the terms *human* and *natural rights,* John Finnis says, the term *human rights* is synonymous with natural or moral rights.[8] Perhaps

1. Alasdair MacIntyre, *After Virtue* (South Bend, Ind.: University of Notre Dame Press, 1981), 67.
2. Willard Van Orman Quine, "The Two Dogmas of Empiricism," originally published in *Philosophical Review* (January 1951): 21.
3. Mark Tebbit, *Philosophy of Law: An Introduction* (New York: Routledge, 2000), 100.
4. Jeremy Bentham, "Principles of the Civil Code," in *Selected Writings on Utilitarianism,* ed. Tom Griffith (Hertfordshire, England: Wadsworth, 2000), 315.
5. Leif Wenar, "The Nature of Rights," *Philosophy and Public Affairs* 33 (2005): 224.
6. W. N. Hohfeld, *Fundamental Legal Conceptions* (New Haven: 1919).
7. Wenar, "Nature of Rights," 229.
8. John Finnis, *Natural Law and Natural Rights* (Oxford: Oxford University Press, 1980), 198–99.

this is because human beings are naturally moral creatures. As such, human beings have a knowledge, however faulty, of right and wrong. Philip Edgecumbe Hughes explains that being made after the image of God means that man is a moral creature.[9] Humans can recognize that certain behaviors are right while others are wrong. Perhaps to be human means to be moral and to recognize our rights, as well as the rights of others. If this is the case, then it is only logical to realize that the state has no right to restrict our beliefs or our religious practices unless they violate the rights of others.

Concerning the source of rights, Alan Dershowitz writes that:

> the source of rights determines their status. If rights come from God, then they are truly 'unalienable,' as our Declaration of Independence asserted and Alexander Hamilton reiterated. If they derive from nature, then they are as immutable as the natural laws of physics and astronomy. . . . But if rights are solely the product of human law-making—if they are inventions rather than discoveries then they are subject to modification, even abrogation, by the same source that devised them in the first place.[10]

In other words, the source of a right determines whether it exists. If rights are simply made by man, then rights talk is a moot point. When the existence of rights is denied, a logical result is that rights can be created or dissolved with any whim of the state. For example, some have argued for the right to an abortion or the right to medical care. And they expect that the state will not only guarantee these rights but that the state will also provide for these rights. I, for one, would like to have the right to pancakes on a Saturday morning, but somehow I don't suppose that the state will provide for it.

We might conclude from all of this that if the Declaration of Independence is right, then the source of rights is God. As such, we can neither create nor abolish rights. At the same time we are left with a question: How does God implement rights and how does he propagate the knowledge of rights? This will be answered in the following section.

9. Philip Edgecumbe Hughes, *True Image* (Grand Rapids: Eerdmans, 1989), 59–61.
10. Alan Dershowitz, *Rights from Wrongs* (New York: Basic Books, 2004), 17–18.

Natural Law

In this section, I intend to explain what natural law is and why it is important. This will be accomplished by explaining its history, the main criticisms of natural law, and how natural law will help interpret the First Amendment in general and religious liberty in particular.

What Is Natural Law?

Natural law is a concept that dates back to ancient Greek philosophers, such as Aristotle and the Stoics. According to Andrew Altman, "Natural law theory claims that a necessary connection exists between positive law and morality. This necessary connection is said to exist by virtue of the very concept of law."[11] Men know the natural law by the faculty of reason. Perhaps the most significant proponent of this idea in the Middle Ages was Thomas Aquinas, who wrote extensively on the subject in his *Summa Theologiae.* Aquinas was followed in the early modern period by Hugo Grotius, who employed natural law as the foundation for international law.

The classical version of natural law depends on a Creator God who has ordered all of his creation in accordance with his good nature. This created order, according to Iain M. MacKenzie, "is seen in terms of God's *oikonomia*—the economy of God. While they [the Elizabethan, Jacobean and Caroline Divines] refer to this generally in Patristic terms as 'the ordering of God's household of creation,' it is primarily seen again in Patristic terms as that 'order' which God is eternally in Himself."[12] The great British legal scholar, Sir William Blackstone, maintained that there are "immutable laws of good and evil, to which the creator himself in all his dispensations conforms; and which he has enabled human reason to discover, so far as they are necessary for the conduct of human actions."[13]

"If natural law is to be defined as real law," writes Russell Hittinger, "a law-giver will need to be brought into the picture."[14] As Hittinger explains, that "natural law needs a lawgiver in order to be placed in the genus of law is not a point that has been overlooked by theologians and jurisprudents. For example, the well known definition given by

11. Andrew Altman, *Arguing about Law* (Belmont, Calif.: Wadsworth, 2001), 49.
12. Iain M. MacKenzie, *God's Order and Natural Law: The Works of the Laudian Divines* (Burlington, Vt.: Ashgate, 2002), 37.
13. William Blackstone, *Blackstone's Commentary on the Laws of England,* Part I, 40.
14. Russell Hittinger, *The First Grace* (Wilmington, Del.: ISI Books, 2003), 39.

St. Thomas, 'and this participation in the eternal law by rational creatures is called the natural law' presupposes the existence of an eternal law in relation to which natural law is defined."[15] By eternal law, Thomas Aquinas means all of the laws that God created, as opposed to temporal laws which are created by men.

Brian Bix explains, "According to Aquinas, (genuine or just) positive law is derived from natural law. This derivation has different aspects. Sometimes natural law dictates what positive law should be: for example, natural law requires that there be a prohibition of murder and settles what its content will be. At other times, natural law leaves room for human choice (based on local customs or policy choices)."[16]

Natural law or the law of nature, when properly understood, is part of general revelation. As such, all men have access to it whether or not they believe it. The Jews held a few conclusions about natural law, according to Marcus Bockmuehl, such as:

1. Moral authority in nature is not distinct from God's moral authority.
2. The law of nature is in keeping with the law of God and vice versa.
3. The idea of a law of nature is well established except in Palestinian scribal circles. The natural law motif is not highly developed in early rabbinic literature.
4. The idea of a law according to nature is well established prior to Philo. This is partially the result of a long-standing tradition within Second Temple Judaism.[17]

While there is some debate over how much can be drawn from it, the New Testament seems to refer to the idea of natural law. Romans 1:20 says, "For since the creation of the world His invisible attributes, His eternal power and divine nature, have been clearly seen, being understood through what has been made, so that they are without excuse" (NASB). In other words, God has so ordered creation that one must know that God exists and what he is like. The rest of the Romans passage relates this knowledge of God with human conduct. When one rejects the truth about God, he cannot help but err in his moral conduct.

15. Ibid., 39–40.
16. Brian Bix, "Natural Law Theory," in *A Companion to Philosophy of Law and Legal Theory,* ed. Dennis Patterson (Malden, Mass.: Blackwell, 1996), 225.
17. Marcus Bockmuehl, *Jewish Law in Gentile Churches* (Grand Rapids: Baker, 2000), 110–11.

Romans 2:14–15 explains that even Gentiles without the law know it instinctively, which is why they are morally culpable. The law written on the heart is the natural law. Some people need glasses to see clearly while others do not. Either way, men are still accountable.

But not everyone who subscribes to natural law requires a lawgiver. Lon Fuller is an advocate of natural law who argues this position. He writes: "These natural laws have nothing to do with any 'brooding omnipresence in the skies.' Nor have they the slightest affinity with any such proposition as that the practice of contraception is a violation of God's law. They remain entirely terrestrial in origin and application. They are not 'higher laws'; if any metaphor of elevation is appropriate they should be called 'lower laws.'"[18] Fuller believes that natural laws are lower laws because they are like the laws of carpentry which a good carpenter will obey if he is to do a good job.[19] As such, these laws are still immutable, are applicable everywhere, and cannot be created by men.

It should now be apparent that there are different approaches to natural law. While these approaches have some things in common, they are clearly not equal. As Baptists, who are concerned with the Word of God, it should be obvious that we may subscribe to the classical view of natural law, which involves a divine lawgiver.

Why Is Natural Law Important?

You might think, *Well, all of this is very interesting, but what is the point of it?* Simply put, natural law provides the foundation for natural rights. To be sure, this view has plenty of detractors, such as Alan Dershowitz. He rejects natural law because he believes it is intellectually bankrupt.[20] He finds natural law a harmful fiction because it "is an invitation to self-righteous lawlessness."[21] Instead of natural law, Dershowitz offers the idea that rights come from human experiences with injustice.[22]

However, Lloyd Weinreb asserts, "Although various theories of rights, or natural rights, appear much earlier, rights are not closely associated with natural law until the seventeenth and eighteenth centu-

18. Lon Fuller, *The Morality of Law* (New Haven: Yale University Press, 1963), 96.
19. Ibid.
20. Dershowitz, *Right from Wrong,* 80.
21. Ibid., 67.
22. Ibid., 8–9.

ries. Even then, the association is mostly only verbal."[23] In spite of all of this, Weinreb admits that "natural law is a philosophy of rights."[24] In the seventeenth century, John Locke made the connection between natural law and natural rights.[25] He generally used the phrase, "law of nature" rather than "natural law." This "law of nature," according to Nicolas Wolterstorff, means, "a law of moral obligation which can in principle be known by Reason."[26] Richard Ashcraft explains that Locke "supposed that God created all men free and equal and that they are under an obligation to obey His will, as expressed in the natural law."[27] Locke also believed that "the municipal laws of countries are only so far right, as they are founded on the law of nature, by which they are to be regulated and interpreted."[28] Finally, Locke emphasizes rights, property rights in particular, as being based upon natural reason and Scripture.[29]

The Main Criticisms of Natural Law

The primary criticism of natural law theory comes from the fact/value dichotomy. This idea has its origins in the writings of David Hume.[30] (The other argument against natural law concerns how we know the natural law. Since the knowledge of the natural law has already been discussed, there is no need to deal with it again.)

Alan Dershowitz, like others, believes in Hume's fact/value dichotomy, which argues that you cannot derive an "ought" from an "is." This means that one cannot know what is right or wrong for a thing based on that thing's nature. Conclusions based on this type of inference are faulty because they are arrived at by induction. Hume showed that knowledge arrived at by induction is, at best, uncertain. The fact/value dichotomy is otherwise known as the naturalistic fallacy.[31] Dershowitz admits that

---

23. Lloyd L. Weinreb, "Natural Law and Rights," in *Natural Law Theory: Contemporary Essays,* ed. Robert P. George (New York: Oxford University Press, 1992), 278.
24. Ibid., 298.
25. John Locke, *Two Treatises of Government,* 2.19:225–30.
26. Nicolas Wolterstorff, *John Locke and the Ethics of Belief* (New York: Cambridge University Press, 1996), 140.
27. Richard Ashcraft, "Locke's Political Philosophy," in *The Cambridge Companion to Locke,* ed. Vere Chappell (New York: Cambridge University Press, 1994), 239. Ashcraft is referring to Locke's *Two Treatises on Government,* 2.2,6–8.
28. Locke, *Two Treatises on Government,* 2.2,9,11–12.
29. Ibid., 2.5,25.
30. David Hume, *A Treatise on Human Nature* (1740), 3.1.1.
31. The analytic philosopher G. E. Moore called any attempt to violate the fact/value dichotomy by basing morality on the nature of a thing the "naturalistic fallacy" in his book *Principia Ethica* (New York: Cambridge University Press, 1903), 90.

nature should be considered in these matters, writing, "Any attempt to build a system of morality that completely ignores nature will fail. Nature has a vote but not a veto on questions of morality."[32] After this admission, he argues that "morality cannot and should not be derived directly from nature."[33] Finally, he writes, "Religious and philosophical approaches are striking examples of human beings recognizing the natural 'is' of selfishness and aspiring to the less natural 'ought' of altruism."[34]

Many assume that the naturalistic fallacy is an unassailable idea. For this reason most ethical theorists will not even attempt any ethical theory that implies teleology. In the last century a few have challenged the concept of a naturalistic fallacy. These include John Finnis and W. V. O. Quine. John Finnis rejects the naturalistic fallacy because he believes that many have misinterpreted Hume. He argues that there are only two plausible interpretations of what Hume actually meant. He writes:

> The first and standard interpretation treats Hume as announcing the logical truth, widely emphasized since the latter part of the nineteenth century, that no set of non-moral premises can entail a moral conclusion. The second interpretation places the passage in its historical and literary context, and sees it as the tailpiece to Hume's attack on the eighteenth century rationalists (notably Samuel Clark), an attack whose centre-piece is the contention that rational perception of the moral qualities of actions could not of itself provide a motivating guide to action.[35]

It is this second interpretation that Finnis finds as the correct one. He concludes, "Hume himself lacked a viable conception of practical reason and practical principles. So he was able to offer no more than a scatter of notoriously inconsistent and puzzling responses to the problem."[36]

Willard Van Orman Quine was the first person to attack the naturalistic fallacy. In his famous article "The Two Dogmas of Empiricism"

32. Dershowitz, *Right from Wrong,* 35.
33. Ibid.
34. Ibid., 38.
35. John Finnis, *Natural Law and Natural Rights* (New York: Clarendon Press, 1980), 37.
36. Ibid., 42.

Quine argued that the fact/value dichotomy rests upon the analytic/synthetic dichotomy.[37] Analycity is a problematic idea because it is essentially meaningless. As such, there is no dichotomy, and so the naturalistic fallacy is shown to be an illusion. Quine used this argument for justifying a naturalistic approach to epistemology, but it can easily be applied to ethics as well. Quine and Finnis demonstrate in different ways that the naturalistic fallacy is both assailable and defeatable. As such, natural law can and should serve as the foundation for the inalienable rights mentioned in the Declaration of Independence.

Religious Liberty

When Baptists think of the First Amendment to the Constitution of the United States, we think of our right to freedom of religion. The First Amendment is found in the Bill of Rights, which should, as a minimum, enumerate the rights that our citizens have. Some argue that the Bill of Rights enumerates only the rights that citizens have. Others argue that the Bill of Rights lists only a few of our rights.

In any case the framers of the Declaration of Independence argued that all men are created equal because they are endowed by inalienable rights granted by our Creator. In other words, the founders of our country believed first that rights exist. They also believed that rights are not created by men or the state. Instead they believed that rights are God created and God given. As such, it is wrong for the state or anyone else to interfere with our rights. Implicit within this is the idea that it would be wrong for the state to create rights.

The Declaration of Independence lists three rights in particular. These are the rights to life, liberty, and happiness. Thomas Jefferson got these ideas from John Locke.[38] In fact, it might be said that Jefferson's ideas are nothing more than footnotes of John Locke.[39] When Jefferson constructed the First Amendment, the order of the rights was not accidental. Stephen Carter writes, "Although one might scarcely know it from the zeal with which the primacy of the other first amendment freedoms (free press, free speech) is often asserted, those protections come after the clauses that

37. Willard Van Orman Quine, "The Two Dogmas of Empiricism," originally published in *Philosophical Review* (January 1951): 21.
38. John Locke, *Two Treatises on Government,* 2.19,225.
39. See Carl Becker, *The Declaration of Independence: A Study in the History of Political Ideas* (New York: Harcourt Brace, 1992).

were designed to secure religious liberty, which Thomas Jefferson called 'the most inalienable and sacred of all human rights.'"[40]

John Locke and Religious Liberty

According to Peter Berkowitz, "In Aristotelian terms, Locke's political theory as a whole shifts attention from the virtues of the human soul to the virtues of a good citizen of a regime based on natural freedom and equality, and to the social virtues that are necessary for the maintenance of any sort of human association."[41] Locke was unique among the modern moral philosophers. He was the last to argue that political and moral philosophy are different parts of the same discipline. Another interesting aspect of Locke is that he was a serious, if at times errant, Christian. Anyone reading Locke's works will find a constant and consistent mention of God and the gospel of Jesus Christ.

John Dunn notes, "The most conspicuous single shift in the structuring of western thought between Locke's birth and the present day has been the erasure of the all-structuring role of a single omnipotent and omniscient Deity (if not necessarily as a contingent focus for personal belief, at least as a publicly avowable premise of cognitive strategy)."[42] Locke believed that natural rights are given by God, and he emphasized the rights of life, liberty and property.[43] These natural rights should not be violated by the state or by anyone else.[44]

Locke's *Letter Concerning Toleration* emphasized the importance of religious freedom. In this work he argued that toleration is the chief virtue. He asserted, "The toleration of those that differ from others in matters of religion, is so agreeable to the Gospel of Jesus Christ and to the genuine reason of mankind, that it seems monstrous for men to be so blind, as not to perceive the necessity and advantage of it, in so clear

---

40. Stephen L. Carter, *The Culture of Disbelief* (New York: Anchor Books, 1993), 106. Carter quotes Jefferson's "Freedom of Religion at the University of Virginia."
41. Peter Berkowitz, *Virtue and the Making of Modern Liberalism* (Princeton, N.J.: Princeton University Press, 1999), 76.
42. John Dunn, "Measuring Locke's Shadow," in *Two Treatises of Government and a Letter Concerning Toleration,* ed. Ian Shapiro (New Haven: Yale University Press, 2003), 268.
43. John Locke, *Two Treatises and A Letter,* 110–121.
44. Ibid., 435–36. According to Richard Ashcraft, Locke "argues that property ownership precedes the establishment of political society and therefore must be understood in terms of moral principles pertaining to rights and duties of individuals and the origins of political society." Richard Ashcraft, "Locke's Political Philosophy," in *The Cambridge Companion to Locke,* ed. Vere Chappell (New York: Cambridge University Press, 1994), 236.

a light."[45] Locke believed that the state should be separated from the church: "Now that the whole jurisdiction of the magistrate reaches only to these civil concernments; and that all civil power, right and dominion, is bounded and confined to the only care of promoting these things; and that it neither can nor ought in any manner to be extended to the salvation of souls."[46]

Locke gave three reasons for this position. "First, because the care of souls is not committed to the civil magistrate any more than to other men. It is not committed unto him, I say, by God; because it appears not that God has ever given any such authority to one man over another, as to compel any one to his religion."[47] Locke's second reason was, "The care of souls cannot belong to the civil magistrate, because his power consists only in outward force: but true and saving religion consists in the inward persuasion of the mind, without which nothing can be acceptable to God."[48] Locke's third reason states that

> though the rigour of laws and the force of the penalties were capable to convince and change men's minds, yet would not that help at all to the salvation of their souls. For there being but one truth, one way to heaven; what hope is there that more men would be led into it, if they had no other rule to follow it but the religion of the court, and were put under a necessity to quit the light of their own reason, to oppose the dictates of their own consciences, and blindly to resign themselves to the will of their governors, and to the religion, which either ignorance, ambition or superstition had chanced to establish in the countries where they were born.[49]

In summary, both the Declaration of Independence and the Constitution have deep roots in the writings of John Locke. Locke related natural rights to natural law. He also based the right of religious liberty on natural law. Consequently, if we are to gain a fuller under-

45. John Locke, *Two Treatises and A Letter,* 217.
46. Ibid., 218.
47. Ibid.
48. Ibid., 219.
49. Ibid., 220.

standing of what is meant by the First Amendment, we need to understand natural law as it is expressed by John Locke.

Contemporary Problems with Religious Liberty

One of the main problems with the contemporary understanding of the First Amendment concerns a particular construal of the separation of church and state. Any simple reading of the First Amendment leads one to the conclusion that the state should not endorse a specific religion. "Simply put, the metaphorical separation of church and state originated in an effort to protect religion from the state, not the state from religion. The religion clauses of the First Amendment were crafted to permit maximum freedom to the religious."[50]

Judge Robert Bork agrees. Like Stephen J. Carter, he thinks that the courts have taken a position that is hostile to religion. "The court has brought law and religion into opposition. The results are damaging to both fields. All law rests upon choices guided by moral assumptions and beliefs. There is no reason to prohibit any conduct, except on the understanding that some moral good is thereby served."[51] Bork adds:

> There is no lack of other evidence to show that no absolute barrier to any interaction between government and religion was intended. From the beginning of the republic, Congress called upon presidents to issue Thanksgiving Day proclamations in the name of God. All the presidents complied, with the sole exception of Jefferson, who thought such proclamations at odds with the principle of the establishment clause. Jefferson's tossed off metaphor in a letter about the "wall" between church and state has become the modern law, despite the fact that it was idiosyncratic and not at all what Congress and the ratifying states understood themselves to be saying.[52]

This shows that even Jefferson was inconsistent and sometimes confused about the ideas that he gained from Locke. With an understanding of natural law, as explained by John Locke, it is clear that Carter and Bork are correct in their understanding of the First Amendment.

50. Carter, *The Culture of Disbelief*, 105–06.
51. Robert Bork, *Coercing Virtue* (Washington D.C.: AEI Press, 2003), 69.
52. Ibid., 66–67.

What John Locke understood is that God's nature is reflected in the created order and that the state must act in accordance with that order. Part of the role of the church is to remind the state of this truth in order to set it back on the right course. This is something that only the church can correctly do. As such, the church needs to be free to speak out on the issues confronting our country and should not be muzzled. It is interesting to note that when Clarence Thomas was nominated for the Supreme Court, many stood against him. The opposition was due to his belief in natural law as explained by Thomas Aquinas. What Judge Thomas's enemies understood was that his religious beliefs would affect the way he would evaluate the law. Once again we have another example of people who are misinterpreting what the First Amendment was intended to be. They want the First Amendment also to mean that an official of the state, whether elected or appointed, should not be allowed to let his religious belief affect his position on any matter of public policy or law.

What is obvious in both of these positions—muzzling the church and dismissing jurists who have religious convictions—is that those who advocate them envision an America without moral foundation to its laws. This is unfortunate because the nation will inevitably fall apart from moral decay without such a foundation. Religious freedom is ultimately what keeps America strong, healthy, and vibrant. While not requiring belief in God, our people and political leaders should acknowledge God and help ensure that America remains a good and moral country. Or, to quote de Tocqueville, there are "two perfectly distinct elements that elsewhere have often made war with each other, but which in America, they have succeeded in incorporating somehow into one another and combining marvelously. I mean to speak of the spirit of religion and the spirit of freedom."[53] He further explained that "freedom sees in religion the companion of its struggles and its triumphs, the cradle of its infancy, the divine source of its rights. It considers religion the safeguard of mores; and mores as the guarantee of laws and the pledge of its own duration."[54]

The First Amendment allows the citizens of America to live in accordance with their consciences. As such, America is a healthier and happier country than perhaps any other place on earth. "The separation of church and State," Carter writes, "is one of the great gifts that American

53. Alexis de Tocqueville, *Democracy in America*, trans. Harvey Mansfield and Debra Winthrop (Chicago: University of Chicago Press, 2000), 44.
54. Ibid., 44-45.

political philosophy has presented to the world, and if it has few emulators, that is the world's loss."[55] If the Supreme Court and others interpret the First Amendment apart from the classical idea of natural law as expressed by, among others, John Locke, it is America's loss.

55. Carter, *The Culture of Disbelief*, 107.

CHAPTER 7

Understanding the Difference Between Religious Liberty and Religious Autonomy

Daniel R. Heimbach

It is difficult to have a casual discussion of religious liberty because discourse on the subject is highly charged and rightly so. The stakes are high and include such fundamental matters as personal conscience, accountability to God, duty to preach the gospel, the role and responsibilities of government, and even questions of social survival. The view we take on religious liberty is shaped by how we think about the relation of morality to law, of ethics to government, and the enormous tension that always exists between necessities that drive and limitations that restrict responsible use of God-assigned power in the hands of governors to accomplish what the Bible calls approving good and avenging wrong (Rom. 13:3–4), or restraining the wicked and favoring the righteous (Ps. 82:3–4; 2 Chron. 19:2; 1 Pet. 2:14).

Religious liberty includes a number of foci that easily lead to opposing (or at least rather confused) views about what it means in the first place. So while debating the merits of religious liberty, parties often talk past each other so completely as never to engage what the other affirms or denies. Lack of clarity at critical junctures about what one means by religious liberty can be dangerous if it leads to concessions that should never be made or hinders agreements that really are essential. So precisely because religious liberty is highly charged, we must approach it with careful attention to what actually is intended in specific circumstances.

While there certainly is a valid theoretical need to clarify what religious liberty means, the need for clarification is not just theoretical but intensely practical as well. Conflict arising from contrary notions of and about religious liberty drives struggles around the world, including some close to home. For example, a major division has arisen among Southern Baptists between those who espouse the sort of liberty from outside interference the Christian community needs to assure fidelity to the Word of God and those who espouse a form of autonomy that severs individuals and congregations from accountability to God through his Word.[1]

Consider also the tension that rises between the pride Baptists have in having helped the American founding fathers to assure religious liberty in the U.S. Constitution and arguments set forth recently by Justice Antonin Scalia regarding the need responsible government has to prohibit using substances dangerous to human life and social order. On the first, historian Joseph Martin Dawson has said that "if researchers of the world were to be asked who was most responsible for the American guarantee for religious liberty, their prompt reply would be 'James Madison'; but if James Madison might answer, he would as quickly reply, 'John Leland and the Baptists.'"[2] That is because Leland and Madison together led the charge that convinced the American founders to guarantee the new nation would honor and protect the independence of religious conviction, expression, and practice.

John Leland, the Baptist, is famous for having once said that "government has no more to do with the religious opinions of men, than it has with the principles of mathematics."[3] And Leland is largely responsible for convincing James Madison, a lifelong Anglican who represented Virginia at the Constitutional Convention, that "religion and government will both exist in greater purity, the less they are mixed together."[4] In line with this heritage, Southern Baptists today affirm in The Baptist Faith and Message that we believe the state not only "has no right to impose penalties for religious opinions of any kind . . . (and)

1. Gregory A. Wills, in an unpublished paper, has analyzed how Baptists in America started with a view of religious freedom that focused on ecclesiastical freedom to determine matters of doctrine and to exercise church discipline independent of state control. He goes on, however, to show that many Baptists over time came to a different view of religious freedom, one that insists, not on freedom *for,* but on freedom *from,* accountability and discipline in church life. His paper is titled: "That Altar to Freedom: Freedom, Authority, and Southern Baptists."
2. Joseph Martin Dawson, *Baptists and the American Republic* (Nashville: Broadman, 1956), 117.
3. Quoted in H. Leon McBeth, *The Baptist Heritage* (Nashville: Broadman, 1987), 275.
4. James Madison, *The Writings of James Madison,* ed. Gaillard Hunt (Temecula, Calif.: Best Books, 2004).

no right to impose taxes for the support of any form of religion," but also that "a free church in a free state . . . implies the right of free and unhindered access to God on the part of all men, and the right to form and propagate opinions in the sphere of religion without interference by the civil power."[5]

But, while maintaining our zeal for religious liberty, how should Baptists say our heritage accords with civil need to restrain religiously motivated activities threatening the common good? The U.S. Supreme Court, in 1990, considered whether government can ever justify restricting religiously motivated conduct, and Justice Scalia, writing the majority opinion, held that, under the U.S. Constitution, the American right to religious expression is not unlimited and that government interference is sometimes warranted. In that case, *Employment Division v. Smith,* the Supreme Court held that states have a right to prohibit using narcotic drugs including peyote, even though some Native Americans have long used peyote for sacramental purposes.

Justice Scalia held that religious beliefs do not excuse individuals "from compliance with an otherwise valid law prohibiting conduct that the State is free to regulate . . . [and] the mere possession of religious convictions which contradict the relevant concerns of political society does not relieve the citizen from the discharge of political responsibilities."[6] He denied unrestricted liberty of religious expression because, he said, such liberty produces "a right to ignore generally applicable laws" and "any society adopting such a system would be courting anarchy."[7] We cannot, Scalia argued, "afford the luxury of deeming presumptively invalid, as applied to the religious objector, every regulation of conduct that does not protect an interest of the highest order."[8]

Third, to further illustrate the need we have to clarify the meaning of religious liberty, consider the volatile and exceptionally dangerous tension we face these days between the sort of religious liberty we have in mind as Baptists, which sees no inconsistency with swearing to "support and defend the Constitution and laws of the United States of America

5. The Baptist Faith and Message, adopted by the Southern Baptist Convention, June 14, 2000 (Nashville: Southern Baptist Convention, 2000), 20–21.
6. *Employment Division, Department of Human Resources of Oregon v. Smith* (17 April 1990).
7. Ibid.
8. Ibid.

. . . without any mental reservation or purpose of evasion,"[9] and a sort of religious liberty that denies civil authorities should ever hinder (or even monitor) the activities of Muslims who believe the Koran requires doing all in their power to impose Islamic rule on the rest of the world. The sort of religious liberty Baptists affirm is completely consistent with defending a Constitution that says, "Congress shall make no law respecting an establishment of religion."[10]

But because the Koran tells Muslims to "make war on the infidels [non-Muslims] who dwell around you" (Sura 9:123) and requires them to "fight . . . until idolatry [non-Muslim religion] is no more and Allah's religion reigns supreme [politically and religiously]" (Sura 2:193), zealous Muslims cannot honestly swear to support the U.S. Constitution "without any mental reservation or purpose of evasion." Autonomy for Muslim activity in the United States means leaving ourselves vulnerable to activities aimed at destroying the American system of government and allowing religious freedom only for followers of the Muslim faith.

Do Baptists believe civil government should absolutely never hinder anything men do in the name of pursuing "access to God"? Are Baptists unexceptionally opposed to government ever restricting religiously motivated activities however interpreted, whatever they involve, and no matter what they threaten? Do Baptists espouse a version of religious liberty that insists on complete unaccountable independence from answering to any external authority at all? Do we defend what might be called religious autonomy? Or do we espouse something more limited, a view of religious liberty that assumes some basic level of common decency sufficient to keep society from trying to avoid chaos at the price of tyranny on one hand and trying to avoid tyranny at the price of chaos on the other? In different terms, the fundamental issue Baptists must clarify when it comes to religious liberty in the face of religiously inspired terrorism is this: *How are we to handle religious liberty for individuals and systems whose religion demands getting rid of the sort of religious liberty we believe in?*

We will proceed now to clarify the meaning of religious liberty by evaluating three questions: Why liberty? What liberty? and Whose liberty? The first question—why liberty?—shows there are two fundamentally contrary approaches to the value of religious liberty touching the

9. Naturalization Oath of Allegiance to the United States.
10. The Constitution of the United States, Amendment I.

role and duties of responsible government. The second question—what liberty?—reveals two mutually incompatible concepts of liberty that affect the way we understand efforts to escape government regulation. The third question—whose liberty?—highlights differences that arise between claiming exemptions that apply to institutions as opposed to individuals. And finally, we will show that combining these distinctions enables us to define four different views about the fundamental meaning of religious liberty.

Why Liberty? Different Views on the Value of Religious Liberty in General

We turn now to consider what distinguishes favoring religious liberty as something valuable and necessary from rejecting religious liberty as something dangerously evil. For Baptists used to biblical categories, it must be said the sort of freedom with which we are dealing in this context is not what Paul had in mind writing to the church in Galatia where he said, "It is for freedom that Christ set us free" (Gal. 5:1). Paul was speaking there of the sinner's spiritual-moral freedom from bondage to the power and penalty of sin, a freedom won for us by Christ's death and resurrection, a freedom that can neither be guaranteed, restricted, nor removed by any human power. Is that the sort of freedom to which we refer in discussing religious liberty in temporal affairs, to the sort of religious liberty granted or denied by civil authorities? No, it is not.

To be sure, that is a very real sort of freedom. And that sort of freedom is certainly religious in nature. But it is not the sort of religious freedom with which we deal when advocating or defending independence from government interference. Spiritual-moral freedom from the power and penalty of sin is something God alone determines. That sort of freedom cannot be given or hindered by men no matter what they say or do. By contrast, the sort of religious liberty for which Baptists have struggled for centuries, on many continents, and against many administrations of human government is an affair of the social and civil order. It is more political than spiritual and refers more to ways in which groups or individuals relate to one another in space-time-material reality than to how they stand before God. And while this sort of religious freedom affects Christians and matters to the church, it has no immediate relation to spiritual-moral freedom from the power and penalty of sin by which sinners escape the wrath of God.[11]

Moving now to what we actually mean by religious liberty in relation to government, our first defining question is, why liberty? Addressed to the state, this question asks whether, and to what extent, government ought to protect and promote moral truth. How we answer sets up a division distinguishing two opposing approaches: one favoring religious idealism in general and the other favoring religious liberty in general.

The Case against Religious Liberty in General[12]

Religious idealism—an approach associated with pre-Vatican II Catholicism,[13] various parts of the Orthodox Church,[14] Saudi Arabia, Islamic terrorist groups linked to Osama bin Laden and Al Qaeda,[15] Japan prior to WW II, and ideological communism—is characterized by a single overarching principle, that *only truth has rights, and error has no rights.*[16] This one key principle is judged to be universal and is thought applicable to social and political, as well as theological, matters. Adherents may pursue this approach in ecclesiastical or secular forms, but all are convinced there is only room for one religious-moral ideology on earth.[17] In secular form, truth is interpreted by an ideologi-

---

11. For a more complete discussion, see John Courtney Murray, S. J., *Religious Liberty,* ed. J. Leon Hooper, S. J. (Louisville, Ky.: Westminster/John Knox Press, 1993), 140ff.

12. Although I employ different terms, I here follow a distinction made by John Courtney Murray. Ibid., 97– 113, and 130–51.

13. At Vatican II, the Roman Catholic Church shifted from traditional-historic commitment to religious idealism to instead favor and support religious liberty. This change was promulgated in "Declaration on Religious Freedom: On the Right of the Person and Communities to Social and Civil Freedom in Matters of Religion" (*Dignitatis Humanae*). *The Documents of Vatican II,* ed. Walter M. Abbott, S. J., trans. Joseph Gallagher (Rome: American Press and Association Press, 1966), 675–96.

14. For example, the Romanian Orthodox Church took the *religious idealism* approach when in 1994 it successfully pressured the Romanian government to cancel, on short notice, several previously approved Easter programs sponsored by the Evangelical Alliance of Romania that were scheduled to be aired on the government-owned, government-operated television station.

15. Documentation of this view can be found in John Kelsey, *Islam and War* (Louisville: Westminster/John Knox, 1993); especially see his chapters on "The Islamic View of Peace" and "Religion as a Cause of War."

16. As an example of this view, Murray cites Pope Pius XII in *Ci riesce, Acta Apostolica Sedis* 45 (1953), 788–89, who states, "That which does not correspond to the truth and the norm of morality has, objectively, no right either to existence or to propaganda or to action." Cited by Murray, *Religious Liberty,* 134.

17. Historic examples include the Catholic pope, the patriarch of the Greek Orthodox Church, the Islamic caliph (before destruction of the caliphate), the ayatollah of Shiite Islam, or the

cal body, like the communist Politburo of the former Soviet Union, that declares what must be applied to everyone else. In ecclesiastical form, truth claims issue from the head of a body of believers, such as the pope speaking for the Catholic Church or Osama bin Laden claiming to speak for the *umma muslima*—the universal community of faithful Muslims.

But whether in secular or ecclesiastical form, religious idealism always assumes that civil government must do all in its power to coerce conformity to one true faith, and it leaves no room for tolerating differences in theology or politics. Religious idealism is completely intolerant of ideological diversity so long as there is power enough to eradicate other views, and it tolerates dissent only so long as adherents are too weak to impose their view on others.[18]

The Case for Religious Liberty in General

The opposite position to religious idealism regarding the role of government in promoting religious-moral truth is, of course, to favor religious liberty in general. This approach—historically associated with Baptists and Anabaptists, and more recently with post-Vatican II Catholicism, the United States, and most western European nations as well—supposes that everyone has a right to some degree of independence from government interference based on some notion of accountability to higher moral authority.[19] Whereas religious idealism in

---

Communist Party Politburo which ruled the former Soviet Union.

18. Murray explains, "The supreme juridical principle for the exclusive rights of truth, and its pendant distinction between thesis and hypothesis, establish a rule of jurisprudence with regard to tolerance and intolerance. This rule prescribes intolerance whenever possible; it permits tolerance whenever necessary." Murray, *Religious Liberty,* 134.

19. Many examples, both theological and philosophical, could be cited in defense of religious liberty. Baptist minister Leonard Busher, in 1614, explained in a petition to King James I of Great Britain, that "kings and magistrates are to rule temporal affairs by the swords of their temporal kingdoms, and bishops and ministers are to rule spiritual affairs by the Word and the Spirit of God, the sword of Christ's spiritual kingdom, and not to intermeddle one with another's authority, office, and function." Anson Phelps Stokes, *Church and State in the United States* (New York: Harper, 1950), 1:113.

John Leland, another Baptist minister, writing at the time of the American Revolution, argued saying, "I now call for an instance, where Jesus Christ, the author of his religion, or the apostles, who were divinely inspired, ever gave orders to, or intended, that the civil powers on earth, ought to force people to observe rules and doctrine of the gospels. . . . There are many things that Jesus and the apostles taught, that men ought to obey, which yet the civil law has no concern in." L. F. Green, ed., *The Writings of John Leland* (New York: Arno, 1969), 187.

In a break from previous Catholic tradition, Pope John XXII, in 1963, defended religious liberty, saying, "The dignity of the human person requires that a man should act on his own judgment and with freedom. Wherefore in community life there is good reason why it should be chiefly on his own deliberate initiative that a man should exercise his rights, fulfill his du-general expects government to use coercive power to eradicate error at all levels, the approach favoring religious liberty in general limits the coercive power of government only to where needed to preserve basic (not ideal) social order.[20]

Proponents of this approach expect governors to be humble enough to recognize their judgments are not God's judgments, even though they should cooperate with God to protect religious liberty within the general duty to preserve civil order. Favoring religious liberty in general does not deny that government has a moral purpose, nor does it suggest that government never punish evil or reward good. It views the legitimate purpose of morally responsible government to be limited only to what is needed to maintain peace with justice in civil affairs.

According to this approach, the duties of responsible government do not include eliminating theological error and do not include matters of religious discipline. These are left to religious institutions and individuals out of desire to honor boundaries making room for freedom of conscience and of religious competition within the civil order. This respect for religious liberty in general within the civil order does not deny the importance or reality of theological truth by which individuals are reconciled with God or the church pursues its mission on earth. But it does give latitude for competition between competing religious convictions within the same civil order. Indeed, this approach presumes such trust in the power of truth over error that institutions and individuals with a strong sense of religious-moral conscience are given room by civil authorities to compete without interference from the government.

---

ties, and cooperate with others in the endless variety of necessary social tasks. . . . [It] is clear that a society of men which is maintained solely by force must be considered inhuman." *Pacem in terras, Acta Apostolica Sedis* 55 (1963), 265; also Murray, *Religious Liberty,* 137–38.

20. Thomas Jefferson, author of the "Bill for Establishing Religious Liberty" passed by the state of Virginia in 1785, argued that "the opinions of men are not the object of civil government, nor under its jurisdiction; [and] . . . to suffer the civil magistrate to intrude his powers into the field of opinion and to restrain the profession or propagation of principles on supposition of their ill tendency is a dangerous fallacy, which at once destroys all religious liberty, because he being of course judge of that tendency, will make his opinions the rule of judgment, and approve or condemn the sentiments of others only as they shall square with or differ from his own; [thus] . . . it is enough for the rightful purposes of Civil Government for its officers to interfere when principles break out into overt acts against peace and good order." Stokes, *Church and State,* 1:334.

What Liberty? For Whom? Different Views on the Meaning of Religious Liberty Itself

The second question we must address to understand what religious liberty actually means is, what liberty? And responding to this question leads to recognizing two incompatible concepts of liberty: one we may call *ordered liberty,* and the other, *autonomous liberty.*[21]

Ordered Liberty

Ordered liberty is a concept of freedom that is restrained by moral obligations. Freedom from human authority is pursued in order to obey some higher moral authority—an authority that is by definition beyond being controlled by the institutions or individuals concerned.[22] This concept of freedom always involves freedom *for* as opposed to freedom *from.* It is freedom to do what we ought, not freedom simply to do what we wish. It is freedom to fulfill higher moral obligations and is not just a matter of avoiding accountability.

Put differently, it is freedom under a higher law, not freedom from any law at all. Ordered liberty presumes that real moral authority is objective, enduring and universal, and is certainly not anything controlled or made up by those living by it. Not only is the source of moral authority considered to be outside and beyond the individual and outside and beyond institutions of religion, it is outside and beyond civil government as well.[23] This is the view of morally responsible religious liberty in relation to human government expressed throughout the Bible.[24] It

21. I am following a distinction described by Michael Novak in *The Catholic Ethic and the Spirit of Capitalism* (New York: Free Press, 1993), 93–99. Novak identifies two contrary concepts of liberty in chapter 4, titled "The Second Liberty." Although he approaches liberty as a component of economic philosophy, he nevertheless takes time to discuss its religious dimensions. Thus the distinction he makes between concepts of liberty does, in fact, pertain directly to the project addressed in this article.

22. Novak calls this the "Anglo-American" conception of liberty and quotes Lord Acton, who said, "The Christian notion of conscience imperatively demands a corresponding measure of personal liberty. The feeling of duty and responsibility to God is the only arbiter of a Christian's actions. With this no human authority can be permitted to interfere. We are bound to extend to the utmost, and to guard from every encroachment, the sphere in which we can act in obedience to the sole voice of conscience, regardless of any other consideration." Novak, *Catholic Ethic,* 94; originally from Lord John Emerich Edward Dalberg-Acton, *Select Writings of Lord Acton,* ed. J. Rufus Fears (Indianapolis: Liberty Classics, 1988), 3:491.

23. Lord Acton said, "With this [religious freedom] no human authority can be permitted to interfere." Ibid.

24. For example, when the Sanhedrin banned Peter and John from preaching in the name of Jesus, they replied, "Judge for yourselves whether it is right in God's sight to obey you rather than God" (Acts 4:19 NIV).

is also the view that has most influenced the formation of English and American law.[25]

Autonomous Liberty

Standing in contrast to ordered liberty is a view we may call autonomous liberty.[26] This is a view of independence that arises from Roman law and that permeates continental European legal traditions.[27] The autonomous liberty view defines freedom as the absence of obligation. It is always freedom from and is never freedom for. Freedom, thus conceived, is defined by what it lacks—no limitations, no responsibility, no accountability—not by what it entails. This is not liberty under obligation to some higher law but liberty that is essentially lawless.[28] According to this view, an individual or institution is never truly free unless independent from, and therefore unaccountable to, any limitation or accountability whatsoever—not merely civil but ecclesiastical, moral, and social as well. Consequently, this view poses a dilemma—law must either deny autonomous liberty in order to maintain social order or allow autonomous liberty to increasingly undermine the rule of law leading eventually to complete social collapse.

The third and final question we must ask to better understand religious liberty is, whose liberty? This leads us to address the fact that religious liberty covers more than one sort of relationship and often involves complex levels of interrelated interests, responsibilities, and authorities. In particular, religious liberty concerns the manner in which individuals and institutions relate to one another and to God. Each party in this complex bears responsibilities and duties in relation to all the others, and lines of relationship must be drawn that order these responsibilities and duties in ways that secure harmony not conflict.

---

25. This view is outlined by Novak and contrasted with European nations whose legal traditions descend directly from the Roman system (as opposed to the Anglo-American common law tradition). Novak, *Catholic Ethic,* 99–101; also see Harold J. Berman, *Law and Revolution: The Formation of the Western Legal Tradition* (Cambridge: Harvard University Press, 1983).

26. Novak describes this as the Roman or Latin concept of liberty and refers to it by the French word *liberté.* Novak, *Catholic Ethic,* 99. I prefer the term *autonomous liberty* because it defines the concept itself.

27. Ibid.

28. Novak says that "those who live in Latin countries in particular are accustomed to thinking of *liberte* as lawless. In Latin countries, many early leaders of the liberal party prided themselves on being anticlerical, atheistic, not infrequently amoral, and metaphysical skeptics. . . . [Thus they] do not conceive of liberty as ordered by law, reason, and conscience, or recognize that, without law, liberty [in the Anglo-American sense] cannot be achieved." Ibid.

Contrasting Views About the Specific Meaning of Religious Liberty

Using the distinctions clarified above, it is possible to identify several specific categories of meaning for religious liberty, and when the distinction between individuals and institutions is combined with the distinction between ordered liberty and autonomous liberty, it yields four distinctly different concepts: (1) ordered liberty for institutions; (2) autonomous liberty for institutions; (3) ordered liberty for individuals; and (4) autonomous liberty for individuals.[29] We shall now look at each in turn.

View 1: Ordered Liberty for Institutions

Ordered liberty for institutions touches many important issues such as freedom of association, freedom of worship, freedom of the church to maintain discipline, freedom to control religious education, freedom to set membership requirements, freedom to hire church workers, and freedom to evangelize. While ordered liberty for institutions is characterized by obligation to a higher moral authority and while standards of truth are treated as objective and enduring, an institution's perception of truth and its understanding of moral obligation—that is, its beliefs—can be either accurate or mistaken. That is, they can be genuinely believed even if they lack a basis in fact.

But, whether beliefs are accurate or mistaken, ordered liberty for institutions means that desire, will, and conduct, at the level of institutional leadership, are subject to convictions of religious-moral conscience; it involves an acceptance of corporate responsibility to be faithful to a higher source of religious-moral authority, a source that transcends the mere wishes of institutional leaders or the passing whims of institutional majorities. In American practice and tradition, this form of religious liberty has proven good and beneficial to society and supportive of civil order.[30]

---

29. Here I develop an original paradigm that goes beyond what is found either in the work of John Courtney Murray or Michael Novak. I rely on Murray's understanding of institutional as well as individual dimensions of religious liberty, and I borrow Novak's insight regarding differing concepts of liberty. But neither of these noted scholars considered the intersection of these particular distinctions.

30. This traditional assessment was expressed by George Washington, partly in a letter of May 1789, sent to the United Baptist Churches of Virginia, and partly in his "Farewell Address." In the first he said, "If I could have entertained the slightest apprehension, that the constitution framed in the convention, where I had the honor to preside, might possibly endanger the

View 2: Autonomous Liberty for Institutions

Autonomous liberty for institutions results from combining the claims of a religious body with the autonomous concept of liberty. This second view addresses concerns similar to the first—freedom of worship, group discipline, and institutional control of religious education and propagation. Nevertheless, the second view differs from the first in that the freedom claimed does not, even in the mind of institutional leaders, entail obligation to an authority beyond or above the personal authority of an institution's leaders. However they are put, standards espoused by institutions holding this view are no more than ambitions, wishes, or desires held by leaders who do not believe they are under any constraint other than what they make up for themselves.

Where this is genuinely the case, one cannot rightly speak of religious-moral conscience or the rights of conscience. That is because religious-moral conscience must by definition entail some sense of obligation to moral authority beyond one's own,[31] and there simply is no ground for claiming obligation to comply with conscience where there is no place for obligation to any authority beyond one's own desires.

Without any sense of obligation to higher authority, the convictions of such institutions cannot be judged accurate or mistaken, and others can only evaluate their conduct as harmful, irrelevant, or helpful as it affects the civil order. We can conclude that institutions claiming to be religious while led under the rubric of autonomous liberty serve

---

religious rights of any ecclesiastical society, certainly I would never have placed my signature to it." Stokes, *Church and State,* 1:495. In the second he added, "Of all the dispositions and habits which lead to political prosperity, Religion and Morality are indispensable supports. In vain would that man claim the tribute of Patriotism, who should labour to subvert these great pillars of human happiness, these firmest supports of the duties of Men and Citizens. . . . Whatever may be conceded to the influence of refined education on minds of peculiar structure; reason and experience both forbid us to expect that national morality can prevail in exclusion of religious principle." Ibid., 1:494–95.

31. The rights of conscience have received critical attention in the defense and affirmation of religious liberty precisely because conscience is deemed to entail obligation to an authority beyond human control and ability to shape or determine. Reinhold Niebuhr, referring to human conscience, calls it "the sense of moral obligation laid upon one from beyond oneself and of moral unworthiness before a judge." *The Nature and Destiny of Man* (New York: Scribner's, 1941), 1:131. Similar to Niebuhr, I contend that conscience is a sense, or awareness, that our actions are known and judged from a standpoint beyond ourselves, beyond our social community, and beyond the realm of contingent reality itself. It is an awareness, at the edges of conscious self-understanding, that our lives, including every particular thought and action, are being examined from a transcendent perspective, by an authority we do not control but cannot ignore because we are in some way being held accountable whether we like it or not.

only the self-interests of institutional leaders. Where self-interests are benign, there is no real threat. But where they are not, the autonomous liberty for institutions view is surely hazardous to social order and civil tranquility. In extreme form the influence and activities of such institutions will erode and not support social cohesion and will inevitably leave less assertive groups vulnerable to more assertive ones. That is because where groups are free to operate with no sense of responsibility to any authority beyond themselves, experience shows it will not be long before the common good comes under attack and the welfare of others is trampled.[32]

View 3: Ordered Liberty for Individuals

Ordered liberty for individuals constitutes a third view regarding the particular meaning of religious liberty. Here we move from what freedom means in the life of religious institutions to the freedom of individuals in matters of religious conviction and religiously motivated conduct. The liberty involved includes such matters as personal choice of association, individual involvement in corporate or private worship activities, one's personal perception of right and wrong, as well as individual accountability to God as judge of every thought and activity. Like ordered liberty for institutions, ordered liberty for individuals also involves religious-moral conscience because an individual understands himself to be under some moral authority higher than himself, a moral authority he cannot himself control and to which he must submit. He is obligated to obey an authority that will not bend to fit personal desires.

This third view argues that human government must not interfere with the obligation individuals have to live up to standards they do not control and to fulfill religious duties they cannot deny. At the same time, the sort of freedom involved in the liberty for individuals view strengthens respect for the moral purposes of government. Indeed, the moral purposes of government are thought to support, and never to oppose, efforts to conform with higher moral duties. Like ordered liberty of institutions, ordered liberty for individuals includes the possibility of honest error. It may involve adherence to genuine convictions that are misperceived. But even where misperception exists, individuals are not denying accountability to moral authority transcending their own.

32. This tendency explains the atrocious behavior of ethnic cleansers in Bosnia, who sensed no moral obligation other than to what served the limited interests of their own select group.

Consequently, this third view of religious liberty, like the first, has also proven to be good for society and supportive of civil order.[33]

But while this view supports the strength of responsible institutions, it also threatens those that are irresponsible. Why? Because individuals are left to scrutinize freely moral failure in their leaders, whether they be leaders of religious institutions or leaders in government. Indeed, ordered liberty for individuals is the view expressed by heroic prophetic witness in the Bible.[34]

View 4: Autonomous Liberty for Individuals

A fourth view of religious liberty—autonomous liberty for individuals—applies the concept of lawless liberty to individuals within the civil order. Like the previous three views, autonomous liberty for individuals also demands a realm of independence for religious belief and expression. But like the second and opposed to the first and third, it involves no real sense of higher moral duty. Indeed, it proposes a more radical concept of religious liberty than even the second. By the rubric of autonomous liberty for institutions, individuals are at least still held accountable under the leadership of a religious body. But individuals claiming autonomous liberty are accountable to no authority at all. They claim a sphere of expression for which any irresponsibility will go unchecked.

For this reason proponents of this view, like those espousing autonomous liberty for institutions, cannot properly claim to be exercising a right of conscience. That is because the notion of autonomous liberty involves no measure by which to legitimize such claims. No one can ever assess whether alleged convictions are either valid or invalid, genuine or

33. This understanding was expressed in the 1866 edition of McGuffey's fifth reader: "Religion is a social concern; for it operates powerfully on society, contributing, in various ways, to its stability and prosperity. Religion is not merely a private affair; the community is deeply interested in its diffusion; for it is the best support of the virtues and principles, on which the social order rests. Pure and undefiled religion is, to do good; and it follows, very plainly, that, if God be the Author and Friend of society, then, the recognition of him must enforce all social duty, and enlightened piety must give its whole strength to public order." William H. McGuffey, ed., *McGuffey's New Fifth Eclectic Reader* (Cincinnati: Wilson, Hinkle & Co., 1866), 306.

34. The prophet Jeremiah offers one of the finest biblical examples of such witness: "Jeremiah said to all the officials and all the people: 'The LORD sent me to prophesy against this house [i.e., the king] and this city all the things you have heard. Now reform your ways and your actions and obey the LORD your God. Then the LORD will relent and not bring the disaster he has pronounced against you. As for me, I am in your hands; do with me whatever you think is good and right. Be assured, however, that if you put me to death, you will bring the guilt of innocent blood on yourselves and on this city and on those who live in it, for in truth the LORD has sent me to you to speak all these words in your hearing'" (Jer. 26:12–15 NIV).

mistaken. Self-generated convictions are so purely subjective they can be evaluated by others only in regard to whether words are consistent with actions.

But even though this view denies individual responsibility to any external authority—any authority outside the control of individuals concerned—the behavior of individuals in this category can still be assessed by others as to how they affect social stability and the welfare of others in the civil order. Being so thoroughly autonomous—even to the level of persons who recognize no moral authority beyond themselves—the autonomous liberty for individuals view serves no higher good at all, whether social, political, or personal. It necessarily upsets theological-moral discipline in the church and directly opposes government responsibility to maintain social-moral accountability in the civil order.[35]

Some Final Remarks

The views we have defined regarding four different ways of understanding the essential meaning of religious liberty each share the idea that matters of religious belief and religious expression should in some sense be left free of government limitation, regulation, or control. And yet these four views do not carry the same level of legitimacy either in traditional Christian understanding or in terms of political-social analysis. Where they affect legitimate duties and responsibilities of civil government, it is clear these views are not equally compatible. Two of these views obviously strengthen and support the functioning of responsible government while two serve only to undermine and threaten responsible government.

Therefore in assessing their practical implications, I conclude by offering four general principles. While these principles will not exhaust needed analysis, they do suggest some ways Baptists might proceed in defending religious liberty without hindering God-assigned functions of responsible government in the face of religiously inspired terrorism.

First, it is not within the competence of governments to distinguish between true or erroneous conscience. Although governments can

35. This view of religious liberty comports with complete anarchy; and, should a government grant this view full protection under law, it would soon find itself helpless to maintain order at any level. Criminals could justify any action as a matter of pressing personal and self-defined religious conviction, while shifting their convictions to what seems convenient from situation to situation.

certainly distinguish institutions from individuals, they are not competent to discern when claims of religious-moral conscience are either accurate or mistaken. That is, they cannot tell when perceptions of duty owed to a higher source of moral authority are in fact true or false.[36] This means governments risk tyranny and oppression where they prefer one religious institution or religious class over others based solely on their own assessment of religious validity.

Second, governments have little, if any, ability to distinguish sincere from insincere claims of religious-moral conscience.[37] I have suggested that the presence of religious-moral conscience is critical for distinguishing ordered liberty from autonomous liberty at all levels and that distinguishing autonomous from ordered views of religious liberty does seriously affect the proper working of legitimate government responsibilities. But while the difference surely matters to government, civil government also lacks competence to recognize the most critical factor setting them apart. It cannot easily discern the difference between convictions of a genuine religious-moral conscience that truly submits to higher authority and insincere appeals to alleged convictions of conscience made only to win license to indulge the desires of those who submit to no sense of higher authority at all.

Together these first two principles mean that government cannot use evaluation of religious-moral conscience to separate between the four views of religious liberty. The best it can do is assume a particular claim is likely to be one variety or the other based on the appearance of sincerity and efforts to verify consistency. This impediment stands even though the different views offer radically opposed risk profiles. This means government efforts to judge the authenticity and validity of as-

36. Government has no way to render judgment between an authoritative or counterfeit experience of spiritual revelation. For example, government has no basis of meaningful authority by which to judge the validity of the vision reported by the apostle Paul to evangelize Macedonia (Acts 16:9) as compared to the spurious visions alleged by Joseph Smith to justify the founding of the Mormon religion. That one might be true and the other false, or that both may be true or both false, are surely conceptual possibilities. But that determination is beyond the competence of government to prove or decide.

37. For example, government cannot genuinely discern by external observation when an objection to participating in war is truly a matter of a claimant's submission to higher moral authority and when it is actually a matter of fear and self-interest cloaked in moralistic rhetoric. That such a distinction exists is clear enough. But where the difference is not readily apparent, the government is bound to grant claimants the benefit of a doubt or risk a serious violation of a genuine moral conviction.

sertions regarding religious-moral conscience cannot completely avoid uncertainty and vulnerability.

Efforts to judge the difference between sincere and insincere religious-moral conscience may be easier in more homogeneous religious environments, but they are still permeated with risk. And, of course, the more diverse the religious environment becomes and the more radically different religious minorities involved happen to be, the more risky and difficult it will be for government officials to make any satisfactory assumption regarding authentic claims of religious-moral conscience.[38]

Third, while governments can distinguish between belief and action, they are not able to distinguish in a reliable way between authentic and inauthentic religious expressions. Governments do not have the competence necessary to separate exercises that genuinely serve a higher authority from exercises that are merely fabrications of an autonomous human imagination.[39] This means that on matters of religious expression, as with claims of religious-moral conscience, civil governments can tell little difference between different views of religious liberty except where it concerns distinguishing individuals from institutions and evaluating consistency between words and actions.

A government may actually feel threatened by the risk of allowing freedom for persons or groups that sense no responsibility for anything beyond themselves. But it has no reliable way to assess the religious authenticity of exercises, the validity of which is subject only to the interpretation of those who engage in them. Because it cannot judge the authenticity of any particular source of religious authority, government cannot reliably use authenticity of religious expression to judge between the actions of ordered and autonomous liberty.

This brings us to the fourth principle for relating government to the various views identified. And it is, I believe, the only principle that offers legitimately functioning governments a way to make meaningful distinctions within their competence to judge. Governments are indeed

38. For example, in early American society differences regarding contrary claims of conscience were for the most part limited to those that could be evaluated within the larger conceptual framework provided by the Judeo-Christian worldview. Hazardous as they are, government efforts to determine sincerity of conscience in such circumstances is easier than in a more radically pluralistic setting that must also evaluate conscience claims raised by Buddhists, secular humanists, atheists, Wiccans, New Agers, and neopagans.

39. For example, civil officials of a secular government are not able to distinguish persons who seek to smoke peyote because they truly think it is religious from persons who make religious claims merely as a stratagem to justify getting high on the drug's narcotic effect.

(or should be) competent to judge between actions and expressions that are benevolent, benign, or malicious as to their effect upon civil peace, order, justice, and safety. Since responsible human governments do have a God-assigned moral mission to punish evil and reward good so far as it concerns their civil responsibilities, they must try to pass and to uphold laws that serve to restrain behavior that is harmful and to promote behavior that is beneficial to the common good (whatever their motives). This means government can discern and should restrain malicious conduct that at times arises from institutional or individual views of autonomous religious liberty, even while it protects and rewards benevolent conduct whatever its origin.

As a practical matter, government must be able to protect the civil order from abuses committed in the name of religious liberty, and such abuses certainly can arise where latitude is granted individuals and institutions who, under no sense of transcendent moral obligation, are guided by nothing more than their own transitory wishes and desires. But where it acts to restrain such abuse, government, if it is to remain responsible, must take care to limit its power to only that necessary to prevent harm. Should it seek to order society by imposing a single view of religious truth, then it oversteps its moral mission, presumes to act as God (in God's place) rather than with God (in cooperation with God, or at least noninterference with God), and makes judgments that only deity can truly judge. When that happens, then not only does government become tyrannical; it also undermines its own success by destabilizing society and marginalizing the moral influence of men and women who truly live by legitimate religious-moral conscience—those who truly live for something more than their own self-centered concerns.

A government that restrains its power out of respect for the ordered religious liberty of citizens will be strong and stable. But a government that tries to control religious belief and expression—either from zeal for religious idealism or for fear of religious autonomy—will soon be tyrannical, however good its intentions. When a government hinders ordered religious liberty, it cannot be stable, and it eventually destroys itself because it loses the respect and support of the responsible, public-minded segment of its citizenry that produces and strengthens social cohesion.

★★★★★★★★★★★★★★★★★★★★★★★★★★★★★

Chapter 8

Conservative Christians in an Era of Christian Conservatives: Reclaiming the Struggle for Religious Liberty from Cultural Captivity

Russell D. Moore

> First of all, then, I urge that supplications, prayers, intercessions, and thanksgivings be made for all people, for kings and all who are in high positions, that we may lead a peaceful and quiet life, godly and dignified in every way. This is good, and it is pleasing in the sight of God our Savior, who desires all people to be saved and to come to the knowledge of the truth. For there is one God, and there is one mediator between God and men, the man Christ Jesus, who gave himself as a ransom for all, which is the testimony given at the proper time. For this I was appointed a preacher and an apostle (I am telling the truth, I am not lying), a teacher of the Gentiles in faith and truth.
>
> I desire then that in every place the men should pray, lifting holy hands without anger or quarreling; likewise also that women should adorn themselves in respectable apparel, with modesty and self control, not with braided hair and gold or pearls or costly attire, but with what is proper for women who profess godliness—with good works (1 Tim. 2:1–10 ESV).

For too long culture mavens have assumed that conservative *Protestant* Christians are just another electoral interest group or identifiable American subculture. That, in itself, is not all that problematic. What is problematic is that many conservative Protestant Christians assume that they are principally another electoral interest group or identifiable American subculture. After a half century of political isolationism, many of our churches seem to identify what it means to be a Christian more in terms of specific policy proposals than in terms of a theological identity.

This is dangerous, not only for the mission of the church but also for the preservation of religious liberty in the Western world. This is because the struggle for religious liberty has never been principally about politics or even principally about culture. The Baptist struggle for religious freedom has been from the beginning first and foremost about the Great Commission calling of the church. If we see religion—or even religious liberty—as principally a cultural or political concern, we will lose not only the resources to protect the "first freedom," but we will also lose the distinctiveness of our Christian witness.

This means that, while we must engage politically to protect our inalienable religious rights and those of our neighbors, we must do so first as conservative *Christians* and not first as Christian *conservatives.* We must call the state to justice, but our ultimate concern should be for a place at the table at the marriage supper of the Lamb, not a place at the table at a political party platform committee meeting. As we find in Paul's discourse in 1 Timothy 2:1–10, our concern for the temporal political order is built on our much more significant concern for the gospel and the covenant community. If we will further our Baptist commitment to religious liberty, we must turn our attention to our theology—specifically our concepts of salvation and the church.

Regeneration, Not Just Reformation

I am not much of a neoconservative. My political philosophy is influenced much more by Russell Kirk, Richard Weaver, and the old Southern agrarian tradition than by some of the more ambitious conservative agendas on the scene today.[1] Nonetheless, I resonate with a few

1. For a sketch of the major emphases of traditionalist conservatism, see Mark C. Henrie, "Understanding Traditionalist Conservatism," in *Varieties of Conservatism in America,* ed. Peter Berkowitz (Stanford: Hoover Press, 2004), 3–30. For a discussion of the agrarian conservative tradition(s) in particular, see Allan Carlson, *The New Agrarian Mind: The Movement Toward Decentralist Thought in Twentieth Century America* (New Brunswick, N. J.:

key components of the neoconservative vision—a sense of morality, not just calculating national interest realism in foreign policy, for example—even while I disagree with some of their specific public policy proposals.[2] Perhaps the most important contribution the neoconservatives have made to contemporary political thought in the post-September 11 era is the reminder that ideas are behind religious movements and regimes, not just economic or cultural factors.

Leading neoconservatives have insisted, rightly, that behind Islamic jihadism there is a particular ideology—grounded in theology—that must be understood before it is confronted.[3] Thus, the reason "they hate us" is not simply economic envy. We cannot rid the world of terrorism simply by supplanting Third-World economies with more money. As a matter of fact, when American capitalism meets Islamic fascism, the result is more terrorism—since the Islamic terror lords conceive of American capitalism in terms of the cultural rot of Eminem music videos and Janet Jackson wardrobe malfunctions. Just as we had to understand the pseudotheological ideology behind Marxist communism, we must understand the ideological theology behind Islamic jihad.

In our own context, however, many look at conservative evangelicalism—particularly the Southern Baptist Convention—through the grid first of culture rather than theology. For much of the nineteenth and twentieth centuries, Southern Baptists could assume a common culture rooted in the relative safety of the Bible Belt South. There was a day when Southern Baptist identity meant that one knew the difference between a GA and an Acteen,[4] a day in which every Southern Baptist meeting would serve sweet tea. Those days are gone and mostly for the good since it means that Southern Baptists are engaging globally in the

---

Transaction, 2000); and Herbert Agar and Allen Tate, eds., *Who Owns America? A New Declaration of Independence* (Wilmington: ISI Books, 1999).

2. For an explanation of neoconservatism, see Irving Kristol, *Neoconservatism: The Autobiography of an Idea* (New York: Free Press, 1995).

3. See, for example, Natan Sharansky, *The Case for Democracy: The Power of Freedom to Overcome Tyranny and Terror* (New York: PublicAffairs, 2004).

4. "GA" refers to "Girls in Action," a missions education program designed for females of elementary school age. "Acteens" is a similar program designed for older girls. "RAs" indicates "Royal Ambassadors," a missions education program designed for boys. These organizations were promoted by the Woman's Missionary Union and the Brotherhood Commission of the SBC. In Southern Baptist churches, RAs and GAs typically met on Wednesday night for activities, fellowship, and lessons on missionaries and cooperative support for the Great Commission. They also served as a Baptist version of Cub Scouts or Campfire Girls, complete with badges, awards, and summer retreats. The organizations are now in decline.

Great Commission task and that we are impacting all of North America, not just Dixie. But it also means that we must take more careful heed in definition—heed to the theological commitments that define us. We must approach religious liberty in a way different from the Anti-Defamation League or the Seventh Day Adventists—even when we share the same policy goals. We must teach our people that religious liberty is not just about self-interest or American constitutionalism. It flows instead from our deepest and most theological commitments.

The apostle Paul's Spirit-inspired communiqué to his young disciple Timothy is instructive here. He called on the church under Timothy's care to pray not simply for people in general but specifically for "kings and all who are in high positions" (1 Tim. 2:2 ESV). It is important that twenty-first-century Southern Baptists understand the reasons behind this interest in political structures. It is not for power or for domination. It is instead because of the Great Commission. Paul noted that kings have much to do with whether "we may lead a peaceful and quiet life." The question for us is, who is the "we"? There is no doubt that, for Paul, the "we" is the church of the Lord Jesus. Moreover, Paul immediately turned from prayers for kings to his central concern—the mediation of Christ who gave himself for all people and the desire of the Father that all persons come to know the gospel. He longed for political tranquility because he wanted the church to be the church and to spread the gospel of the kingdom across the creation. Caesar's decisions make a difference about whether we have access to the nations to baptize, whether we can meet in freedom to worship our King Jesus. That is for what we must be praying.

Now Paul's admonition has a special application to citizens of a democratic republic. We are not only the church in this context; we are also those who are kings and in authority. Christians have a responsibility to be politically engaged and civically active. But we must not forget that religious liberty is about the Great Commission and not the other way around. If we blur this reality, we will become just another political interest group. And we will lose religious liberty along the way.

This is something our Baptist forebears from Isaac Backus to John Leland to George W. Truett understood well. For years the Baptist left has sought to copyright religious liberty and separation of church and state—importing into these terms the content of the latest platform of the Democratic National Committee or the latest fund-raising letter of the American Civil Liberties Union. And yet, any historical investigation will reveal that the trail of blood was left by persecuted Baptists and Anabaptists crying out for a free church in a free state who were *not* posing against the "religious right." They *were* the "religious right." They insisted on religious liberty precisely because they believed in personal regeneration, a regenerate church, the convicting authority of the Holy Spirit, and the supernatural origins of Christianity.

If we abstract religious liberty and political engagement from the Great Commission and the gospel of personal regeneration, we will have taken off down a dark and treacherous path. There are right now scads of "evangelical" political parachurch organizations with detailed policy proposals and virtually no theological consensus. They stand united on same-sex marriage and a pro-life ethic, but they haven't a clue why. Some pro-family organizations say far more about George W. Bush than Jesus of Nazareth.[5] Indeed some of our churches have more of a consensus on foreign policy than on the inerrancy of Scripture.

Evangelical groups find themselves uniting for conferences on saving America with the likes of evangelist Joyce Meyer. Yes, Meyer is right on abortion and on voluntary prayer in schools and so forth, but she is theologically aberrant to the core.[6] Some evangelical Christians align themselves in pro-Israel causes with the likes of John Hagee—without qualms that Hagee has remained notoriously unclear about whether Jewish people can be saved apart from faith in Christ. This is not to say that we cannot unite with those who disagree with us theologically for specific policy purposes, especially for religious liberty. We can work with Mormons, for instance, to work against zoning laws that unfairly penalize churches. But we make sure that our churches understand that our understanding of religious liberty flows from our understanding of the gospel—and then we spend years of discipleship and teaching to make sure they grasp the content and glory of that gospel.

As we do so, we make clear that religious liberty and political engagement is not incidental to our calling as the church. Our Chinese

5. For a further discussion of how Christian theism must be theologically grounded in order to avoid being politically identified, see Russell D. Moore, *The Kingdom of Christ: The New Evangelical Perspective* (Wheaton, Ill.: Crossway, 2004).

6. Joyce Meyer is among the most successful contemporary manifestations of the "prosperity gospel" movement popularized in the twentieth century by preachers such as Oral Roberts, Kenneth Copeland, and Fred Price. For an analysis of the "word faith" movements, see D. R. McConnell, *A Different Gospel: Biblical and Historical Insights into the Word of Faith Movement* (Peabody, Mass.: Hendrickson, 1995).

and Sudanese brothers and sisters in Christ cannot send missionaries to the nations because they are hunted like animals by predatory governments.[7] In the "free world," religious liberty means more than simply making sure no one goes to jail for preaching the gospel. It also means understanding that political decisions often transform culture and that culture then transforms the context in which we preach the gospel.

The abortion issue, for instance, is about more than saving the lives of babies (although that would be reason enough to obligate us to stand against it). How are we to preach the gospel of everlasting life in a culture that celebrates death? You change minds about abortion because the abortion culture is more than a political problem. It is a satanic conspiracy that drives people away from wisdom and toward death itself (Prov. 8:36). This means that if we are going to make a difference on the abortion issue, we need to cultivate more than pro-life voters. Too often people assume that we oppose abortion because we want to vote Republican. Rather, for most of us, we so often vote Republican because of the abortion issue and the issues that cluster around it. To fight for religious liberty and Christian freedom, we must cultivate churches that are in love with the gospel itself.

There may well be a resurgent isolationist stream in the Southern Baptist Convention. Some Baptists have embraced some of the postmodern cynicism of the emerging church movement in American evangelicalism. The "pomo-Baptists" criticize some of the naively political rhetoric of conservative Christianity—often with justification. We should heed the warning to flee a collapsing of the church's witness and any political party. And yet there is the danger of some in the emerging church who call us to be "missional" and "incarnational" by being politically ambiguous as a strategy for Great Commission effectiveness. This is not accidental since some of the same people call us to be theologically ambiguous—uniting with those who deny biblical inerrancy or the exclusivity of Christ or the objective nature of biblical truth.[8]

7. For a discussion of persecution of Christians across the world, see Allen D. Hertzke, *Freeing God's Children: The Unlikely Alliance for Global Human Rights* (Lanham, Md.: Rowman and Littlefield, 2004).

8. See, for instance, the heterodox theology of Brian D. McLaren on issues of the reality of hell, the meaning of truth, the doctrine of Scripture, and so forth. Among Southern Baptists, Houston pastor Chris Seay turns to postmodernism while embracing views of an errant Scripture in precisely the same terms of Southern Baptist moderates a generation ago. Chris Seay, *Faith of My Fathers: Conversations with Three Generations of Pastors About Church, Ministry, and Culture* (Grand Rapids: Zondervan, 2005), 81–87.

Yes, we must be sure that our churches are not co-opted by any political party or agenda, but a biblical concept of mission and incarnation has to do with clarity—not ambiguity. The pomo-Baptists criticize "culture warriors" for treating American culture as a battlefield instead of a mission field—again, sometimes with justification. But most of the leaders they criticize are speaking to believers, understanding that political and cultural trends are transforming the minds of church members and must be countered with a more Christian way of seeing reality. A church member who embraces white supremacy or a pro-choice position on abortion isn't principally a political statistic but a failure of Christian discipleship. Likewise, a Christian who longs for a coercive state church or who doesn't care about religious persecution in the Islamic world doesn't just have a skewed political ideology but an apathetic heart for the nations, a heart that doesn't understand the freeness of the gospel or the task of the Great Commission.

Only with a firm grasp of the gospel, what Paul explains in mysterious glory to Timothy, can we motivate regenerate hearts to press for religious liberty. We come to Caesar not as supplicants seeking our rights. We come to Caesar, when he obstructs the freedom to worship or evangelize or live peaceably, with a warning, "No sir, you will not come this far." The reason we do so is that we, more than anyone else, understand that Caesar's authority is derivative and strictly limited (Rom. 13:1–7). We also understand that religious liberty—or even constitutional rights as citizens—are not ends in themselves; they are means to an end. They enable us more freely to preach and persuade and pray and worship and live in ecclesial community. "Just as I Am" is a religious liberty anthem.

Counterculture Peace, Not Just Culture Wars

In order to preserve our heritage of advocacy for religious liberty, we must protect the centrality of the church. Many contemporary Christians argue that social and political engagement is for individual Christians, not for churches. The problem with this argument is that there is no understanding of a Christian in the New Testament who is not ecclesially located. A churchless Christian is, for the apostles, simply lost (1 John 2:19; Heb. 10:23–31). All of the Christian life is situated within the life of the community, a covenant community that models for the world the realities of the coming kingdom of Christ. The fight for religious liberty means more than just advocacy by Christians for protection from the government. It means maintaining the freedom for churches to be the church before the watching culture.

This is why Paul, after commanding the church to pray for ruling authorities in the context of the free offer of the gospel, turned the question of precisely what it looks like for a free church to live "godly and dignified in every way" (1 Tim. 2:2 ESV). He meant that the men of the congregation must not be quarrelers. They must be holy. They must be praying diligently. He meant that the women of the congregation must likewise not be conformed to the culture around them. They must not be entranced by outward beautification. They must not usurp the headship of men. He calls on the church not only to attend to the culture, chiefly through prayer, but also to attend to forming through the Spirit and the Word a counterculture.

If we are to preserve our commitment to religious liberty, we must confront within our own people the notion that they are getting perpetually from the culture and from the state, the notion that they are autonomous individuals living individual stories and claiming individual rights. Too often even Christians see themselves as isolated individuals who come together at the voting booth to decide who runs the Congress and who come together at a congregational business meeting to decide whether to buy a lawn mower. Is it any wonder that we often find community more in our political commonalities than in our lives together in the church?

Jim Crow fell in Southern Baptist churches not because civil rights activists appealed to the Fourteenth Amendment. White supremacy fell because they appealed to Ephesians 2 and Ephesians 3 and Galatians 3—the unity of the people of God in the church. This carries the weight not of a political agenda but the weight of the authority of God himself as revealed in his inerrant Word. We need not only to claim the religious liberty to live out the calling of the church; we need actually to live out that calling. We need not only to claim the rights to have crisis pregnancy centers; we should have them. We need not only to claim the rights of elderly people and orphans to live; we should take them in and care for them. We need not only to maintain that the welfare of the impoverished is principally the role of the church and not the state; we as churches need to take care of the poor. We need not only to express outrage when a renegade court forbids students from freely gathering to pray; we need to engage our churches to teach teenagers to be praying men and women.

As in the first century, one key aspect of this countercultural church reality is focused on the creational orders of gender. Right now Southern Baptists, along with very few others, are standing virtually alone for male headship in the church and home against a cultural tsunami of feminism.[9] Some suggest that a proclamation of biblical patriarchy may one day be persecuted as a hate crime. Will we have communities so submissive to the will of God that our churches will order themselves biblically no matter what Caesar (or, for that matter, Jezebel) says about it?

The first step is not just teaching religious liberty but teaching biblical authority and the church as the primary locus of the glory and kingdom of Christ in the present age. Just as for Timothy's Ephesian context, this means cultivating godly patriarchs to teach, lead, and pray protectively (1 Tim. 2:8). It means equipping women who have a modesty and dignity and godliness that causes the culture to look askance and to wonder why (1 Tim. 2:9–10). Just as for Timothy's congregation, the first question for religious liberty right now is not whatever Britney Spears and Madonna are doing to each other at the MTV awards show. It is why in our own congregations our preteen daughters look like Britney Spears and Madonna.

Creating countercultural Christian churches also implies that our political alignments will be provisional and loosely held. It also means that we will never be comfortably at home with any political movement or even with American culture itself. If Christian conservatism is going to "conserve" a Christian counterculture, we must understand the ways in which our interests are subverted not only by an overreaching government but by an overreaching socioeconomic culture as well.[10] After

9. See the Baptist Faith and Message articles 6 and 18 on "The Family" and "The Church," which define the biblical pattern of male headship in the home and a male-only pastorate. For a fuller exploration of the "complementarian" position, see John Piper and Wayne Grudem, eds., *Recovering Biblical Manhood and Womanhood: A Response to Evangelical Feminism* (Wheaton, Ill.: Crossway, 1991).

10. For an excellent survey of the social and economic factors involved in family breakdown, see Brian C. Robertson, *Forced Labor: What's Wrong with Balancing Work and Family* (Dallas: Spence, 2002); and Allan Carlson, *The Family in America: Searching for Social Harmony in the Industrial Age* (New Brunswick, N.J.: Transaction, 2003).

all, tax policy alone is not causing hordes of evangelical and Roman Catholic mothers to go into full-time careers while their children sit in day care centers watching *VeggieTales*. And don't be deceived, it will take much more than a weekly hour of Sunday school and moralistic lessons from singing vegetables to transform the character formation built in by two parents chasing the corporatist vision of the American dream into the fruits of the Spirit.

Most conservative Christians would concede that there is more to life than what is advertised on the high-definition television screens at Wal-Mart. But do our churches and our pastors lead them to ask whether there might be something *different* to life than this? Yes, we believe that children are a gift from the Lord. But do our own congregants roll their eyes in dismay at the godly Christian husband and wife who actually seek to raise a multitude of Christian children, or at least a "multitude" as defined by our antiseptic contraceptive culture? Why rail against Planned Parenthood when Planned Parenthood is shaping the way our own churches view family size and parenting and our pastors say nary a word (1 Tim. 2:15)?

If we're to be a church that maintains religious liberty, we need to love the religion as much as the liberty—indeed more so. And that means we'll be increasingly odd in American culture. And we may have less and less in common with libertarian Republicans and libertine Democrats. If the outside culture pronounces this anathema, so be it; it always has. And if Caesar decides to add his sword to the disapproval of the culture, so be it; he's done it before. The church still stands. We will claim our mantle of dissent not simply by standing in the public square demanding our rights—though we must sometimes do that. We claim it first of all by being an alternative community, the people of Christ.

Conclusion

Maintaining religious liberty has more to do with Vacation Bible School than with the Supreme Court. If we are to ensure that the next generations of churches have liberty, we must remember why we claim that liberty: for the gospel and for the church. And we must therefore rear a generation of children and grandchildren who so love the gospel, who so love the church, that they are willing, when soldiers with AK-47s line them up against the walls for the faith, to go to their deaths for the Christ who is alone King. They won't do that through a weekly diet of how-to sermons and moralistic Sunday school drivel. They won't do that for a political party or even a cultural way of life.

They will do it through identification with the same gospel and same churches that our ancestors carried in their hearts as they were drowned for insisting that they would baptize the way Jesus ordered, not the way the state church commanded. They will find religious liberty—and every kind of liberty—not in the word of the Constitution or in the "natural rights" of humanity, but by being hidden in Christ and living together in his body. They will be free only if they realize that they must be conservative Christians, not just Christian conservatives.

★★★★★★★★★★★★★★★★★★★★★★★★★★★★★

Chapter 9

Fantasy or Possibility: Can Religious Liberty Be Created in Islamic Countries?

Emir F. Caner

Worldviews and Table Manners

The scene is still vivid in my mind. More than twenty years ago I found myself sitting at a dining room table having what was supposed to be a normal meal with my devout Muslim father. But a few months earlier my life had changed; indeed, it was transformed. This once follower of Allah had walked into the Stelzer Road Baptist Church in Columbus, Ohio, and, at the end of the service, professed faith in Jesus Christ. Though as a young Muslim I knew some of the potential consequences of that weighty decision, I did not have the foresight to see that my life was in some limited sense a microcosm of the worldviews that are now colliding on the center stage of history.

While many watched as the epic battle between two superpowers reached its climax in the 1980s, there I was sitting across the table from my hero, who had just asked me to recite the normal Islamic prayer before eating. Though an embryonic theologue to say the least, I knew I could not prostrate myself to a false god and be captured in idolatry. I informed my father of my decision to follow Jesus as the Son of God and my Savior, thereby admitting that Muhammad was a fraud and a false prophet. Without flinching, my father[1] disowned me, declaring me dead in his eyes.

1. This one event does not presume upon my father that of an absentee father. I found out later in life how much my father cared for me. Unbeknownst to me, he would sometimes show up at my baseball games or keep tally of my life by documenting accolades I received at school like the honor roll. Nevertheless, he felt compelled to adhere to the precepts of Muhammad and consider me as dead.

Later, when asked by so many people where my father would get such a notion to disown his own son, I would inform the curious yet cynical inquisitors of what are, in my estimation, the most important words ever uttered by Muhammad: "If a Muslim changes his Islamic religion, kill him" (Bukari hadith 9.57).[2] I was de facto dead to him, and memories were the only items that remained.

My father interpreted this saying of Muhammad as allegory and not as literal. It goes without saying how grateful I am that my father was much more a Muslim counterpart to Origen, without the sharp ascetic tendencies, than he was to John Chrysostom. Consulting with his imam and other Islamic leaders, my father viewed the statement of Muhammad in stark contrast to millions of contemporary purist[3] Muslims around the world. In the years which followed, I realized how important hermeneutics is to the conversation on religious liberty.

The question of whether religious liberty is possible within Islamic contexts ultimately will not be answered by mulling through Islamic theology or history but will be answered through biblical interpretation. In reality, the Holy Scripture is the only avenue that will lead to a viable and optimistic answer, for if one attempts to find justification for religious liberty within the Qur'an, he will be sorely discouraged.[4] If one

2. The Hadith (sayings of Muhammad) is the second source of authority in Islam after the Qur'an. Bukhari's (b. 816 A.D.) edition is one of four compilations by Islamic scholars in the Middle Ages and is universally considered the most respected and accurate. All four versions of the Hadith are available online at http://www.usc.edu/dept/MSA/reference/searchhadith.html. See also Muhammad Muhsin Khan, *The Translation of the Meanings of Sahih Al-Bukhari* (Riyadh, Saudi Arabia: Darussalam, 1997), 9:46. Khan translates the verse above, "Whoever changed his Islamic religion, then kill him." It should also be noted that the verses subsequent to this expression document the slaughter of a Jew who reverted from Islam back to his roots.

The Qur'an is also explicit on rejecting those who reject the faith. Surah 3:85 stipulates, "If anyone desires a religion other than Islam (submission to Allah), never will it be accepted of him; and in the Hereafter he will be in the ranks of those who have lost." Surah 4:89 informs, "They but wish that you should reject Faith, as they do, and thus be on the same footing (as they); so, take not friends from their ranks until they flee in the way of Allah (from what is forbidden). But if they turn renegades, seize them and slay them wherever you find them; and (in any case) take no friends or helpers from their ranks."

3. I use the term *purist* and not *radical* or *extremist* for two reasons. First, *purist* connotes the meaning that these Muslims wish to go back to the roots of their faith and follow the principles of their founder Muhammad. The other two terms imply they go *beyond* the boundaries set forth by Muhammad. Second, the terms *radical* and *extremist* need to be used for those who do go beyond the goals and principles of Muhammad, such as female *mujihadeen* (holy warriors), who were never allowed by Muhammad.

4. Many Islamic commentators point to surah 2:256 as demonstration of Islamic toleration. It reads, "Let there be no compulsion in religion." But one must differentiate between forced

endeavors to find acceptance of liberty within Islamic history, he will be unquestionably disappointed. In fact, the present resurgence of Islam is not moving toward a moderation of faith but a desire to traditionalize the faith. Millions of Islamists across the world desire to regress to an Islamic faith much closer to Muhammad and much farther removed from the West. At present more than a dozen countries have reinstated forms of Islamic laws in their constitutions.

With the rising tide toward traditional Islam, and with many Western societies moving away from the tenet of religious liberty as well,[5] the fight for freedom has become elusive to say the least. It is easy to become contemptuous in one's outlook on the future of religious liberty and its survival. In the end the answers as to the possibility of religious liberty are found within three camps which offer their solutions to the complicated matter.

Moderates/revisionists are willing to accept that the Islamic world will not adopt an essentially Western-style democracy or its freedoms and redefine terms such as *freedom* and *democracy* while conceding defeat to some extent. Liberals/pluralists still hold to the notion that Islam has always been a peaceful religion and simply needs to be nudged from its extremism back toward its alleged tolerance. Conservatives/exclusivists, the view I hold, believes that religious liberty is not based on the actions, attitudes, or ambitions of man but on the eternal Word of God.[6] Through adherence to its doctrines, liberty can be created in an otherwise oppressive society.

---

conversion, which this verse seems to disallow, and religious liberty, which this verse does not deal with. As can be seen through the Pact of Umar, the resignation that some will remain Christians after being conquered does not conclude that those Christians have freedom to express their faith. Other scholars argue that this verse was abrogated when Muhammad gained the upper hand in Medina. Also, this verse says little about the punishment for apostasy, that is, someone who is a Muslim and converts to another religion. For a solid study on the history and theology of apostasy, see Samuel M. Zwemer, *The Law of Apostasy in Islam* (London: Marshall Brothers, 1924).

5. In recent days France has passed a law prohibiting the public display of crosses, yarmulkes, and Islamic headdress within the governmental school system. At the same time countries such as Belarus are limiting evangelistic activity of foreigners through laws which require a license to proselytize. Laws against "hate speech" have also passed through the court systems in countries such as Australia.

6. In order to be grounded in absolute truth, Christians must not base their epistemology (which answers the question, how do I know what I know?) in man-centered terms. If one's knowledge is founded on human reason, emotion, or experience, then one's knowledge is subjective and relative in its scope. The understanding that God has revealed himself provides the Christian with a reality based in the Sovereign, who is both immutable and omnipotent.

Moderate/Revisionist Reappraisal: A Quiet Resignation of Realistic Compromise

Admittedly, it is difficult to delve into an intelligent and informed discussion with someone on the issue of religious liberty within Islamic history. In fact, it would be easier to find a Mormon at a Starbucks than it is to find an Islamic scholar at an American university willing to objectively and substantially tackle the issue of religious liberty and persecution within the nearly fourteen-hundred-year history of Islam. Few ever seriously broach the questions: "Did Muhammad intend for his statement in hadith 9.57 to be taken literally? Did Muhammad's disciples carry out executions of apostates?"

Instead, modern knee-jerk reactions from Islamic scholars and polemicists usually are expressed in statements such as, "Christians have their own bloody history,"[7] or the ever popular, "There are fundamentalists on both sides." Disregarding for a moment the fact that the former comment only lends credence to the potential dismissal of both religions while the latter disallows any passionate and traditional adherence to a faith, these comments cannot be given any credence since they lack intellectual integrity.

This is not to say that such topics have not been introduced by some. Scholars, such as Ivy League professor Bernard Lewis, have done commendable work in the area of historical dogma and its ramifications for Islamic societies in the present.[8] But there seems to be an inherent admission from moderate/revisionist scholars that religious liberty is, to a great extent, foreign to the traditional Islamic mind-set. Indeed, John Esposito, who studied under one of the foremost Islamic experts, Isma'il R. al Faruqi, admits as much when discussing whether democracy itself is possible in Islamic contexts. He explains that democracy can work only

7. For an open discussion on Christian militancy during the Crusades, inquisitions, and modern times, see Emir Caner and Ergun Caner, *Christian Jihad: Two Former Muslims Look at the Crusades and Killing in the Name of Christ* (Grand Rapids: Kregel, 2004). The authors argue that Christians went to war not because of biblical theology but because they adopted Muslim theology. Popes as early as A.D. 847 asserted that those who went to war for the sake of the Roman Church would be guaranteed heaven if they died. Of course, this promise is absent in the Bible though it is explicit in the Qu'ran (surah 3:169–71).

8. Two books in particular, *Islam in Crisis* (New York: Modern Library, 2003), and *The Middle East* (New York: Scribner, 1996), give a succinct yet substantial overview on Islamic history in what was once a Christian stronghold. However, the latter book gives ample illustration that even the best of scholars do not give much space to Islamic history subsequent to Muhammad's death.

if not defined in a "highly restricted way and is viewed as possible only if specific Western European or American institutions are adopted."[9]

Furthermore, democracy is promising solely if Islamic principles are not defined "in a rigid and traditional manner."[10] One is left with the impression that if a strict minimalist approach to democracy must be given, little hope is left that religious freedom can be implemented within a Muslim-dominated society. Ibn Warraq, a former Muslim turned secularist who now lives in the United States, is even less optimistic on the compatibility of Islam with religious freedom. He surmises, "The Islamic God is not a democrat; we cannot get rid of Him as we can a human representative elected by the people in a representative democracy. . . . Democracy depends on freedom of thought and free discussion, whereas Islamic law explicitly forbids the discussions of decisions arrived at by the infallible consensus of the *ulama* [Islamic scholars]."[11]

The question of possibility is further confused by scholars who disregard the difference between "religious toleration" and "religious liberty." Not one Islamic country has religious liberty. Not one. However, other than Saudi Arabia, most Islamic nations bestow some degree of toleration upon religious minorities. In fact, the Pact of Umar, a seventh-century document written by and named after the second caliph succeeding Muhammad, illustrates the extent of acceptance given to Christians after a land was conquered in the name of Islam. Christians were required to adopt the document, which acted as an official surrender treaty. It reads in part:

> We shall not build, in our cities or in their neighborhood, new monasteries, Churches, convents, or monks' cells, nor shall we repair by day or by night, such of them as fall in ruins or are situated in the quarters of the Muslims.[12]

9. John Esposito and John O. Voll, *Islam and Democracy* (Oxford: Oxford University Press, 1996), 21. Esposito and Voll, expounding on the hope of a new breed of democracy, quote favorably one scholar and his hope of democracy, explaining, "The theocracy built up by Islam is not ruled by any particular religious class but by the whole community of Muslims including the rank and file. . . . If I were permitted to coin a new term, I would describe this system of government as 'theo-democracy.'" They then give Iran as a good example! (24).

10. Ibid., 23. For further discussion of militancy in Islam from the perspective of Esposito, see his works *Unholy War: Terror in the Name of Islam* (Oxford: Oxford University Press, 2003) and *The Islamic Threat: Myth or Reality,* 3rd ed. (Oxford: Oxford University Press, 1999).

11. Ibn Warraq, *Why I Am Not a Muslim* (New York: Prometheus Books, 1995), 180–81.

12. To this day, countries such as Egypt use this statement against religious minorities and thus build new mosques in obscure places, thereby prohibiting any other religious structure

> We shall not manifest our religion publicly nor convert anyone to it. We shall not prevent any of our kin from entering Islam if they wish it.
>
> We shall not display our crosses or our books in the roads or markets of the Muslims. We shall use only clappers in our churches very softly.[13]

One must take note that the entire community was obligated to hold fast to their promise, a crucial reminder that community always trumps individuals (and individual rights) within the Islamic community (Ar. *umma*). If Christians were guilty of breaking any of the promises found within the document, protection afforded to them via the Islamic government was forfeited. They were to be considered traitors and enemies of the state.[14] Moreover, the document privatizes the Christian faith, a notion which is both antithetical to the essence of Christianity as well as in opposition to democratic freedoms. In particular, Christians living under an Islamic regime must not evangelize Muslims, though Muslims were commanded to evangelize Christian families.

In his book *Their Blood Cries Out,* Paul Marshall explains the modern consequences for perpetuating such doctrines. He segregates the Muslim world into categories according to their record on liberty. Nations such as the Sudan and Saudi Arabia are labeled as Advancing Jihad, characterized by the desire to implement Shari'a law through outright persecution of other religions.[15] Alongside Iran and Egypt, these countries are the greatest culprits of terror, instituting laws that allow for the forced conversions of some and the execution of others. Yet, even the freest of Muslim-dominated nations in the world's eyes, countries that have democratic processes in place, such as Turkey, are open violators of freedom. Marshall reminds the reader, "Persecution of the Assyro-Chaldean minority has intensified within Turkey itself.

---

from being erected.

13. Paul Halsall, ed., "Medieval Sourcebook: Pact of Umar, 7th Century?" at www.fordham.edu/halsall/source/pact-umar.html; accessed 7 September 2005.

14. This is a major reason that Christians and Jews who share their faith in Islamic countries are considered traitors. As such, these people are considered guilty of treason and are subject to capital punishment under Islamic law, which is based on surah 5:33.

15. Paul Marshall, *Their Blood Cries Out* (Dallas: Word, 1997), 15–40. Marshall rightly points out that Pakistan must be considered among the worst violators of religious freedom. In 1986, the government passed section 295–C in their penal code, which called for the death, imprisonment, and/or fine of anyone who "by imputation, innuendo, or insinuation, directly or indirectly, defiles the sacred name of the Holy Prophet (peace be upon him)" (33).

They cannot build new churches, have no schools, and are banned from public service."[16]

With such a track record in the country where secularism has been given the greatest chance to succeed, one can see why so many do not believe there is any possibility for liberty to thrive within traditional Islamic countries. Recognizing the overwhelming challenge within Islamic societies, moderates/revisionists conclude that Americans should take what they can get in terms of politics and freedoms. Examples such as Kuwait illustrate a government elected by the people that nonetheless institutes mandatory Islamic education for children and bans public expression of the Christian faith. The greatest amount of freedom possible still falls far short of the hope of liberty, yet partial freedom is better than no freedom.

The Liberal/Pluralist Solution: Utopia in Mecca

But all is not lost, according to liberal scholars such as Carl W. Ernst. He is a professor of Islamic studies at the University of North Carolina-Chapel Hill and perfect poster child for postmodern liberal thinkers who have high aspirations that modernism will save Muslim societies and integrate freedom much as the Enlightenment allegedly helped free Europe from the ravages of traditional fundamentalist Christianity. In his recent book *Following Muhammad,* Ernst raves, "One should recall that democracy does not have much of a profile in the history of Christianity, but that it belongs instead to the modern Enlightenment together with the separation of church and state."[17]

---

16. Ibid., 50. For further discussion on the future of Turkey, see Marvine Howe, *Turkey Today: A Nation Divided over Islam's Revival* (Boulder, Colo.: Westview Press, 2000). In her work she documents the rise of Islamists in the 1980s against the secularists. Though it is obvious she is pulling for the secularists, she nonetheless concludes, "The integration of a vibrant Islamic movement under a fully democratic Republic of Turkey would be a powerful and positive experience for the Islamic world" (263). Ironically, she assumes these two theories are congruent.

Turkish history itself is marred in military coups and religious battles. In 1453, the Ottomans captured the Christian stronghold of Constantinople. In the process of Islamization, the Turks transformed St. Sophia Orthodox Church into a mosque. One other notable event worth mentioning is the Armenian holocaust during World War I in which nearly two million Armenian Christians were slaughtered at the hands of Muslims. In fact, on April 24, 1915, more than 600,000 were killed in that one day. I believe this immense persecution was, in part, the reason Turkey was willing to become a secular state.

17. Carl W. Ernst, *Following Muhammad: Rethinking Islam in the Contemporary World* (Chapel Hill, N.C.: University of North Carolina Press, 2003), 140. Like many other scholars,

Manifesting his own prejudice against traditional Christianity, which he displays innumerable times in his work, Ernst maintains, "The continuing export of fire-breathing Christian missionaries to Muslim countries provided a new example of how one can use the authority of scripture to bash one's opponents."[18] Therefore, the hope of freedom within Islam is likewise to free that religion from the fundamentalists and extremists and grant "liberal Islam" and its foremost thinkers the ability to argue against authoritarian Islam via Islamic texts, Islamic philosophical tradition, and Western pluralistic thinkers such as Immanuel Kant and Georg Hegel.

Ernst's inflammatory and bigoted comments are borne out of a classical liberal mind-set that views traditional forms of exclusivist faiths as the enemy and modern pluralism as the friend of freedom. He parallels fundamentalist Islam with fundamentalist Christianity, both militant and dangerous to the health of society.[19] On the other hand, he believes that if liberal Muslim voices gain a hearing, common Muslims who live in ignorance will accept indisputably the pristine voice of academia.

But Ernst's arguments are replete with inaccuracies. First, he believes that the liberal/pluralist can isogete the Qur'an for his own advantage while ignoring all of the more than one hundred militant verses of the Qur'an, not to mention numerous hadiths that are clear as to their context. Second, he is in utter denial of the militancy of formative and developing Islam. He seems to forget the way Islam spread, especially during its first one thousand years, or at least believes it should have no impact as to how Muslims think today. This negation of history may work in the West where most citizens suffer from historical amnesia, but Muslims honor their history and consider it part and parcel of their life and thought. Third, the inaccurate statements and suppositions dispose of any hope that his thesis can become a reality. For example, Ernst states with unqualified certainty, "Religious dogma plays a much

Ernst has accepted the myth of the monolithic church. He fails to mention that many Christian groups such as the fourth-century separatist church of North Africa, also known as the Donatists, disassociated themselves from the organized church due to the Constantinian synthesis between church and state.

18. Ibid., 67.

19. Ernst forgets that the Protestant Reformation was a return to the grammatical-historical interpretation of the Scripture, lost since the days of Origen, Clement of Alexandria, and Augustine. This hermeneutic led the Anabaptist (free church) of the Reformation to herald the doctrine of religious liberty nearly three centuries before it was enacted into law in America.

smaller role for Muslims than it does for Christians."[20] Additionally, Ernst believes that religions "are not timeless, eternal essences."[21]

In the end the reader is left to accept the theory that a Muslim can be convinced that religion is no more than a neoorthodox religious experience, that Muhammad was a misunderstood pluralist lost within the historical doldrums of anti-Islamic hate speech from Christians, and that the Islamic world is one voice away from seeing another Woodstock break out in Mecca. Sadly, the reader also goes away with the idea that Christian fundamentalists are the enemy of freedom. And in Ernst's view, the more evangelistic one is, the more fascist he is as well.

The Conservative/Exclusivist Solution: A Hermeneutic of Hope

Countering these two opposing views, the Christian worldview believes liberty is borne out of the courage to stand firm on principles regardless of the cost. It goes without saying that both Islam and Christianity are exclusivist faiths which believe that their sacred text is the absolute Word of God. The Qur'an internally argues for its preservation: "We have, without doubt, sent down the Message; and We will assuredly guard it (from corruption)" (surah 15:9). The Bible, too, internally argues for its inspiration (Matt. 5:17–18; 2 Tim. 3:16; 2 Pet. 1:19–21). As such, both texts assert that their word is the final word. In Islam, Muhammad is the final prophet and his word on salvation is the final word on salvation (see surah 23:101–103). In Christianity, Jesus is the final and superior Word (Heb. 1:1–8), and his word on salvation is the final word on the subject (John 14:6).

Yet the two sacred texts differ greatly on how to handle someone who leaves the faith or is considered apostate. Whereas, it has been demonstrated that Muhammad employed the death penalty for apostates (Ar. *murtad*; see also hadith 4.260),[22] Christianity acknowledges that

20. Ibid., 45. For a good explanation of the importance of dogma within Islam from a devout Muslim scholar, see Seyyed Hossein Nasr, *Islam: Religion, History, and Civilization* (New York: HarperCollins, 2003), 7–15.

21. Ibid., 50.

22. The subsequent verses to hadith 9.57 show the result of Muhammad's statement. A Muslim convert from Judaism who decided to return to his Jewish roots was executed as an apostate. Hadith 9.58 reads in part, "There was a fettered man beside Abu Muisa. Mu'adh asked, 'Who is this (man)?' Abu Muisa said, 'He was a Jew and became a Muslim and then reverted back to Judaism.' Then Abu Muisa requested Mu'adh to sit down but Mu'adh said, 'I will not sit

God, and God alone, will judge those who are his enemies. Forbidding his disciples to take punitive action against those who do evil, Christ stated in the famous parable of the wheat and the tares that believers, "the wheat," and unbelievers, "the tares," should coexist in this world. He explained, "Allow both to grow together until the harvest; and in the time of the harvest I will say to the reapers, 'First gather up the tares [unbelievers] and bind them in bundles to burn them up; but gather the wheat [believers] into my barn'" (Matt. 13:30 NASB).

Additionally, the believer is called to care for and sacrifice one's rights on behalf of those who are more likely to stumble in the faith. Paul explained, "But beware lest somehow this liberty of yours become a stumbling block to those who are weak" (1 Cor. 8:9 NKJV). Finally, the ultimate penalty for those who are rebellious in the faith is wholly separate from the state and its sword (Rom. 13:4). Instead, church discipline is the method prescribed by the New Testament writers. Removal from the fellowship of the saints is the final act of punishment for those who are unwilling to repent of their rebellion against Christ and his church (Matt. 18:15–18), and even then Christians are to hope for restoration of that believer through repentance.

Thus, with the doctrine of liberty firmly established within the Scripture, the first step toward implementing religious liberty must be to state clearly and courageously biblical guidelines. The apostle Paul said as much when giving a defense of his faith to King Agrippa. He noted, "I am not out of my mind, most excellent Festus, but I utter words of sober truth. For the king knows about these matters, and I speak to him also with confidence, since I am persuaded that none of these things escape his notice; for this has not been done in a corner" (Acts 26:25–26 NASB).

A Christian must base his actions solely on the Scripture and not react hastily according to another person's beliefs. Balthasar Hubmaier (A.D. 1480–1528), the formative theologian of the sixteenth-century Anabaptist (free church) movement, heralded religious liberty during some of the darkest days of religious oppression within Europe. In his work *On Heretics and Those Who Burn Them,* Hubmaier was the first

---

down till he has been killed. This is the judgment of Allah and His Apostle (for such cases)' and repeated it thrice. Then Abu Musa ordered that the man be killed, and he was killed. Abu Musa added, 'Then we discussed the night prayers and one of us said, "I pray and sleep, and I hope that Allah will reward me for my sleep as well as for my prayers."'"

Reformation author to argue for complete religious liberty. In doing so, his thirty-six-point thesis included the following four articles:

> Article 3: Those who are such should be overcome with holy instruction, not contentiously but gently, even though the Holy Scripture also includes wrath.
>
> Article 15: Yea, we should pray and hope for repentance as long as a person lives in this misery.
>
> Article 21: Every Christian has a sword [to use] against the godless, namely the [sword of the] Word of God (Eph. 6:17f), but not a sword against the evildoers.
>
> Article 29: If to burn heretics is such a great evil, how much greater will be the evil, to burn to ashes the genuine proclaimers of the Word of God, without having convinced them, without having debated the truth with them.[23]

More than two centuries ahead of his time, Hubmaier believed that to have an option to love God, you must have an option to hate him. To persecute someone who disdains God is to diminish or destroy any chance of voluntary and sincere repentance.

Hubmaier insisted that persecution of the infidel would also wreak havoc on the church, putting genuine believers in jeopardy. Ironically, Hubmaier's life became a remarkable example of his point. Considered a heretic by the organized church, he paid the ultimate price for stating his views publicly and boldly. Along with his wife, Elizabeth, who was thrown in the Danube River with a rock around her neck, Hubmaier was condemned to death and burned at the stake in Vienna by the Catholic King Ferdinand in March 1528. Even then, his final prayer exemplified his heart of liberty: "O dear brothers, if I have injured any, in word or

23. H. Wayne Pipkin and John H. Yoder, *Balthasar Hubmaier: Theologian of Anabaptism* (Scottdale, Pa.: Herald, 1989), 58–66. The term *Anabaptist* (from a Latin word meaning "re-baptizer") was a derogatory label given to men and women of the dissenting free church who were unwilling to accept the marriage of church and state. Instead, they believed in a visible, local church comprised exclusively of believers who had voluntarily professed faith in Jesus Christ and followed that decision in believer's baptism.

deed, may he forgive me for the sake of my merciful God. I forgive all those that have done me harm."[24]

Yet his martyrdom serves to illustrate how liberty has historically come to oppressive regions across the world. Persecution, along with its close allies of proclamation and perseverance, are the three necessary ingredients for freedom. Liberty is borne out of a Christian community that is willing to proclaim the gospel at any cost, be persecuted to any extent, and persevere for countless years. To modify a popular quote from the early church father Tertullian (160–220), the blood of the martyrs is not only the seed of the church; it is the bedrock for freedom.

A brief panorama of the history of Christianity proves the point. After the death of Christ, the New Testament church endured the painful persecutions of leaders such as Stephen, Peter, and Paul. Later, infamous Roman rulers such as Nero (54–68), Domitian (81–96), Decius (249–251), and Diocletian (284–305) slaughtered sporadically and systematically those of the Christian faith. At the beginning of the fourth century, Roman citizens were, as church historian Bruce Shelley explained, "sickened by so much bloodshed."[25] In Britain, Emperor Galerius, who openly admitted his failure to exterminate Christianity from the region, quashed the harassment of Christians. "Even the throne could no longer take the risk of continuing the torturing, maiming, and killing," Shelley wrote.[26] Soon after, Constantine himself, in response to the commitment of Christians as well as through a mystical experience in battle, enacted the Edict of Toleration across the empire.

The doctrine of liberty had seemingly won the day, though sadly, since the edict only guaranteed the freedom of worship for Christians, history took an ironic twist as the persecuted became the persecutors. Most Christians were convinced that the state should not only provide freedom for the church; it should provide favor and prestige as well. Anyone who stood in the way of such privileges was considered anathema.[27]

---

24. Emir Caner, "Truth is Unkillable: The Life and Writings of Balthasar Hubmaier, Theologian of Anabaptism" (Ph.D. Thesis: University of Texas at Arlington, 1999), 40–41.
25. Bruce L. Shelley, *Church History in Plain Language* (Dallas: Word Books, 1982), 108.
26. Ibid.
27. The most influential theologian in the history of the Western Church, Augustine (354–430), believed that dissenting Christians must be punished in order to sustain unity in the church. He thereby agreed that persecution of the Donatists was prudent and necessary. His stance gave Reformers like Luther and Calvin the justification they needed to persecute other "heretical" Christians.

By the sixth century the death penalty was instituted as punishment for those unwilling to accept the official doctrines of the emerging Roman Church, in particular infant baptism. Though dissenting Christians survived, and at times flourished, the Middle Ages was, in regard to liberty, a time of incredible pessimism. Fear gripped most of the European continent. Nonetheless, dissenting groups such as the Waldensians persevered during the height of the era. The most important council of the age, the Fourth Lateran Council (1215), called for the inquisition of the denomination, asserting: "The [Waldensians] began by trying to recapture what they conceived to have been the simplicity of the Apostolic Church; but they, like many other groups who started with this aim, tended towards an intransigent sectarianism. . . . Although the discipline of the Church does not carry out bloody retributions . . . still it is aided by the regulations of catholic princes."[28]

As Dutch martyrologist Thieleman J. van Braght amply illustrates in his work *Martyrs Mirror,* tens of thousands of these free-church followers were imprisoned, fined, ostracized, and executed.[29] But they persevered powerfully and stood firm, even against the greatest of pains. One Waldensian martyr contended, "The priests actuate the secular arm and then think to be free from murder and they wish to be known as benefactors. Yes, just as did Annas and Caiaphas and the rest of the Pharisees . . . they refrained from going into the house of Pilate lest they be defiled and in the meantime delivered Jesus up to the secular arm."[30]

In the end their voices were heard and their immense sacrifice did not go unnoticed. Though their suffering spanned more than a millennium, the free churches of the Middle Ages created an environment that would lead to a considerable discussion of liberty within Protestant Christianity. Even defenders of persecution such as Martin Luther doubted the validity of persecution. He articulated, "I am really distressed that these poor people should be so pitifully murdered, burned, and horribly put to death. Everyone should be allowed to believe what he likes. If

28. Henry Bettenson, ed., *Documents of the Christian Church,* 2nd ed. (London: Oxford University Press, 1963), 132–33.

29. Other books which retell the stories found within the *Martyrs Mirror* include John S. Oyer and Robert S. Kreider, *Mirror of the Martyrs* (Intercourse, Pa.: Good Books, 1990); Dave and Neta Jackson, *On Fire for Christ: Stories of Anabaptist Martyrs* (Scottdale, Pa.: Herald, 1989). The author of this article has recently published a book on the modern-day persecution of Muslims who convert to Christianity entitled *The Costly Call* (Grand Rapids: Kregel, 2005).

30. Leonard Verduin, *The Reformers and Their Stepchildren* (Sarasota, Fla.: Christian Hymnary Publishers, 1964), 44.

he is wrong, he will be punished enough in hell fire."[31] Unfortunately, Luther was convinced by colleagues such as Phillip Melanchthon to reevaluate his open position, and he caved in to the supposed necessity of persecution to keep order in society.

After more than a millennium of severe persecution, many Anabaptists settled in parts of the New World and found greater freedom. This is, or course, not to say the persecution ended, for Puritan Congregationalists in New England and Anglicans in the middle and southern colonies recreated a system which favored their denomination while excluding others and forbidding many religious practices. In his work *An Appeal to the Public for Religious Liberty,* Isaac Backus (1724–1806) pleaded with his fellow countrymen finally to enact religious liberty for America, a dream which was centuries in coming. He concluded:

> Suffer us a little to expostulate with our fathers and brethren who inhabit the land to which our ancestors fled for religious liberty. You have lately been accused with being disorderly and rebellious by men in power who profess a great regard for order and the public good. And why don't you believe them and rest easy under their administrations? You tell us you cannot because you are taxed where you are not represented. And is it not really so with us?[32]

Ultimately, men such as Backus, John Leland, and Roger Williams not only paved the way for religious freedom in America today; they stood on the shoulders of giants and used centuries of sacrifice beforehand for inspiration and illustration. America was the ultimate answer of Providence to centuries of dissenters who hoped that one day they could worship freely and were willing to give their all so that it would come to pass.

Therefore, when someone asks whether liberty is possible in Islamic countries, the Christian worldview answers loudly in the affirmative. To do otherwise would not only be un-American, it would be un-Christian. But the road to freedom in countries that have been immersed in tyranny

31. John Oyer, "The Writings of Luther Against the Anabaptists," *Mennonite Quarterly Review* 27 (April 1953): 108.
32. Isaac Backus, "An Appeal to the Public for Religious Liberty," in Curtis W. Freeman, James Wm. McClendon Jr., and C. Rosalee Velloso da Silva, ed., *Baptist Roots: A Reader in the Theology of a Christian People* (Valley Forge, Pa.: Judson, 1999), 165–66.

and theocracy for centuries can be a tough and long one. The contemporary Christian should check his character and see if he is able and ready for the sacrifice it may take to accomplish around the world what is true in America today. The Christian should not answer in the affirmative unless he is willing to pay the ultimate price for others to hear the gospel of Jesus Christ, a gospel which will not only set you free but is based in liberty itself. He should prepare himself for a long journey, something most Americans are not willing to consider. He should make himself more than a mere spectator on the world's scene but boldly defend the cross of Christ and those who suffer for his sake. He must not confuse toleration with liberty, pragmatism with principle, or prosperity with blessing.

In order to succeed, he must view the world's scene and see where God is working. He is acutely aware of historical religious persecution in places such as the Korean peninsula, which in its southern region is now a haven for millions of evangelicals today. He is reminded of the tyranny which once consumed former Soviet republics such as Romania but now is replaced with a thriving movement of Baptists across the country. He should find those places where persecution is greatest and know that liberty may be around the corner in years to come. But blind optimism this is not. It is, instead an understanding of how God has used persecution to lift up liberty. Brief optimism it can never be, for truth is eternally vigilant.

The General

By now many of those engaged in the question of fantasy or possibility are perhaps quite cynical of this extreme optimism. One may be thinking that the author has lost his mind and is living in fantasyland, less realistic than people who attend a Star Trek convention.

But this author has at least one ally in his belief that liberty is not out of the reach of the Middle East and other Muslim countries. A few months ago I ate lunch with General George Hormis Sada, a retired Iraqi air vice marshall (the equivalent of a three-star general). During Desert Storm, Sada, a Christian who attends the National Presbyterian Church in Baghdad, served under then-president Saddam Hussein. After more than two dozen coalition force airmen were shot down during the conflict, Sada was ordered by Hussein himself to execute the men for alleged crimes against humanity. Knowing his faith would not allow him to do so, he acted as a mediator and was able to convince the regime that the prisoners were more valuable alive than dead. When Iraq was liberated in 2003, Sada, an inspiration to so many, was asked to work within the newly formed interim government. During the past few years, Sada has served as the personal advisor to the interim prime minister Iyad Allawi as well as advising the new emerging Iraqi army.

Thus, he is eminently qualified to understand the situation in Iraq and to give intelligent counsel about the future of the country. I wondered to what extent democracy and religious liberty had a chance of being implemented within the newly freed nation. Acknowledging the absence of liberty within Iraq since it was captured by Caliph Umar in 636, I asked about the chances for liberty to take root in the country. He swiftly answered, "Yes." The reason for his extreme optimism was profound: Americans have shed so much blood in the conflict that Iraqis are willing to listen. As active participants who are witnessing this paramount shift in the world's order, may Christians recognize the value of suffering and the worthiness of sacrifice, uniting the inspiration of the past with the hope of the future.

Chapter 10

Contemporary Religious Liberty and the Judiciary in America: A Southern Baptist Jurist's Personal Perspective

Paul Pressler

We must learn from the past so that we can understand the future. In this presentation I will discuss briefly the history behind statements in our nation's founding documents concerning the right to religious liberty. The one clause granting religious liberty is not actually in the Constitution; it is in the Bill of Rights. We hear a great deal of talk about "separation of church and state." This expression exists neither in the Constitution nor in the Bill of Rights. Thomas Jefferson used this phrase in a letter he wrote to Baptists in Danbury, Connecticut, seeking to encourage ratification of the Constitution with the Bill of Rights.

Jefferson stated:

> Believing with you that religion is a matter which lies solely between man and his God; that he owes account to none other for his faith or his worship; that the legislative powers of the government reach actions only, and not opinions, I contemplate with sovereign reverence that act of the whole American people which declared that their legislature should "make no law respecting an establishment of religion, or prohibiting the free exercise thereof," thus building a wall of separation between church and State.[1]

1. Adrienne Koch and William Peden, *The Life and Selected Writings of Thomas Jefferson* (New York: Random House, 1944), 332.

Jefferson referred to and quoted the First Amendment of the Bill of Rights, which reads, "Congress shall make no law respecting the establishment of religion or prohibiting the free exercise thereof, or abridging the freedom of speech, or of the press; or the right of the people peaceably to assemble, and to petition the government for a redress of grievances."[2]

Special notice should be taken of the sentence, "Congress shall make no law respecting the establishment of religion or prohibiting the free exercise thereof." What were our founding fathers thinking when they wrote this into the Bill of Rights? It is interesting to review the condition of religious liberty at that time. The Puritans settled in New England to escape religious persecution in England by Anglicans. After they left, Oliver Cromwell had Charles I executed, took power in 1652, and reigned until 1660. The reign of Oliver Cromwell, an evangelical Christian, was as despotic and cruel as the reign of any other tyrant in Europe. He ruthlessly suppressed people who did not agree with him. No religious freedom existed under Oliver Cromwell or under the other sovereigns of England.

What did the Puritans do when they came to New England?[3] They established regulations requiring membership in a Congregationalist church in order to vote. They denied religious freedom to the people in their communities. That is why Roger Williams founded the colony of Rhode Island. Roger Williams was a Baptist and had to leave Massachusetts because he did not have the freedom to worship there. The Quakers were also persecuted in England. Roman Catholics who did not have freedom to worship in England settled in Maryland where they found freedom. William Penn founded Pennsylvania. He was a Quaker and wanted to provide religious freedom for Quakers.[4]

Virginia became a haven for Episcopalians, and they did not allow religious freedom. My wife is descended from Richard Cave, a member of a Baptist church in Culpepper, Virginia. In order to preach in Virginia, one had to get a license from the state which was controlled by the Episcopalians. The local Baptist preacher could not get a license to preach, and when he kept on preaching, they put him in jail. The preach-

2. The Constitution and Bill of Rights may be accessed online at http://www.archives.gov/national-archives-experience/charters/constitution.html. Accessed 20 March 2006.
3. For a discussion of the role of religion in American colonization, see Clifton E. Olmstead, *History of Religion in the United States* (Englewood Cliffs, N.J.: Prentice-Hall, 1960).
4. Melvin B. Endy Jr., *William Penn and Early Quakerism* (Princeton, N.J.: Princeton University Press, 1973), 348–77.

er was a friend of Daniel Boone, so the whole congregation migrated to the Kentucky territory under Boone to obtain religious freedom. They became known as the "Traveling Church."

South Carolina was a haven for Huguenots. The Huguenots had a rough time. On St. Bartholomew's Day, August 24, 1572, there was a tremendous persecution and many deaths of Protestants.[5] They received some relief when Henry IV established the Edict of Nantes, which guaranteed religious toleration for the people of France in 1598. The Huguenots (French Protestants) had grown greatly, and many in the middle classes in France had become Huguenots, forsaking the Roman Catholic Church. The grandson of Henry IV, Louis XIV, would revoke the Edict of Nantes eighty-seven years after its establishment, making Protestantism illegal. This revocation of the Edict of Nantes, officially known as the Edict of Fontainebleau, did not start new wars, but it did result in a mass exodus of French Protestants.[6]

I have some ancestors from Sedan, France who were named Rochet. During this persecution the father was separated from his wife and daughters, except for one daughter, Suzanne. The mother and the daughters fled to Germany without Suzanne. Many of their friends were massacred in Sedan. The Catholics demanded that Suzanne be placed in a convent so she would be reared Catholic. The father gained passage for his daughter, hidden in a wine barrel, and she was shipped from France to freedom in Holland.

There are more German surnames in America today than there are of any other ethnic group. The Germans had been through the Thirty Years War, from 1618 to 1648. This was a war in which the Hapsburg Empire in the south was supported by the Roman Catholic Church, and they tried to retake all of Germany for Roman Catholicism. They retook Silesia and Austria. We have friends who have a castle in the Wachau Valley, west of Vienna. The church in their town was built as a Protestant church, and when the Counter Reformation came, the Catholics took it over. Protestant worship was restricted in Austria beginning in the 1640s. The Thirty Years War was bitter. It left Germany divided with Lutherans denying religious freedom in their part

5. For a discussion of the massacre, see Henry White, *The Massacre of St. Bartholomew* (New York: Harper & Brothers, 1871), 404–45.

6. Excerpts from the Edict of Nantes can be viewed online at http://www.stetson.edu/~psteeves/classes/edictnantes.html. Accessed 20 March 2006. For the revocation of the Edict of Nantes, see J. H. Robinson, ed., *Readings in European History* (Boston: Ginn, 1906), 2:287–91.

of the country, and Catholics denying religious freedom in their part.[7] My ancestors fled Silesia in order to worship freely.

All of these events occurred within 100 to 150 years of the writing of the Constitution of the United States and the Bill of Rights. That might sound like a long period of time, but it is really not. When I was brought up, everybody talked about "The War." It was not World War I. It was not World War II. It was the "unpleasantness" between 1861 and 1865. That war was personal because our ancestors lived through it and died in it. My generation included many who were the children of people who lived through Reconstruction. They often talked about "The War" and the privations of Reconstruction. That was a little over 150 years ago, and it is still planted firmly in my mind.

Article I of the Bill of Rights is a prohibition not on worship but on action by the Congress of the United States. There were worries about establishing a central government. The colonists feared that the central government might establish a religion or prohibit worship or observances by certain religious groups, such as was done in Culpepper, Virginia. In the June 2005 issue of *Baptists Today,* there was an interesting article about a historic church on Martha's Vineyard, an island off the Massachusetts coast. On December 21, 1780, a group of Baptists on Martha's Vineyard petitioned their town council, saying, "We the undersigned . . . are of the mind to have a Baptist minister to preach the Gospel to us as Baptist principles are most agreeable to our opinion, and we desire to be exempt from paying taxes to said town to support the orthodox ministry [the established clergy.]"[8] Their petition was denied in 1780, four years after the Declaration of Independence. Until 1804, this town on Martha's Vineyard required the payment of taxes by Baptists to support the Congregationalist minister.

This occurred after the Bill of Rights was approved. Obviously, if this could be done after the Bill of Rights was approved, it was not considered in violation of the Bill of Rights. So here you have it clearly said that "Congress"—not the "town council on Martha's Vineyard," or the "State of Virginia in Culpepper"—but "Congress shall make no law respecting an establishment of religion or prohibiting the free ex-

7. For more information, see S. H. Steinberg, *The Thirty Years War* (New York: Norton, 1966).
8. For the original story, see E. St. John Vineyard, *The Martha's Vineyard Times,* 5 May 2005.

ercise hereof." It is simple. A judge should be a person who takes the Constitution or a law, reads it, accepts it, and takes it at face value. That is what happened in the courts of our nation for a number of years. It was clear that this did not prohibit a state or municipality from establishing religion. If they had done that, possibly the Bill of Rights would not have been accepted by the states.

The Fourteenth Amendment to the Constitution states that "no state shall make or enforce any law which shall abridge the privileges or immunities of citizens of the United States." Adopted after the War Between the States, this amendment was the first which asserted that states must abide by the same restrictions which are placed on Congress.

Something else happened in the late 1930s that fundamentally changed our nation. President Franklin Roosevelt was upset that his programs were being overturned by the Supreme Court of the United States. He proposed that the number of justices on the Supreme Court be increased so that he would have the right to name additional justices. He wanted the court increased so that he could appoint enough justices to have a liberal majority on the court. The court-packing attempt was voted down, even by a heavily Democratic Congress under Franklin Roosevelt, who was a popular president. It was considered too much of a manipulation of the third branch of our government. However, some of the justices retired or died. By filling vacancies, Roosevelt accomplished what he could not with legislation.[9]

Let me give you an illustration of the thinking of this new Supreme Court. The Commerce Clause in the Constitution says that the federal government has the right to regulate commerce. What does this mean? A person had a private vegetable garden. He raised all the vegetables for himself and for his family. He did not sell any vegetables. He harvested them by himself, used them for his family, and they never went off his property unconsumed by a member of the family. Now the question was: Was he engaged in interstate commerce? His activities were as local as anything can be. However, the court ruled that if he had not been eating his own produce, he would have been buying it in the marketplace. If he bought it in the marketplace, that would affect commerce, so the government had the right to control him as he raised his own crops although they were in his own garden for his own consumption.

9. For a book dedicated to the discussion of this topic, see Merlo J. Pusey, *The Supreme Court Crisis* (New York: MacMillan, 1937).

This type of construction is the problem we have in church-state relationships. This type of interpretation of the Constitution by a liberal court with roots in the late 1930s has caused lots of changes. The Lemon case was decided in the early 1970s. It provided that religion could be involved in the public sector if its engagement was primarily for a nonreligious purpose, there was no excessive entanglement with the government, and it did not breach the principle of separation of church and state. This rule may still be applied where the property is leased by a government to a religious organization.[10]

We should briefly consider what is happening in the two other branches of government. In the executive branch, our current President is a person who believes that we should not discriminate against religion. He has made this clear in his pronouncements. He has said that funds that are given for human assistance should not be denied to a religious organization solely because it is religious.[11] That's revolutionary! It does not, in my thinking, bind together church and state, but it allows religious organizations such as the Salvation Army and similar groups to take federal funds and use them for their nonreligious purposes. The problem is: Does taking federal funds allow federal control to be exercised over the entire organization?

Lyndon Baines Johnson knew how to operate the legislative process. There has never been a majority leader like him. He was insulted in the early 1950s by the way some of the pastors in Texas treated him and campaigned against him when he ran for election to the United States Senate. He, therefore, inserted into an Internal Revenue bill a rider which provided that if a church endorsed a political candidate, it would lose its tax-exempt status. What he had done was not discussed. The legislative process is interesting because so much goes on that members of the legislative body cannot pay attention to everything. Legislators are always slipping things in. As people in Dallas and Fort Worth know, Jim Wright was a master at doing that. He had a provision included in a bill concerning Love Field that no plane from Love Field could transport passengers beyond a state contiguous to the state of

10. *Lemon v Kurtzman,* 403 U.S. 602, 614 (1971). This ruling is available online at http://caselaw.lp.findlaw.com/cgi-bin/getcase.pl?court=us&vol=403&invol=602#612. Accessed 20 March 2006.

11. "Bush Urges Government, Foundations to Fund Faith-Based Groups," *Baptist Press,* 10 March 2006. For the White House perspective, see http://www.whitehouse.gov/government/fbci/. Accessed 20 March 2006. See also "Bush Enacts Faith Based Measure," *Fox News,* 12 December 2002.

Texas.[12] This limited Love Field and made Dallas-Fort Worth International Airport much more important economically.

When I was in the Texas legislature, a friend of mine who was also from Houston wanted to run for the state senate. He saw me as a possible threat to him. He proposed a constitutional amendment, which would have raised the minimum age for a member of the state senate so that I could not run for the senate when he wanted to run. I was twenty-seven years of age. I was on the constitutional amendment committee and had an amendment to the constitutional amendment adopted providing that the amendment would not go into effect until several years later. Therefore, it would not apply to me. It infuriated him, but I thought, *I'll show him he can't get away with this.* When he noticed my amendment, he dropped his bill because it was not any help to him anymore. It is easy to slip in an amendment.

Lyndon Johnson similarly slipped his provision into the Internal Revenue bill. Congressman Walter Jones from North Carolina has a bill before Congress at the present time to repeal the Lyndon Johnson rider and to give greater latitude to pastors and churches to express themselves in political activity.[13] It has not passed, and prospects for its passing in the immediate future are not good. Therefore, there is not much activity on church and state matters in either the executive or the legislative branches. The action is in the judicial branch where many interesting cases are pending which will affect church and state matters.

A very interesting case, which the Supreme Court decided in 2005, has received much comment. The rule has always been that a state can exercise its power of imminent domain to build highways and to serve other public purposes but only when there is a public use made of the property that will be taken under the exercise of imminent domain. The Supreme Court ruled that a town in Connecticut could take private property from a person and turn it over to a private developer because there would be an economic advantage to the city in doing so.[14] Therefore, if

---

12. Keith L. Alexander, "Southwest, American Due to Spar over Wright Amendment," *Washington Post,* 10 November 2005, D03. See also http://www.setlovefree.com/historyof-wright.html. Accessed 20 March 2006.

13. See Joe Plecnik, "The Free Speech Congressman: Walter Jones v. Lyndon Johnson," *The Conservative Voice,* 31 December 2004. For more information, see http://www.hr235.org/, which discusses the bill in detail. Accessed 20 March 2006.

14. *Kelo v. New London,* (04–108) 268 Conn. 1, 843 A. 2d 500, affirmed. A discussion of this case and various opinions can be viewed at http://www.law.cornell.edu/supct/html/04–108.ZO.html. Accessed 20 March 2006.

there is a lower socioeconomic area in a city that has churches scattered through it ministering to the people, the local authority could come in, condemn the whole area, and build a residential or commercial community any way it wanted which could be completely devoid of churches. This appears to be a dangerous precedent.

Our legislature shortly after this decision passed a law that says this cannot be done in the state of Texas, and our governor has signed it into law. Other states are getting ready to amend their state laws so that it cannot be done there, but the Supreme Court has created a dangerous precedence.

A important case was argued before the Supreme Court of Texas in January 2005 (*HEB Ministries v. Texas Higher Education Coordinating Board*).[15] This case concerns whether the Texas Higher Education Coordinating Board can require that before a seminary can operate in the state of Texas, it has to comply with certain licensing requirements of the board: it must have so many library books, must have so many people who are psychologists on their faculty, must have their courses approved, must have the board of trustees of the seminary approved, etc. The state has thus attempted to take over the licensing and control of new seminaries.

Think of the ramifications. It does not presently concern a school like Southwestern Baptist Theological Seminary because Southwestern is such a strong school. But once the principle is established that the state controls a seminary, it could require diversity in teaching and on the board of trustees—even diversity in theology. Here there was a small seminary backed by a small religious group that granted thirty-four diplomas in Bible. It was fined $173,000 by the state of Texas for granting these diplomas in Bible because they did not have a license from the state Board of Education to do this. The Seminary sued.

At this time, none of the courts in the state of Texas has ruled for the seminary. It has been argued before the Texas Supreme Court. I have a compact disk record of the arguments. It is exciting. One justice lit into the state of Texas and asked, "What right do you have to do this? How can you do that? Where is this within your authority?" The representative of the state of Texas was stammering and stuttering by the time this

15. Allie Martin, "Texas High Court Agrees to Hear Critical Church-State Case," *Agape Press*, 9 December 2004. The appellant court opinion is available online at http://www.3rdcoa.courts.state.tx.us/opinions/htmlopinion.asp?OpinionId=12008. Accessed 20 March 2006.

justice finished. Then the other Supreme Court justices joined in and were asking similar questions. Currently, we do not have an opinion, as it takes about a year to get an opinion out of the Supreme Court of Texas. We anticipate a complete victory in that case because regulating religion is not a function of the Texas Board of Education. We have to win that case; it is so important.

Martha Gallien is a lady in my Sunday school class. She came up to me after class one Sunday and told me that she was studying to get a degree in counseling. The professor showed a violent, prohomosexual film to the class, and she got up and started to walk out. The professor blocked her way and would not let her leave. She was told that if she did not watch the video, she would flunk the course, and the professor would not allow her to take any other courses at the University of Houston—Clear Lake branch. She is suing, and I think she will win.

At Texas Tech a professor wrote recommendations for students to medical schools. He posted a statement on his Web site stating that if a student does not believe in evolution, that student will not get a favorable recommendation to medical school from him. After the problem was brought to light, the United States Department of Education got involved and started an investigation. The professor was thus forced to reverse his policy.[16] That victory was won.

Balch Springs is a community east of Dallas. About twenty or thirty senior citizens meet in a city recreational facility. The city council, by a vote of four to two, told them that they could not sing hymns or any songs that were Christian, they could not pray before meals, and they could not have a sermon or devotional delivered to them on public property. All of these things had been done for twenty to thirty years in this same recreational center in Balch Springs. The senior citizens with signs in hand picketed the city council. This brought public attention to the matter. The case went to trial, and the city council was ruled in error. The plaintiff was awarded $73,000 as reimbursement for his attorney's fees. The citizens of Balch Springs were so angry that they recalled the four members of the city council who tried to enforce their policy on the senior citizens. All four council members were

16. Megan Rooney, "Biology Professor's Policy of Linking Recommendations to Belief in Evolution Prompts Federal Probe," *The Chronicle of Higher Education,* 3 February 2003. See also Sebastian Kitchen, "Texas Tech Professor's Evolution Policy Prompts U.S. Justice Inquiry," *Avalanche-Journal,* 30 January 2003; and Larry Taylor, "Biology Professor Alters Evolution Statement for Recommendations; Justice Ends Probe," *Skeptical Inquirer,* 27, no. 4 (July-August 2003).

recalled and replaced by people who had a different view of church-state relationships.[17] These senior citizens did not take it lying down.

In the Plano school district a young boy, eight years old, took candy canes to his school's "Winter Festival"—no longer called "Christmas." The candy canes told the story of the candy cane and had a Christian message with them. He was told he could not hand out those candy canes in the Plano school district. Other children were told they could not hand out pencils that said "Jesus" on them, could not write "Merry Christmas" on their letters to the soldiers in Iraq, or invite their friends to church. A case was brought forward (*Morgan, et al v. Plano ISD*). The court entered an injunction against the Plano school district right before Christmas to keep them from prohibiting that young man from handing out his candy canes with the Christian message.[18]

Santa Fe, south of Houston, has a strong Christian community. There is a wonderful Baptist church in that town which practically everybody attends. They conducted prayer during the high school football games for many years. Somebody objected and brought suit (*Doe v. Santa Fe I.S.D*). The federal district judge enjoined having prayer at the football games. He also enjoined having any sectarian prayer at graduation. The district judge edited the prayer of the valedictorian of the high school.[19] How can there be any more of an entanglement of state with religion than a judge editing the prayer of a student?

I believe that Jesus Christ is the only way to heaven. Every religion of the world, except Christianity, is a methodology of doing things to make ourselves acceptable in the sight of God. Christianity says that it is not by works of righteousness that we have done but only because of the grace of God that we are saved. There is no compatibility between a religion that believes in redemption by faith in the blood of Christ and a religion that believes in redemption through individual efforts and good works.

---

17. "Seniors May Pray Again at Texas Senior Center," *Religious Freedom in Focus*, vol. 1 (February 2004). Available online at http://www.usdoj.gov/crt/religdisc/newsletter/focus_1.htm. Accessed 20 March 2006. The Civil Rights Division of the Department of Justice also investigated this incident. Their concluding report is available at http://www.usdoj.gov/opa/pr/2004/January/04_crt_006.htm. See also "Dallas Suburb's Mayor Pro Tem, 3 Council Members Recalled," *Tyler Morning Telegraph*, 17 May 2004).

18. Michael Foust, "Lawsuit: School Bans Christmas Colors, Christian-Themed Gifts," *Baptist Press*, 16 December 2004. See also Emanuella Grinberg, "Parents Sue to Allow Religious Holiday Messages in Public Schools," *CNN*, 27 December 2004.

19. *Santa :Fe Independent School Dist. v. Doe*, (99–62) 530 U.S. 290 (2000) 168 F.3d 806, affirmed. A discussion of the case along with the opinion and dissenting opinion is available at http://supct.law.cornell.edu/supct/html/99–62.ZS.html. Accessed 20 March 2006.

Do we have a problem with the state establishing religion? I think so, but it is not a danger of establishing Christianity. It appears that we have a concerted effort in our nation to have a national secular religion that brings together everything at its lowest common denominator and establishes a religion of humanism, a religion that says that everything has equal value. When a judge starts writing or censoring prayers, he is establishing his religion and forcing it on the person praying.

I have been distressed at the horror with which certain people react when it is suggested that "intelligent design" be taught in our schools. The earth had to be created either by chance or by a system or person who was intelligent. All that intelligent design affirms is that what has happened in the development of the universe and all that lives in it could not have happened accidentally or by chance. This is not necessarily theistic. It is not the establishment of a religion. It is not giving favor to a certain religion. It is just a theory of origins. What is happening is that the scientific community is up in arms and will do everything they can to prevent the teaching of an alternative theory to their belief in Darwinism. Why is that? Because the key point of their religion is evolution and their belief that there is no Creator. Everything just evolves, and all created beings are animals.

Did you see what happened recently in the London zoo? They had a cage with human beings in it to try to demonstrate that people are just another form of animal. They put six or eight people in a cage among the cages for animals. Human beings were part of the exhibits. That was done with public money in England paying for the exhibit. Before long, we are going to see things like that in America if we are not diligent. This religion of secular humanism will be promoted with our money if the liberals have their way. It is going to be done through promoting evolution and secularism. That is why they are so afraid of the teaching of an alternative to Darwinism. When Darwinism is undermined, their established religion is undermined. The promotion of their religion of secular humanism is far more dangerous than prohibiting a few seniors from singing hymns in a public building in Balch Springs.

The city of McKinney, Texas, decided that a church could no longer meet in a home (*Grace Community Church v. City of McKinney*). The city was defeated, and the church can now meet there.[20] A female

20. McKinney, Texas, "Ordinance NO–2004–12–124." The results of the city council meeting are available online at http://www.mckinneytexas.org/agendas/councilmeetings/2005–

church member in Fort Worth had an unbiblical relationship with a man and sought to divorce her husband for an unbiblical reason. The church member refused to repent when confronted by the leaders of the church. The church, in accordance with its disciplinary procedure, sent a letter to the congregation advising it of the woman's unrepentant attitude. This former member sued the church, the elders, and the pastors, claiming that she was maligned by them although they stated the truth about her adulterous relationship.[21] The court should not be involved in something like that.

In San Antonio in the Northeast Independent School District, they observe the "Winter Holiday Season." They have songs about Hanukkah, Kwanza, Santa Claus, La Fiesta, and Winter Solstice, but they did not allow songs about Jesus to be sung or any reference to the Christian faith. Why is that? Why is there discrimination against Christians? It is because we believe there is only one way to heaven, and that is through the Lord Jesus Christ. We are exclusive. We will do everything within our power to allow a person to practice whatever religion he wants to practice, but we cannot say that all religions are of equal value. That policy was changed.[22]

In Waco the public library made a deal with Planned Parenthood to incorporate the proabortion literature of Planned Parenthood into the Waco Public Library. Some Christians wanted to see this part of the Waco Public Library. The librarians excluded them from seeing what they had incorporated into the public library because they knew these people were pro-life and not proabortion. Complaints were filed, and the city of Waco ultimately removed all of the Planned Parenthood lit-

---

January4_files/3.%20Consent%20Agenda/3.1%20Minutes/05–003%20CC%20&%20P&Z%20Joint%20WS%20Minutes%20December%2015,%202004.doc. Accessed 20 March 2006.

21. *Penley v Westbrook*, 2–02–260–CV (2d Cir. 2002). The opinion is available online at http://www.2ndcoa.courts.state.tx.us/opinions/htmlopinion.asp?OpinionId=15626. Accessed 20 March 2006. For the complete case history including the current standing of the case, see http://www.2ndcoa.courts.state.tx.us/opinions/case.asp?FilingID=16526 (*Penley v Westbrook*). Accessed 20 March 2006.

22. See http://www.libertylegal.org/cases.htm. Accessed 20 March 2006. "Encino Park Elementary put on a play to celebrate the Winter Holiday Season that included songs and dialogue about Hanukkah, Kwanzaa, Santa Claus, La Fiesta, Winter Solstice and the birth of Jesus. All references to a Christian church or the birth of Jesus were deliberately removed from the play by the principal. After being contacted by a parent and learning of this intentional discrimination against Christians, LLI sent a letter to the school district demanding that the district take action to correct this problem and ensure that such discrimination never occurs again. The district took action to correct the situation and prevent further discrimination against Christians in the future."

erature from the public library rather than give access to pro-lifers.[23] How could a public library keep a portion of the public from access to a part of the public library because of their convictions?

We could go on and on. There are many cases out there at the present time. When you look at the statement in the First Amendment of the Bill of Rights which says, "Congress shall make no law respecting the establishment of religion or prohibiting the free exercise thereof," it seems so simple. That is all it says.

Some courts are emphasizing the disestablishment of religion and not the free exercise of religion. This has sent wrong signals to schools and cities. The city council prohibited the free exercise of religion by the Balch Springs seniors. This was reversed. School boards have refused to rent space in school buildings to Christian groups although they lease them to other groups. This is improper. Christians need to be treated on the same basis as any other group. These are the types of problems we have today.

These are difficult times, but fortunately a number of groups throughout the country are providing their free services to fight this encroachment on freedom of religion. I am a member of the board of the Free Market Foundation.[24] All of the Texas cases referred to in this chapter are cases in which Free Market has represented the individuals who were discriminated against. I am close to groups located in Arizona, California, Virginia, Georgia, Florida, and elsewhere who are doing the same as the Free Market Foundation. Clients are represented without charge, but often the defendants are required to pay legal fees to these groups which represent the plaintiffs and defend their freedom of religion.

It appears that the tide is turning partly because of these groups. Intolerance is being exposed in many places, and the American Civil Liberties Union is now opposed by more rational lawyers. Free Market has not lost a case in three years, and with President George W. Bush's appointments to the Supreme Court, it appears that the proper balance might return. We shall see!

---

23. See Michelle Hillen, "Planned Parenthood Deal with Libraries Protested," *Waco Tribune-Herald,* 29 October 2002, 1B, and Cindy Culp, "Suit Splits Library Planned Parenthood," *Waco Tribune-Herald,* 14 May 2003, 1A, 4A.

24. See http://www.freemarket.org/portal/index.php. Accessed 20 March 2006.

★ ★

About the Contributors

Emir F. Caner (Ph.D., University of Texas at Arlington) is dean and professor of history at The College at Southwestern. He is author of *The Costly Call: Worldwide Testimonies of Muslims Who Have Become Christians* (Kregel), *The Sacred Desk: Presidential Addresses of the Southern Baptist Convention Presidents* (Broadman & Holman), and *More Than a Prophet: An Insider's Response to Muslim Beliefs About Jesus and Christianity* (Kregel).

Jason G. Duesing (Ph.D. candidate, Southwestern Baptist Theological Seminary) is chief of staff in the office of the president, Southwestern Baptist Theological Seminary.

Barrett Duke (Ph.D., University of Denver) is vice president for research and director of the Research Institute of The Ethics & Religious Liberty Commission. He is author of many pamphlets addressing ethical issues available through the Ethics & Religious Liberty Commission.

Daniel R. Heimbach (Ph.D., Drew University) is professor of Christian ethics at Southeastern Baptist Theological Seminary. He is the author of *True Sexual Morality: Recovering Biblical Standards for a Culture in Crisis* (Crossway).

Richard D. Land (D. Phil., Oxford University) is president of the Southern Baptist Convention's Ethics & Religious Liberty Commission. He is author of *Imagine! A God-Blessed America* (Broadman & Holman), *Real Homeland Security* (Broadman & Holman), and executive editor of *Faith & Family Values,* a national magazine.

Craig Mitchell (Ph.D., Southwestern Baptist Theological Seminary) is assistant professor of Christian Ethics at Southwestern Baptist Theological Seminary. He is author of *Charts for Philosophies and Philosophers* (Zondervan) and *Charts of Christian Ethics* (Zondervan).

Russell D. Moore (Ph.D., Southern Baptist Theological Seminary) is dean of the School of Theology and senior vice president for academic administration at The Southern Baptist Theological Seminary. He is the author of *The Kingdom of Christ: The New Evangelical Perspective* (Crossway) and serves as a contributing editor for *Touchstone: A Journal of Mere Christianity.*

Paige Patterson (Ph.D., New Orleans Baptist Theological Seminary) is president of Southwestern Baptist Theological Seminary. He is the author of numerous articles and monographs including *The Troubled Triumphant Church: An Exposition of First Corinthians* (Wipf & Stock) and *A Pilgrim Priesthood: An Exposition of First Peter* (Wipf & Stock); and he served as managing editor of *The Believer's Study Bible* (Thomas Nelson).

Paul Pressler (J.D., University of Texas) served as a member of the Texas legislature, judge of the 133rd district court, and justice for the 14th court of appeals. He is the author of *A Hill on Which to Die: One Southern Baptist's Journey* (Broadman & Holman).

Thomas White (Ph.D., Southeastern Baptist Theological Seminary) is vice president for student services, provides direction to the Smith Center for Leadership Development, and is a faculty member at Southwestern Baptist Theological Seminary. He is author of "James Madison Pendleton and His Contributions to Baptist Ecclesiology" in volume 1, *Selected Works of James Madison Pendleton* (Paris, Ark.: Baptist Standard Bearer, 2006) and editor of *Selected Works of James Madison Pendleton*, 3 volumes (Paris, Ark.: Baptist Standard Bearer, 2006).

Malcolm B. Yarnell III (D. Phil., Oxford University) is assistant dean for theological studies, director of the Center for Theological Research, director of the Oxford Study Program, and associate professor of systematic theology at Southwestern Baptist Theological Seminary. He is the author of "Are Southern Baptists Evangelicals? A Second Decadal Reassessment," in *Ecclesiology*; "Changing Baptist Concepts of Royal Priesthood: John Smyth and Edgar Young Mullins," in *The Rise of the Laity in Evangelical Protestantism*; and *The Development of Doctrine* (forthcoming, Broadman & Holman).

Index

A

B

C

D

E

F

G

H

I

J

K

L

M

N

O

P

Q

R

S

T

U

V

W

Y

Z